Also by Lawrence J. Greene

Kids Who Hate School
Getting Smarter (with Leigh Jones-Bamman)

Kids Who Underachieve

by Lawrence J. Greene

SIMON AND SCHUSTER • New York

The author gratefully acknowledges permission to reprint from
Gestalt Therapy Verbatim by Fritz Perls, M.D., Ph.D. Copyright
© 1969, Real People Press. Reprinted by permission of the
publisher.

Published by Simon and Schuster
A Division of Simon & Schuster, Inc.
Simon & Schuster Building
Rockefeller Center
1230 Avenue of the Americas
New York, New York 10020
SIMON AND SCHUSTER and colophon are registered trademarks
of Simon & Schuster, Inc.

Designed by Irving Perkins Associates

Manufactured in the United States of America

10 9 8 7 6 5 4 3 2

Library of Congress Cataloging-in-Publication Data
Greene, Lawrence J.
    Kids who underachieve.

    Bibliography: p.
    Includes index.
    1. Underachievers—United States—Case studies.
2. Learning disabled children—Education—United
States—Case studies.   3. Problem children—Education—
United States—Case studies.   4. Achievement motivation
in children—Case studies.   I. Title.
LC4691.G74   1986   371.92′6   85-27775
ISBN: 0-671-55235-X

Acknowledgments

Many people have contributed to the creation of this book. I am indebted to them for their encouragement, criticism, and ideas. Particular thanks go to Susan Whittlesey, Robbie Dunton, Estella Lacey, Candice Jacobsen, Douglas Harper, M.D., and Alison Lucas.

All the men of genius that we have ever heard of have
triumphed over adverse circumstances, but that is
no reason for supposing that there were not
innumerable others who succumbed in youth.

—Bertrand Russell,
The Conquest of Happiness

Contents

Introduction   15

Chapter 1. The Instinct to Achieve   19

Tamara: She Wouldn't Let Herself Achieve   19
Learning to Achieve   21
Achievement and Survival   24
The Pluses and Minuses of Achievement   26
Environment and Achievement   27
The Symbolic Nature of Goals   28
Equating Achievement with Health   30
Parenting Suggestions   31

**Chapter 2. Identifying Achieving and
Underachieving Children**   32

Collin: He Had Crossed the Bridge   32
Zest and the Achieving Child   34
The Path to Achievement   36
The Role of Parents in Assessing Their Child   38
Is My Child an Underachiever?   40
Underachievement Checklist   40
The Complacent Underachiever   42

Different Types of Underachievement   45
The Four Common Sources of Underachievement   46
Parenting Suggestions   47

Chapter 3.   **How Children Achieve**   48

Erik: He Refused to Accept His Counselor's Advice   48
The Ability to Achieve   51
Transforming Potential Ability into Developed Ability   53
Learning Efficiency   54
Differentiating Potential Ability from Developed Ability   55
Intelligence   57
Aptitude   58
Measuring Intelligence and Aptitude   59
The Achieving Child Model   61
Smartness and Achievement   61
Parenting Suggestions   63

Chapter 4.   **Self-Image and Achievement**   64

Devon: Punishment Wasn't the Answer   64
Self-Image/Self-Esteem Loop   67
Bradley: Giving Himself Permission to Succeed   71
The Desire to Achieve   74
The Ego Factor   76
An Expanded Model for the Achieving Child   78
Identifying Jam-ups   80
Parenting Suggestions   81

Chapter 5.   **When Children Don't Achieve**   82

Carey: She Wasn't Sure She Wanted to Be Promoted   82
Frustration and Underachievement   85
Allowing Children to Confront Challenges   88
Checklist of Attitudes on Challenges and Frustration   91
Ego Damage   92
Deserving to Achieve   93
Paying the Price for Success   95
Wendy: The Lamb Who Became a Lion   99

Acquired Helplessness   101
Parenting Suggestions   104

Chapter 6.   Early Recognition of
Underachievement   106

Seth: A Tragedy Averted   106
Figuring Out What's Wrong   110
Parental Intuition   111
Early Identification—The First Step   112
Persistence and Perseverance   116
Critical Questions and Critical Choices   118
Parenting Suggestions   119

Chapter 7.   The Underachiever with Learning
Problems   121

Benjamin: He Lived Under a Microscope   121
The Problematic Diagnosis   125
Underachievers in the Gray Area   125
Slipping Through the Diagnostic Screen   128
Educational Testing and Treatment Priorities   130
Defining a Learning Disability   131
Early Indications   133
Impediments to Early Identification   135
Acquiring Essential Information   136
Learning Problems Checklist   138
Parenting Suggestions   141

Chapter 8.   Underachievers with Poor
Study Skills   143

Marci: "I Can't Figure Out What the Teacher Wants Me to
    Know"   143
The Implications of Poor Study Skills   146
How the Good Student Differs from the Poor Student   148
Identifying the Student with Poor Study Skills   152
Study Skills Checklist   153
Learning Styles   154

Adjusting to the System 156
Helping the Inefficient Learner 158
Effort Without Reward 162
Parenting Suggestions 162

Chapter 9.   **Strategies for Resolving Learning Problems** 164

Craig: Putting the Pieces Back Together 164
Remediation Options 167
Hoping the Learning Problem Will Go Away 168
Programs Within the School System 171
Effective Remediation Checklist 174
Private Programs 175
Retention 184
Parenting Suggestions 187

Chapter 10.   **Communicating with the Underachieving Child** 189

Michelle: It Was More Than Laziness 189
The Function of Parent-Child Communication 195
Barriers to Communication 197
Communicating with Younger Children 199
Communicating with Adolescents 205
Effective Communications Checklist 208
Expressing Disapproval and Criticism 210
Self-Defeating Parental Criticism 214
Parenting Suggestions 216

Chapter 11.   **Performance Standards for the Underachieving Child** 219

Peter: Too Nice to Discipline 219
Establishing Limits 223
The Function of Parental Power 225
The Indecisive Parent 228
Establishing Standards 229
The Guilt Factor 232

Problem Ownership 233
Emotionally Charged Encounters 237
Parenting Suggestions 242

Chapter 12. **Emotional Problems and Underachievement** 245

Mark: He Had Placed His Fears in a Cigar Box 245
Nonachieving Children with Emotional Problems 247
Emotional Overlay 249
Misbehavior 251
Identifying Emotional Problems 251
Emotional Disturbance Checklist 252
Gina: Life Was Very Boring 255
Diagnosis and Treatment 258
Chronic Active Resistance 261
Chronic Passive Resistance 261
Emotional Shutdown 262
Family Problems and Underachievement 263
Family Problems Checklist 267
Parenting Suggestions 271

Chapter 13. **Orchestrating Achievement** 273

Danny: Doing Cartwheels in Class 273
Comfort Zones 276
Achieving Perspective 279
A Healthy Foundation for Achievement 281
The Family's Position on Success 282
Creating Opportunities for Achievement 284
Intentionality 285
Competition 287
Feeling Worthwhile 289

Bibliography 290

Index 291

Introduction

A kindergartener complains of stomachaches, but the pains occur only on school mornings. Each morning at 6:45 her mother must begin the ritual of coaxing the six-year-old out of bed.

A nine-year-old struggles to keep up with his class. He starts his homework promptly at 3:30 and works until dinner time. Despite his efforts and despite an IQ of 132, the child has been placed in the lowest reading and math groups in his class.

An eleven-year-old who has been identified as mentally gifted is convinced that she is incapable of doing better than C work. She does the minimum amount of homework necessary to pass. Most of her time is spent watching television or talking on the phone with her friends.

A thirteen-year-old hands in his assignments late. The work is invariably incomplete, sloppy, and illegible. Certain that their son is lazy, unmotivated, and irresponsible, the teenager's desperate parents take away his bicycle and forbid him to watch television on school nights. Yet his work does not improve.

A fourteen-year-old with subtle reading and math problems concentrates exclusively on sports. No amount of parental prodding can get him to devote sufficient time to his schoolwork. The grades on his report card are all C's and D's.

The children described above are underachievers. They are

15

part of a vast population that includes as many as 50 percent of all school-age children. Although these youngsters have average, above average, or superior intelligence, they function below their potential in school and, often, in other areas of their lives.

The underachiever falls into a gray area in the field of education. Those who manifest specific, identifiable learning problems may qualify for special help. Unfortunately, in most states special education programs are reserved for those with serious learning disabilities. Many underachieving children with subtle and nonspecific problems receive little or no meaningful assistance.

Underachieving children with subtle problems are rarely evaluated for underlying learning problems. They are excluded from testing because their learning deficits are not considered to be sufficiently incapacitating to warrant remedial assistance. Those underachieving children with subtle, intermittent, or nonspecific learning problems who *are* tested are frequently misdiagnosed or simply slip through the gaps in the standard diagnostic screening procedures.

Resolving underachievement has never been a particularly high priority in our society. Teachers are preoccupied with the needs of the average or gifted student. Mental health specialists direct their efforts toward children with serious emotional or family problems. Learning disabilities specialists generally focus on the child who has incapacitating, identifiable learning deficits.

The presence of thirty children in a classroom permits the teacher little time to provide support for the underachieving child. The needs of the group must take priority over the needs of the individual student. Although federally funded programs such as Title I are designed to help the educationally disadvantaged student, such programs are often not available to underachieving children in middle-class school districts.

In most cases, the underachieving child is simply allowed to muddle through school. He performs below standard, and because his accomplishments are marginal, he receives little or no affirmation and acknowledgment. To protect himself from disappointment and failure, the child begins to accept his limitations and lowers his expectations accordingly. The habit of not trying or of giving up becomes an entrenched component of his personality. By the age of six, many underachieving children have already established and accepted a pattern of substandard effort and performance that will persist throughout their lives.

Psychiatrists, psychologists, and learning disabilities specialists know all too well that a child's behavior and attitudes about himself and about the world are profoundly influenced by his experiences during the formative years. Positive life experiences tend to produce "positive" children. These children are easily identified: they are confident, they like themselves, they are motivated, and they are achievement oriented.

Repeated experiences of failure, frustration, and futility, on the other hand, tend to produce "negative" children. These children are also easily identified. They generally don't like themselves, and this lack of self-esteem is reflected in their lack of self-confidence. Typically, negative children never quite figure out who they are and what they want out of life.

Parents and educators should not be surprised when nonachieving and underachieving children evolve into troubled teenagers and poorly functioning adults. A report that appeared in 1983 in *Barrister*, the journal of the American Bar Association, cites research done by the Association for Children with Learning Disabilities, in which children with learning problems were found to have a 220 percent greater chance of becoming juvenile delinquents than their non-learning-disabled peers.

Fortunately, the cycle of poor performance, poor self-esteem, and poor self-confidence can be broken. But first, the parents and teachers of the underachieving child must understand the specific emotional and academic needs of the child. This book has been written with these goals in mind.

1

The Instinct to Achieve

Tamara: She Wouldn't Let Herself Achieve

Tamara was quite charming. With her disarming smile and quick wit, the thirteen-year-old was able to deflect most of my questions about the deterioration in her schoolwork.

I asked her why she wasn't handing in her assignments on time, and she replied that she was often confused about when her assignments were due. I then asked her why the work she did hand in was often incomplete or sloppy. She responded that she had felt the work was acceptable. She expressed surprise that her teachers were not satisfied with its quality.

She explained that it was difficult studying at home with three brothers and a sister making noise and pestering her. At this point her father interjected. With exasperation, he reminded Tamara that she was the youngest in the family and that her older brothers and sister were serious students and seldom made any noise in the evenings. All of them were straight-A students. Tamara giggled and said they must have inherited their daddy's brains. Her father smiled and his anger immediately dissipated.

My diagnostic testing revealed that Tamara had some subtle learning deficits. She did not have a classic learning disability. Her responses to my questions indicated that she was extremely bright and that she had the aptitude and academic skills not only to succeed in school but to excel. There had to be another explanation for her poor performance. Tamara's best grade on her last report card had been a C+. She had also received two D's.

Tamara's father was the president of an electronics company. Her mother was a highly respected interior designer. Both parents were intelligent, achievement oriented, assertive, and opinionated. They reported that Tamara was becoming increasingly irresponsible and unmotivated, but they were quick to add that their daughter was "a joy to be around." My observations of the family dynamics and my discussion with Tamara and her parents convinced me that she had become a master at manipulating them. She was able to "play" them like instruments. When she perceived that they were challenging her or becoming angry, she would charm them into resignation.

Tamara's parents were perceptive enough to realize that they were being conned. They felt that their only recourse was either to monitor Tamara's work constantly or to nag her into getting the work done. This system was proving increasingly ineffectual. The phrase "Well, that's our Tamara..." had become their stock response to her irresponsibility.

I sensed that Tamara felt it was impossible to compete with her brothers and sister. I also suspected that she feared she could never fulfill her parents' expectations if she were to be judged on the basis of performance.

Despite her resistance to her parents' wishes, Tamara desperately wanted their acknowledgment. Unfortunately, she had concluded that charm and manipulation were the only means she had to achieve this recognition.

Tamara's excuses served an important pragmatic function. They permitted her to avoid having to confront an issue which terrified her: Tamara was afraid to achieve. Perceiving herself as unable to compete with her brothers and sister, she had created an alternative achievement system for herself. She had chosen to be cute instead of diligent. She used her manipulative behavior to control others and to protect herself from feeling inadequate. Yet the protection was illusory, and the system had begun to break down. Her manipulative behavior did not work as well outside her home as it did within. Her teachers refused to accept her excuses, and her schoolwork had deteriorated to the point where she was actually in danger of failing several of her courses.

Although Tamara's parents were distressed by her academic performance and behavior, they had "bought into" her manipulation. They rationalized that their daughter would somehow be able to make it through life on the strength of her personality. Tamara was smart enough to sense her parents' ambivalence. This ambivalance encouraged her to remain manipulative.

Tamara's behavior was transparent. She resorted to it because she did not feel safe and secure being herself. Before she would be willing to stop manipulating, she would have to convince herself that she was capable of achieving on the basis of ability and effort. She could then begin to redefine her role in the family. The pressure would dissipate, and Tamara could let go of her compelling need to control others. Once she discovered how bright and talented she actually was, she could simply be herself. The challenge was to help her make this discovery.

Learning to Achieve

With his very first breath of life, the newborn infant proclaims his achievement. He has survived! As he emerges into the world, the infant demands his rights. He cries out, "I'm here! I made it. I want to survive. I want nourishment and attention. You had better provide for my needs because I deserve good treatment. If you do not take care of me, you'll hear about it."

At conception, the genetic foundation for the child's potential achievement is already in place. Although complex biological forces define the child's inherited characteristics, these forces cannot prescribe what a child will do with his genetic raw material. Before the child's resources can be actualized, his genetic potential must be shaped and molded by environmental forces and life experiences. The child must be trained and then educated. He must be taught how to develop, apply, and refine his resources. If he is fortunate, he will be exposed to an environment which encourages achievement and self-actualization.

Tamara's self-defeating actions and attitudes underscored the breakdown in an environmental system which should have stimulated and supported her natural desire to achieve. Distortions in perception, inadequate communication, and scripted manipulative behaviors siphoned off the energy that she would normally have devoted to developing her potential. The energy was directed instead toward making excuses and playing games.

During the early developmental years, a child's primary job is to learn how to use his resources. The learning process begins at birth. The newborn soon discovers the phenomenon of cause and effect: if he cries, he receives attention. This basic principle will be continually reinforced throughout the child's life.

As the child's world expands, his opportunities to learn also expand. The six-month-old discovers that purposeful movement will get him from here to there. The one-year-old learns that his fingers can turn a light on and off or open a cabinet and that his hand can knock over a glass.

A child's curiosity about how things work and his realization that he has the power to cause things to happen is the primary impetus for learning. From the child's curiosity and wonderment evolves the higher-level creative problem-solving ability that is uniquely human.

As he interacts with other children, the toddler confronts other examples of cause and effect. If he takes another child's toy, he discovers that the other child will probably cry. If he takes his older sister's toy, he discovers that she will probably hit him and *he* will cry.

At five years of age, the primary educational arena shifts from home to school. The kindergartner learns how to read words and begins to master the conventions and rules which govern the use of these words. At the same time, the child is provided with a laboratory for exploring the process of socialization. This laboratory is the classroom, where thirty distinct personalities react to one another like chemicals in a flask held above a Bunsen burner. School tests the child's physical and intellectual capabilities. Can she multiply fractions? Can he do twenty push-ups? Can she get an A on the history midterm? School offers the child a continuing opportunity to compare his accomplishments with those of his peers. As he compares himself to the other children, the child will begin to develop an identity. His perceptions of his own abilities will have a profound impact on his evolving sense of himself.

The achieving child is typically the one who pushes himself to the limits of his abilities. He not only accepts the challenges inherent in the educational system, but he also intentionally creates his own challenges.

Some children become compulsive overachievers. Early in their lives, they manifest a profound need to excel and to push themselves beyond their limits. Driven by psychological and environmental forces to reach for goals that are seemingly unattainable, they become obsessed by their goals. Were they not so consumed, such barriers as the four-minute mile would never have been broken. Swimming records and college football rushing records would not be assailed, and the Bruce Jenners, Chris Everts, and Bobby Fischers would never become champions.

Compulsive overachievers are not necessarily happier or better adjusted than those who are less driven. In fact, the converse may be true. Many achievement-oriented people who push themselves unrelentingly experience great psychological stress and inner turmoil because they can never achieve total perfection. These compulsive achievers, however, frequently become our heroes and role models. While their accomplishments are admired, overachievers often pay a high physical and emotional price for their fame and success.

At the other end of the spectrum are the compulsive underachievers and nonachievers. Although many compulsive underachievers actually have the ability to succeed, they are driven by unconscious psychological forces to reject success. Tamara was a classic example. Academic achievement had become entangled with her conflicting emotions about her position in the family, her relationship with her parents, and her feelings about herself. In order to allow herself to achieve, she would first have to confront and break down the barriers she herself had erected against achievement.

Achievement and Survival

One need only read the daily newspaper to see evidence that achievement is no guarantee of happiness. The pages are full of examples of highly successful people who are unhappy, who have difficulty sustaining their marriages, who drink themselves into a stupor, or who stuff white powder into their noses every evening.

At the same time, the antitheses of achievement—nonachievement and, to a lesser degree, underachievement—do not guarantee unhappiness. They do, however, increase the probability of unhappiness. Human beings who are unable to establish and attain goals are rarely content with themselves and with life.

Certain children are selective achievers. They are willing to accept challenges and achieve only in areas which interest them or in which they have talent. For instance, a child may spend hundreds of hours perfecting his ability to dribble a basketball but may be totally unmotivated to learn algebra. Although the child may be considered an achiever by his peers, he may be regarded as an underachiever by his parents and teachers.

Other children will reject all challenges because they have doubts either about their ability or about their "right" to achieve. These children are destined to become underachievers or nonachievers.

The nature of a person's goals can offer a profound insight into that person's "sense of self." One man may aspire to be a tycoon. Another may want only sufficient money to permit him to go fishing on weekends and to retire in relative comfort at the age of sixty-two. Although these goals are clearly divergent, they both serve a vital psychological function. They establish a system of priorities, and they function to orient each person's energies.

By establishing and attaining our goals, we are able to exert a degree of power and control over our destiny. Goals also provide us with a sense of identity. We are aspiring artists, mechanics, athletes, mothers, fathers, ministers, "A" students, cosmetologists, or teachers. The attainment of our goals is a requisite to the development of self-esteem.

A human being's need for power and control over his or her life is universal. Wars and revolutions occur when the need is thwarted. By having and exercising the option to do what we want to do with our lives, we are able to take charge of our destiny.

This existential power in which we take pride is, in part, a delusion. Each person's value system and goal orientation are profoundly influenced by early childhood experiences. What happens to a child in school, at home, and on the playground can either enhance or distort the child's perceptions about himself and about the world. The child who does poorly in school, who is in conflict with herself and her parents, or who experiences little or no social acceptance must inevitably make life choices which reflect the influence of these negative experiences.

Many adults who disavow goals and reject achievement do so because of painful lessons they learned when they were five or six years old. If as children they concluded that they could not or did not deserve to achieve, they will probably carry this negative mind set with them throughout their lives. Although they may believe that they are in control of their choices about careers and goals, in reality they have unconsciously adjusted their value system so that it is congruent with their perceptions about themselves.* Tamara was a perfect case in point. Her

---

*Throughout this book I consistently use the term "unconscious." In specific instances "subconscious" might actually be more precise. The subconscious mind is defined in Webster's Third New International Dictionary as "mental activities just below the threshold of consciousness." The unconscious mind is defined in the same dictionary as "the greater part of the psychic apparatus accumulated through life experiences that is not ordinarily available to consciousness yet is manifested as a powerful motive force in overt behavior."

manipulative and self-defeating behavior reflected her fears and insecurities and not her conscious choice.

Goals serve to focus and direct intellectual, emotional, and physical energies. The nature of a person's achievement orientation helps the person to define his own identity. In tandem, goals and achievement function as a sort of psychological adhesive that binds the diverse energies of the human spirit together and permits that spirit to soar.

The desire to achieve is one of the more powerful forces programed by nature into children. The instincts to survive, to procreate, to learn, to create, and to achieve guarantee the continuation of the species. The child who cannot learn to control, balance, and channel these forces is at risk physically and psychologically.

The Pluses and Minuses of Achievement

The need to achieve can impose a heavy burden on a child. Although the potentially capable child has many advantages, he is often on the receiving end of a great deal of pressure. Parents and teachers tend to raise their level of expectations when they perceive untapped talent in a child. Sometimes they overreact and establish a standard of performance which is excessive and unreasonable.

The potentially capable child is expected to achieve, and his accomplishments are usually closely monitored. Should his performance slip, he becomes the immediate object of attention and concern. While the high expectations of parents and teachers can be an inspiration, they can also be the source of serious emotional stress.

Children at both ends of the achievement spectrum are particularly vulnerable to emotional stress. Just as the achieving child is acutely aware of the positive expectations of his parents, teachers, and friends, the underachieving child is equally aware of the often negative expectations of parents, teachers, and friends. External pressure typically triggers internal pressure. If extreme, this pressure can motivate a child or debilitate him.

Some children respond positively to external or internal pressure, and others respond negatively. The more intense the pressure, the greater is the potential for achievement and, at the same time, the greater the risk of emotional damage. Certain children appear to respond to pressure by developing an almost obsessive need to achieve. They are driven to push themselves to the limits. Other children respond differently to intense pressure: they simply shut down.

Environment and Achievement

A close examination of a child's environment often illuminates the nature of a child's achievement orientation. The value system of a child's family, community, and peers invariably influences the child. Usually, a child will orient himself toward achievement when the environmental conditions support achievement. We are not surprised when the daughter of a judge decides to apply to law school or when the son of an actress decides to become an actor.

There are, however, glaring exceptions to the environmental explanation for achievement. In their autobiographies, many highly successful people have described conditions during their formative years which should have theoretically discouraged achievement. Some were the children of alcoholics or physically abusive parents. Others grew up in abject poverty or in ghettos where education was not highly valued. Despite these negative environmental conditions, and perhaps in response to them, these people developed a strong goal orientation during childhood and ultimately became leaders in their respective fields.

These exceptions notwithstanding, the influence of family and environment on a child's achievement orientation cannot be discounted. Although a child may reject his family's value system or recoil from parental pressure, the typical child assimilates these values. A seven-year-old girl from a success-oriented family, for example, may demonstrate a natural facility in tennis. Her parents and coach may conclude that she has the potential to become a superstar, and they strongly encourage her to work toward this goal. Recognizing her own natural talent and influenced by her parents and coach, the child decides to devote herself to tennis. She throws herself into her training program. Ultimately, she becomes a successful and admired athlete who makes millions of dollars and whose picture appears on cereal boxes.

Although the seven-year-old's decision to become a professional tennis player may have been made freely, the decision was undoubtedly strongly influenced on an unconscious level by the child's desire to please her parents and coach. Young children crave acknowledgment and affirmation from the adults they most love and admire, and they are often driven to make these adults proud of them. The accomplishments and success of many dentists, physicians, attorneys, accountants, and musicians can undoubtedly be attributed to family value systems and to a child's natural desire to please his parents. Ironically, some ostensibly successful professionals have been disillusioned and dissatisfied with the payoffs of the career choices they made for the express purpose of pleasing others.

Children's goals are not and should not be chiseled in stone. As children mature, their perceptions change and evolve. Their goals also change and evolve. Very few of the millions of six-year-olds who aspire to be astronauts or professional baseball players will ever actually achieve these goals.

The Symbolic Nature of Goals

Children's goals can become enmeshed in those of their parents. When goals do become enmeshed, they often assume symbolic importance with profound emotional implications. A father, for instance, may have always fantasized about becoming a professional athlete. Although he may have lacked the talent, the size, or the coordination to attain his objective, he may become convinced that his child can achieve what he was unable to achieve. The parent may become obsessed with instilling his own thwarted goal in his child.

When a parent superimposes his own repressed desire onto his child, he turns that desire into a symbol. Realizing the symbolic importance of the goal, the child may feel compelled to fulfill his father's expectations so that he can be worthy of his father's love and respect.

Symbolism, even parentally imposed symbolism, can of course serve as a powerful motivational force. Were it not for the symbolic importance of goals, few children would be willing to spend four hours a day practicing the violin or swimming laps in a pool. But symbolism can also warp a child's perceptions. Failure to achieve a goal that the child feels is important to a parent can be devastating. The child may feel that the parent's acceptance is conditional on his achieving the goal. The fear of failure may inspire him or paralyze him. If he does fail, he may become convinced that he is worthless.

The child who abandons a goal which he perceives as important to his parents or to other respected adults often experiences anxiety and pain. He may perceive this defection as a defeat, not only for him but also for his parents. If he is convinced that he has let down the people most important in his life, he may be tortured by guilt.

Although a child's fear about disappointing his parents may be exaggerated or imaginary, in many cases the fear is altogether justified. Many parents identify so strongly with their child's goals and achievements that they construe the child's abandonment of a goal as a personal failure.

The goal-oriented child who concludes that he has let down his parents, teachers, or coaches is at risk emotionally. He may become convinced that he deserves to be loved for what he achieves and not for who he is. When the child fails to achieve, he will probably experience a gamut of conscious and unconscious emotions which may range from guilt and frustration to resentment and depression. Anger is often the emotion underlying all of these feelings. Although the child may not be consciously aware of his anger, it will profoundly affect his perceptions of himself and the world. If he expresses his anger, he will probably misbehave. If he represses the anger, he will probably sabotage himself.

Children may be intentionally or unintentionally coerced or manipulated by parents, teachers, or coaches. These adults may conclude that the child has potential that would otherwise be wasted unless his energies are properly channeled. For example, a child may have excellent mathematical aptitude, and his parents and teachers conclude that he should become an engineer. Although the child may enjoy literature, music, and the arts, he accepts that becoming an engineer is what he should do with his life. He studies math and physics in college and avoids the humanities. Ultimately, he becomes a successful engineer. At the age of thirty-five, however, he discovers that he doesn't enjoy engineering. In fact, he discovers that despite his facility in math and science and despite his accomplishments as an engineer, he has always hated engineering. He realizes that what he really wants to do is to go back to graduate school and earn a degree in literature. His wife and friends conclude that he is going through a midlife crisis.

Equating Achievement with Health

The capacity to achieve can create the illusion of social and emotional health. Parents and teachers may assume that the child who can achieve is necessarily happy, well adjusted, and confident. Unfortunately, achievement does not always yield these benefits. Some children who achieve in one arena are not able to achieve in others. One child may be successful academically but be socially inept. Another child may have great athletic skills but struggle academically. To assume that the achieving child is always in harmony with himself is a mistake. Although proficiency and achievement in a particular area can bolster a child's self-esteem and self-confidence, and sustain the child when he encounters setbacks, they do not guarantee self-esteem and self-confidence. The academic superstar may be distraught because he has no friends, and the athletic superstar may be convinced that she is stupid.

The parental instinct to orient a child toward achievement is normal and natural. Providing guidance, support, and encouragement for a child is one of parenting's most important responsibilities. Most parents recognize that academic skills, confidence, and desire are essential components in the equation which produces achievement and self-actualization. Most parents also recognize that the child who achieves and actualizes himself will enjoy more of life's rewards.

Encouraging a child to achieve, however, is quite distinct from encouraging a child to become obsessive about achieving. And encouraging a child to establish goals is also quite distinct from coercing a child into striving for goals which fulfill the parents' needs, but not necessarily those of the child. Children who acquire the capacity to achieve have acquired a powerful resource. Perceptive parents and skillful teachers can play a vital role in developing this resource. But like most resources, the ultimate efficacy hinges on how the resource is cultivated and applied.

● **PARENTING SUGGESTIONS**

● *Resist the temptation to impose your fantasies on your child.*

You are serving your child when you encourage her to establish and attain goals. When you coerce or manipulate her into striving for the goals that have eluded you in your own life, you are doing your child a disservice. Encourage her to establish goals which are compatible with her own talents and desires.

● *Beware of equating obsessive achievement with happiness.*

For most people in Western society, the capacity to achieve is integral to happiness and self-esteem. When the need to achieve becomes an obsession, it may produce the opposite effect—unhappiness and precarious mental health. Parents who overtly or covertly encourage their children to become obsessive achievers may be imposing a great emotional burden. Although some superachievers may be happy, others appear to derive little enjoyment from the fruits of their efforts.

Identifying Achieving and Underachieving Children

Collin: He Had Crossed the Bridge

The nine-year-old stuck his head through the doorway to my office and smiled.

"Can I show you something?"

"Sure. Come in, Collin."

"Look at my report card."

"You received all A's and B's!"

"I know. My mom and dad are so proud of me."

"You should be proud too."

"I am. The teacher put me on the honor roll. She says I've made more improvement than anyone in the class. Dad is going to take me on a river rafting trip this summer as a reward."

"Do you remember how much difficulty you were having six months ago?"

"I know. School is fun now. I'm the best math student in the class. I usually get my problems done first. And I don't make mistakes with subtraction. Even multiplication is easy. I know up to my ten tables. And reading is easy too. I can't wait to start long division. I'm going to go to Stanford like my dad. And I'm going to be an engineer too. Or maybe a racecar driver."

"I'm really proud of you, Collin. Thanks for sharing your

report card with me. It's obvious that you need to graduate from our program. You no longer need our help. We're going to miss you. Because you've worked so hard and done so well, I know that your teacher will want me to give you the Outstanding School Improvement Medal."

"That means I've won all the medals that you guys have."

"You've deserved all of them. Collin, we have to graduate you because we can't afford to buy any more medals. We're going broke."

After Collin left, I leaned back in my chair and savored the moment. I remembered the shy, uncertain little boy who had first entered my office six months earlier with his parents. He had sat dejectedly at the table attempting to be as inconspicuous as possible. He refused to make eye contact with me, and his answers to my questions were almost inaudible. When I asked him if he was single or married, he looked at me incredulously, smiled, and then started to giggle. "Boy, my mom would kill me." The ice had been broken, and I knew we would be friends.

Collin had shut down in school. He was convinced that he was dumb. His parents recognized that their son was bright, and they had insisted that he be tested for a learning problem. With reluctance, the school authorities agreed to do so. The tests revealed some subtle skills deficits, but no specific symptoms of a learning disability. The school psychologist explained that Collin did not qualify for special assistance because he had scored approximately six months below grade level in math and reading. Children had to be a minimum of two years below grade level before they could be considered. Most of the other students in the class, however, were functioning two years above grade level, and Collin was losing the battle to keep up.

At first, his parents were only mildly perturbed about their son's difficulties in school. They became alarmed when the teacher suggested retention. They knew that Collin had an IQ of 141. During first and second grade, he had been anxious to learn and positive about school. Now, he had begun to dislike school intensely, and his teacher was suggesting that he was immature and unmotivated.

My tests confirmed the school's assessment. Although Collin

did not have a significant learning problem, he did have difficulty concentrating and he had subtle memory, reading, and math deficits. Collin was clearly floundering. He had not figured out how to compensate for the deficits, and he was becoming increasingly demoralized.

I recommended a two-hour-per-week program that would focus on shoring up Collin's deficiencies. I knew that the prognosis was excellent because his learning deficits were not severe, but I also realized that the success of the remediation program would hinge on our ability to build up Collin's self-confidence. We needed to convince him that he could succeed. Once he realized how bright and capable he was, I was certain that there would be no stopping him.

The teachers challenged and prodded Collin. They clearly communicated that they expected him to prevail over these challenges. They insisted that he succeed at every task he undertook. An almost immediate transformation occurred. Collin was taught practical memory techniques, and he soon realized that he could not only do what we asked, he could do the projects better than anyone in the class. He ultimately developed memory skills which surpassed those of the teachers. Each achievement was acknowledged with lavish praise, and Collin would beam as he left class.

Within a month, this fourth grader was creating his own challenges. He wanted the hardest math problems we could make up. When he did well in class, he insisted that we reward him by giving him seventh-grade materials to read. The tentative, insecure child emerged from his cocoon as a beautiful Monarch butterfly, and he began to soar.

Zest and the Achieving Child

A special fuel propels achievement-oriented children. The fuel contains a powerful additive called zest, and this unique quality has the capacity to reproduce itself. Achievement produces zest, and zest in turn produces achievement. By the time Collin graduated from our program, his tank was filled with zest.

A child's ZQ (zest quotient) is distinct from his IQ (intelligence quotient). Whereas a child's IQ is a theoretical measure of his potential to achieve academically, his ZQ is a measure of his self-perception. Although there are exceptions, the greater the child's awareness of his ability and potential to achieve, the higher his zest quotient.

Zest manifests itself in the free-flowing energy, spontaneity, and joy characteristic of people who like themselves and who enjoy life. It derives from emotional harmony, confidence, self-acceptance, self-esteem, and self-fulfillment.

Zest is intrinsically linked to achievement. The child with a high ZQ typically establishes and reaches for goals. His willingness to do so derives from a basic faith in himself. He recognizes his ability, and this recognition permits and encourages him to take calculated risks in order to attain his goals. Although he may not be consciously aware of his innate talent, he at least has an unconscious awareness of his capacity to achieve. The child may not analyze why he is goal oriented, but he knows intuitively that he can do what he sets out to do.

When he first entered my office, Collin was at the opposite end of the emotional spectrum from the child who is convinced he can succeed. His high IQ was offset by a virtually nonexistent ZQ. Having concluded that his learning deficits were insurmountable and that he was incapable of achieving, this nine-year-old boy had unconsciously resigned himself to a futile struggle. This sense of futility had destroyed his zest. Success and achievement ultimately permitted him to develop a new perception of himself, and his resignation was replaced by zest.

Zest manifests itself in many forms. One child may be enthusiastic about writing a poem. Another may be intent on perfecting her tennis serve or solving a difficult algebraic equation. The primary characteristics that distinguish achievement-oriented children with a high ZQ from other children include:

1. Orientation toward goals
2. Positive expectations
3. Confidence
4. Resiliency

   5. Self-discipline
   6. Pride in accomplishment
   7. Academic proficiency
   8. Endurance
   9. Courage

   Some exceptional children seem to exude these characteristics almost from birth. These are the naturally gifted youngsters who recognize their own abilities at an early age; they
perceive that they have a mission and sense intuitively that
they are destined for success. If exposed to environmental
conditions that are nurturing and supportive, these children
may become the Nobel Prize–winning scientists, the com-
posers, novelists, and statesmen who someday make significant
contributions to society.
   Most children are not endowed with such exceptional genetic gifts. In order to achieve, these less gifted children have
to work harder. Their extra effort compensates for whatever
they may lack in natural talent. Ironically, many children who
have only average natural ability ultimately contribute as much,
if not more, than those who have superior natural talent.
   Millions of other potentially capable children fail to discover
that they too possess the ability to achieve. Because of their
marginal performance, the parents and teachers of these children may conclude erroneously that poor or mediocre work is
the best that can be reasonably expected. Perceiving the lowered level of expectations of their parents and teachers, the
children accordingly lower their own level of expectations.
Lacking evidence to the contrary, they learn to accept their
"limitations" and, as a consequence, they never develop the
desire to achieve.

The Path to Achievement

The universal desire of all parents is that their children be
happy, self-actualized, and self-confident. A child's capacity
to achieve is a prerequisite to attaining these objectives.
   The first opportunities and payoffs for achievement occur

very early in a child's life. The infant recognizes his parents, takes his first tentative steps, and utters his first words. These major developmental milestones are greeted with acclaim and joy. Later, in kindergarten, other accomplishments are acknowledged. The child's drawings, his attempts at printing his name, his newly acquired reading and arithmetic skills provide repeated opportunities for praise and affirmation. This vital recognition and acknowledgment create the psychological cornerstones of self-acceptance, self-esteem, and self-confidence.

The need to achieve and the need for affirmation are two of the basic sources of human motivation. The beaming face of a toddler as his parents clap in appreciation of a newly acquired skill testifies to the psychological importance of recognition. A child quickly learns to associate achievements with the positive acknowledgment he is given by parents, teachers, and friends.

The child's realization of his power to elicit a response occurs during the first moments of life. The newborn infant discovers that when he is hungry or in discomfort, he need only cry for his mother in order to have his needs satisfied. The infant's realization that he can cause his mother to respond imprints the phenomenon of cause and effect on his unconscious mind. The child has begun to develop a sense of his own power to attain his desired goals. The foundation for achievement is established.

Later, the child will discover that he need not cry in order to open the floodgates to acknowledgment, affirmation, and praise. All he has to do is smile, and he will be appreciated. If he takes a step, the praise will be even more effusive. The child's realization that he can elicit these responses will have a profound impact on his emotional development. His association of achievement with affirmation creates a powerful incentive for continued achievement.

When parents acknowledge their child's efforts, they are helping him recognize and appreciate his own intrinsic value. During the early formative years, parents serve as both judge and jury. Their appreciation and confirmation of their child will profoundly influence the child's evolving sense of his own self-worth.

When teachers acknowledge a student for his accomplishments, they too are helping the child to develop an appreciation of his own intrinsic value. The teacher's judgments about the quality of the child's work can profoundly affect the child's feelings about his own value and efficacy as a person. Like the child's parents, the teacher must also bear the awesome responsibility of serving as the child's judge and jury.

Achieving children have the luxury of an ongoing support system. Because they achieve, they are usually the recipients of praise and affirmation. This acknowledgment of their accomplishments encourages them to continue achieving.

Although underachieving children have a special need for affirmation, they generally receive few positive strokes. The denial of affirmation by parents and teachers is seldom intentional. Because the accomplishments of underachieving children are typically meager, parents and teachers may find little to applaud.

Without positive reinforcement, there is a real danger that the struggling child may conclude that he is incapable of success and unworthy of appreciation. Both the immediate and long-term psychological consequences of this conclusion can be disastrous. Negative expectations have an unfortunate tendency to become self-fulfilling and self-perpetuating.

The Role of Parents in Assessing Their Child

The parents of children who are struggling to achieve have four major responsibilities. The first is to find out why their child is underachieving. The second is to procure help for the child. The third and fourth responsibilities overlap and involve strategic planning. The parents of a struggling child must purposefully create contexts in which the child can experience success. They must then make a conscious effort to acknowledge the child for even meager accomplishments. This acknowledgment is essential to the formation of self-esteem. (Methods for structuring success and building self-esteem in underachieving children will be examined in Chapter 13.)

The first step in the process of redirecting the negative expectations of the underachieving child is to identify the source of the child's underachievement. This identification process may be difficult, especially if the underlying problems are nonspecific or subtle. Blatant problems are generally easier to identify than more diffuse problems.

Early identification of underachieving children is at best tentative. Some children who lag behind developmentally are simply slow starters. Distinguishing these children from those with more serious developmental delays can be difficult, even for professionals.

Developmental immaturity (age-inappropriate behavior), perceptual deficits (difficulty remembering or associating new information with already learned information), motor skills deficits (poor coordination), concentration deficits (inability to focus and pay attention for reasonable periods of time), and hyperactivity (excessive or frenetic body movement) can pose significant barriers to achievement. These symptoms are usually clear indications that a child is not processing sensory information efficiently and effectively. Although perceptive teachers, parents, and professionals may be able to identify blatant deficiencies in preschool and kindergarten children, they may fail to detect or disregard more subtle symptoms. These symptoms may not begin to trigger alarms until second or third grade. By that time, the child may have already established an entrenched pattern of underachievement or nonachievement.

Despite the difficulty inherent in detecting potential underachievement in younger children, detection *is* possible in preschool or kindergarten. Clearly, the more obvious and specific the child's deficits, the greater the chances of early recognition.

The word "struggle" is the key in the identification process. An alarm should go off when parents and teachers see that a child is struggling to keep up with his classmates or to complete projects that are reasonable and age-appropriate. Sloppiness, inattentiveness, poor gross-motor coordination (climbing, jumping, skipping, etc.), and poor fine-motor coordination (printing, coloring, cutting) are all clues to possible developmental delay that may lead to subsequent underachievement.

To defer finding help for the struggling child in the hope that he may simply be a slow starter is risky. Although it is possible that the child may resolve his problems without assistance and ultimately pick up momentum, it is also possible that without help the child may never achieve at a level commensurate with his potential.

Is My Child an Underachiever?

The following Underachievement Checklist is designed to help you determine whether or not your child is manifesting symptoms of underachievement. Place the appropriate number after each characteristic and then total the points. A chart at the end of the checklist will help you interpret your child's score.

The checklist is intended primarily for children in grades one through twelve. You will note that most of the characteristics described on the checklist relate to behaviors and attitudes associated with academic performance, and consequently the checklist has limited value in assessing children in preschool and kindergarten. The checklist may have more predictive value in the case of younger children who are enrolled in highly academic kindergarten programs.

UNDERACHIEVEMENT CHECKLIST

CODE: 0 = NEVER   1 = SOMETIMES   2 = OFTEN   3 = ALWAYS

---

1. My child's schoolwork is sloppy and illegible. _____

2. My child's projects are often incomplete. _____

3. My child procrastinates. _____

4. My child is having difficulty keeping up with his or her class. _____

5. My child's work is not handed in on time.　　　————

6. My child is disorganized at home.　　　————

7. My child is disorganized at school.　　　————

8. My child is irresponsible.　　　————

9. My child is forgetful.　　　————

10. My child lacks pride in his or her work.　　　————

11. My child shows little motivation.　　　————

12. My child avoids academic work.　　　————

13. My child makes excuses for poor performance.　　　————

14. My child avoids challenges.　　　————

15. My child lacks self-confidence.　　　————

16. My child becomes easily discouraged.　　　————

17. My child abandons difficult projects.　　　————

18. My child is easily frustrated.　　　————

19. My child appears to be functioning below his
    or her potential.

　　　　　　　　　　　————

　　　　　　　　Total Points　　　————

INTERPRETING THE CHECKLIST

**Total
Score**

0–2　Your child is not manifesting symptoms of underachievement.

3–7　Your child is manifesting subtle symptoms of potential underachievement. His or her school performance should be monitored. The Underachievement Checklist should be used periodically to reassess your child.

8–20　Your child is manifesting moderate symptoms of underachievement and, perhaps, a learning problem. The score should be considered a dan-

ger signal. Your child's school performance should
be very closely monitored, and the checklist
should be used periodically to reassess your child.
(See Learning Problems Checklist on page 138.)

21–57   Your child is manifesting significant symptoms
of either underachievement or a specific learning
disability. He or she is at risk academically and
emotionally, and active intervention is recommended. You should request that your child be
evaluated by the school psychologist. (See Chapters 6 and 7 for specific recommendations and
strategies. See also Learning Problems Checklist
on page 138.)

In some cases, a child's initial score on the checklist may
be relatively low, but his parents may subsequently detect a
deterioration in his school performance. Parents perceiving
such a deterioration should use the checklist to reassess their
child.

Parents who conclude that counterproductive patterns of
behavior and performance are persisting are advised to initiate
a conference with the child's teacher. Ideally, the school psychologist and the principal should participate in this conference.

The identification of potential underachievers below the age
of six can be difficult. Parents should be alert to patterns
of behavior and performance which could later interfere with
academic performance. Primary symptoms include distractibility, irresponsibility, impulsivity, disorganization, sloppiness, poor motivation, and resistance to learning.

The Complacent Underachiever

Not all underachieving children struggle. Some children appear quite complacent about meager success in school or on
the playing field. An extremely bright child, for instance, may
seem satisfied with B's or even C's on her report card. Another

child may appear unconcerned about the fact that the soccer coach rarely uses him during games. There are several possible explanations for these reactions:

1. Some children have personal interests which preoccupy them and are uninterested in the more traditional concerns and pursuits of other children.
2. Some children decide at an early age that they do not like to work hard.
3. Some children unconsciously accept their deficiencies and adjust their level of expectations accordingly.
4. Some children appear temperamentally unsuited to strive intensely for goals and to compete.
5. Some children identify with social groups that reject the traditional means of achievement.

Achievement requires a mixture of egoism (sense of self), desire, intensity, and commitment. The easygoing child may eschew achievement and avoid challenges that involve risks, emotional intensity, and effort because his individual value system is not oriented toward achievement. It is also possible that the seemingly easygoing child may reject challenges and achievement because of unconscious psychological factors.

For example, a high school sophomore with demonstrated scientific aptitude may choose not to apply herself in science and may prefer to devote herself to swimming or to French. Her decision to pursue swimming and to reject science may reflect a well-reasoned value judgment or esthetic judgment. When she established her priorities, science was not high on the list.

The same student, however, may choose to reject science without establishing alternative priorities and goals. She may appear to be content to do nothing. Each afternoon she comes home from school and spends hours talking on the telephone or watching TV. A close examination of her underlying motives for not developing any personal goals will probably reveal psychological factors that have nothing to do with values or esthetic judgments. She may be afraid to fail, or she may be afraid to succeed. If she takes a risk and tries to achieve, she might not do well. On the other hand, she may realize that if she applies herself and begins to achieve, she would then be expected to continue to work hard and achieve. Her unwillingness to establish goals might also reflect a lack of self-confidence and a reluctance to compete. Unwilling to confront the underlying issues, she may rationalize that her decision to avoid achievement reflects a conscious choice.

Some children choose to underachieve because of social pressure. A teenager may identify with a certain peer group that rejects academic achievement. His friends may value sports, motorcycles, surfing, or fast cars and have little respect for those who study and strive to achieve academically. If a bright, academically capable child wants to be accepted by a non-academically-oriented peer group, he may feel compelled to underachieve.

Certain children identify with social groups that reject all forms of achievement. Those children usually share feelings of inadequacy, alienation, insecurity, and resentment toward adults. They are typically highly impressionable and easily influenced. Their behavior and their dress reflect how they perceive themselves. The group dynamics reinforce their alienation and provide them with an alternative value system and social identity.

Parents who are concerned about their child's level of achievement must wrestle with several crucial issues before they can effectively intervene. These include:

1. Is our underachieving child content and at peace with himself?
2. Do we perceive his lack of achievement orientation as a reflection of an underlying psychological problem?
3. Do we see our child as suppressing his desire to achieve?
4. Are we convinced that our child would be happier if he were more intensely achievement directed?
5. Do we feel that our child is wasting his potential?
6. Are we concerned that our child will one day regret his complacency about or rejection of achievement?

Deciding whether or not an underachieving child requires assistance demands intuition and judgment. The implications of this judgment call can be profound. Parents who become convinced that their child is wasting valuable potential and will ultimately regret this waste later in life are justified in intervening. If, on the other hand, parents conclude that their child is basically content with himself and with his level of achievement, they must be willing to examine their own attitudes about achievement, performance standards, and expectations. Before they attempt to influence their child, they must decide whether or not they have the right to impose their achievement values on the child.

The complacent underachiever who likes himself and who is not impeded by underlying emotional or academic problems has the option to become more intensely achievement oriented later in life. Many highly successful people do not begin to achieve until they are inspired. The timetable for this inspiration can vary significantly from person to person.

Making a proper judgment call about whether or not to intervene demands good parental instincts. In order to acquire these instincts, parents must not only understand their child, they must also understand themselves.

Different Types of Underachievement

Underachievement manifests itself in three basic forms:

Generalized underachievement. The child who manifests generalized underachievement functions at a level below his potential in many areas of his life. He may have athletic ability, academic ability, and/or artistic ability, yet fail to perform commensurate with his potential. Although he may "get by," he seldom excels. Typically, parents and teachers attribute his underachievement to laziness, irresponsibility, or insufficient motivation.

Selective underachievement. The selectively underachieving child develops his ability in one or more areas but functions marginally in other areas. He may choose to perfect his musical skills because he has natural musical talent but avoid athletics or specific academic subjects because he lacks natural facility or interest in these subjects.

Nonachievement. The nonachieving child typically has poor academic skills, poor social skills, and low self-esteem. The problems of the nonachieving child are often compounded by irresponsibility. This self-defeating behavior functions as a psychological defense mechanism. The chronically irresponsible child is attempting to protect himself from frustration and failure. The defense mechanism offers little protection; it simply guarantees continued failure. The child himself does not perceive this paradox. Before the nonachieving child will risk establishing goals and seeking success, his learning and/ or emotional problems must be resolved.

The Four Common Sources of Underachievement

Learning problems. The child who cannot learn efficiently must function at a level below his potential. Poor reading skills, poor math skills, poor writing skills, poor concentration, poor study skills, and poor organizational skills can pose seemingly insurmountable obstacles to achievement.

Family problems. The child who experiences dissension and stress at home will have difficulty functioning efficiently in school. The strain created by family problems is carried to the classroom and can interfere with academic achievement. Emotionally charged conflicts at home distort a child's perspective about himself and his ability. The effects of a messy divorce or a bitter child custody proceeding, for example, generally manifest themselves in school and on the playground.

Emotional problems. Children who are experiencing emotional turmoil are seldom able to work at a level commensurate with their potential. Fear, insecurity, anger, and depression divert the emotional energy required for achievement. The unhappy child who is in conflict with himself seldom possesses the self-esteem and self-confidence requisite to achievement.

Cultural influences. Certain subcultures do not provide support systems that encourage traditional achievement. For example, children who belong to gangs rarely achieve at the same level as children who have joined the science club or the school newspaper in high school. Children from poverty-stricken ghettos may also lack realistic role models for traditional achievement. If they feel that it is futile to establish goals and to strive for success, they will either accept underachievement or nonachievement as their fate in life or will strive for those symbols of achievement that are realistic in their subculture.

The many factors and variables which can cause or contribute to underachievement make it difficult to generalize about the "typical" underachiever. Before parents can help their underachieving child, they must first understand how and why children achieve. These are the subjects of the next chapter.

● PARENTING SUGGESTIONS

● *Be alert to indications that your child is struggling.*

Monitor your child's performance and ask penetrating questions of the teachers and other professionals who work with your child.

● *Attempt to identify the source of your child's underachievement.*

Before you can intervene effectively, you must understand not only your child, but also yourself and your own value system.

● *Acknowledge and affirm your child.*

Structure opportunities in which your child can succeed. Don't hesitate to give praise.

3 How Children Achieve

Erik: He Refused to Accept His Counselor's Advice

The sixteen-year-old entering my office was clearly depressed.
He made no attempt to project his normal charm and friend-
liness. We were meeting at the request of Erik's father. He
had called to tell me that Erik had suffered a serious setback
in school and that he was very discouraged.

Erik had been receiving learning assistance at our center for
approximately six months. Prior to enrolling, he had been
tutored privately for eleven years. Because of this help, he had
somehow been able to meet the stiff requirements of the private
school he had attended. But his academic performance had
always been marginal. Now a sophomore in an academically
accelerated private high school, Erik was still struggling.

Erik had always been conscientious, and he persevered despite his barely passing grades. He seemed to have accepted
the fact that he would have to work harder than the other
students. In spite of his efforts, the struggle had become increasingly acute, and his parents asked me to evaluate him.
My diagnostic tests revealed a profile of moderate learning
deficiencies. His skills were approximately a year below grade
level in most areas, and his deficiencies were quite incapacitating given the school's college-preparatory curriculum.

After testing Erik, I recommended a comprehensive re-mediation program that emphasized basic academic skills and study skills. An individualized tutorial program was designed to help with his French, English, and biology courses. Within two months Erik had begun to show remarkable improvement. Everyone—the clinical staff, the tutors, Erik's parents, and Erik himself—was thrilled with his progress. For the first time in his life, Erik was receiving B's and occasional A's on some of his tests and reports.

Erik had decided that he wanted to go to a four-year college. In order to qualify for admission, he had chosen college-preparatory courses as opposed to the less rigorous general education courses offered at his school. Although the advanced courses were difficult for him and increased the pressure, he never complained.

Erik had just completed the second semester of his sopho-more year. Algebra I and biology had been a real struggle for him, but he was determined to take algebra II and chemistry during his junior year. When he discussed his proposed courses with his counselor, the counselor vetoed the plan. He pointed out to Erik that he had received a C— in both algebra I and biology. He felt that it was unrealistic for him to expect that he would be able to pass the more difficult algebra II and chemistry courses. He also told Erik that he might not be college material and advised him to be more realistic about his goals.

Erik tried to explain to the counselor that he was now re-ceiving intensive tutorial assistance. School was becoming less difficult for him. He expressed his conviction that he would not only make it through the courses, but might actually be able to get B's in both classes. The counselor was unconvinced. It was the school policy not to permit students to take advanced courses unless they received grades of C or better in the less advanced courses. In order to contravene this policy Erik would need the written authorization of his biology and math teach-ers.

Erik produced these authorizations, but the counselor then insisted that the heads of the math department and the science department provide authorization. Because of the counselor's attitude, Erik began to have misgivings about his goals. He had also begun to have misgivings about himself.

As we talked, I could see the devastating effect of the counselor's intransigence. The following is an approximate recounting of my conversation with Erik.

LJG:	You slammed against a wall, didn't you?
ERIK:	It all seems worthless now. All the work. The counselor has made up his mind that I am not college material.
LJG:	You feel he's put you in a little cubby-hole.
ERIK:	Yeah. What's the sense of fighting.
LJG:	You're tempted to give up, then. You'll accept what your counselor said.
ERIK:	I got authorization from the teachers. Now he's saying that's not good enough. It's like the counselor doesn't believe that I can do it.
LJG:	I guess you have no alternative but to accept his opinion. You might as well just accept the fact that he's decided you shouldn't go to a four-year college.
ERIK:	What right does he have to tell me what I can do and can't do? How does he know how smart I am or how hard I'm willing to work?
LJG:	Two good questions.
ERIK:	I've made progress. For the first time I'm getting decent grades. The only reason I got a C− in both courses is because of the work I did at the beginning of the semester. My recent grades on quizzes and tests were much better. I got a C on the algebra final and a C+ on the biology final. The tutoring is helping. I finally am beginning to understand algebra. The study skills

	class taught me how to study for the biology tests.
LJG:	Then you feel the counselor is being unfair?
ERIK:	Yes!
LJG:	Do you have any options?
ERIK:	I could take the easier courses.
LJG:	Do you really think you could handle chemistry and algebra II?
ERIK:	It would be rough. But I could do it.
LJG:	Have you spoken to the department chairmen?
ERIK:	Not yet. I'm afraid they'll say no.
LJG:	And if they do?
ERIK:	I'd have to take the easier courses.
LJG:	What about convincing them? Do you think you could do that?
ERIK:	Maybe.
LJG:	Do you want me to talk to your counselor? There's no question in my mind that you can pass those courses. Now the question is, What do you want to do about this setback?
ERIK:	I'm going to fight.
LJG:	Good. Let's prepare your case.

Because he persisted, Erik was finally permitted to take algebra II and chemistry. He received a B− in both courses. He is still planning to go to a four-year college.

The Ability to Achieve

Predicting a child's ability to achieve is akin to predicting the weather. Despite satellite photos and sophisticated equipment, meteorologists still make mistakes. It sometimes rains when it's supposed to be sunny, and it is sometimes sunny when it's supposed to rain.

Despite highly refined testing procedures, educators' predictions about children's potential can be mistaken. There are countless examples of potentially capable students who fail to live up to the expectations of their parents and teachers, while seemingly less able students achieve a level that far exceeds everyone's expectations.

As Erik clearly demonstrated, effort and determination can enable a child to overcome or compensate for seemingly insurmountable deficiencies. In spite of his learning difficulties and in spite of the barriers erected by his counselor, this highly motivated teenager not only passed the advanced courses, he actually received a B – in each class. By basing his assessment of Erik's potential ability exclusively on his past record, the counselor neglected to consider Erik's personality.

An important distinction must be made between a child's potential ability and his developed ability. Potential ability does not always transform itself into developed ability. This inconsistency raises serious questions about the predictive value of measuring a child's potential ability.

In attempting to determine a child's potential, educators usually focus on intelligence, personality, and environmental influences. A child of above-average intelligence who has the "appropriate" temperament and who is exposed to conducive environmental influences would be expected to have high potential. Conversely, a child of normal or below-normal intelligence who does not have the appropriate temperament and who is not exposed to conducive environmental influences is usually considered to have low potential. Although these predictions have general validity, they may prove to be inaccurate in specific cases. There is an inherent difficulty in predicting the intensity and impact of a particular variable in the achievement equation. For instance, a child of average intelligence who is exposed to an environment which does not encourage achievement may, nevertheless, become highly motivated and achieve far more than might normally be anticipated.

In fairness to Erik's counselor, it must be pointed out that his assessment formula was not capricious. The guidelines were undoubtedly developed as a result of past experiences with thousands of students. The school administration knew that most students who perform marginally in basic college-preparatory courses usually do poorly in more advanced courses. The assessment formula was, nevertheless, flawed because it had become inflexible. In Erik's case the formula failed to take into consideration three important factors: his desire, his intensive learning assistance program, and his progress.

Transforming Potential Ability into Developed Ability

Potential ability may be symbolically represented as the product of a "chemical" equation:

**Genetics + Environment + Psychological factors =
Potential ability**

Imagine pouring into a flask all of the genetic characteristics with which a child is endowed. Then imagine pouring in all the learned psychological characteristics. The cultural and family influences to which the child will be exposed are then added. Finally, the flask is heated over a flame and a chemical reaction occurs. Potential ability is created.

Two new elements—desire and effort—can then be poured into the bubbling flask. These two elements are the catalysts that convert potential ability into developed ability. This reaction can also be represented by an equation:

Potential ability + Desire + Effort = Developed ability

Unless desire and effort are added to the flask, developed ability will not be produced. Once these elements are added, however, the full reaction can occur.

Sometimes the sequence that produces developed ability is aborted, and only the first phase of the reaction occurs. The child never develops his ability, and his potential is wasted. In other cases the second phase of the reaction is so powerful that the child develops abilities that far exceed predictions based upon the first equation. Erik was a perfect example. His desire and effort enabled him to overcome his learning deficiencies.

Both phases of the ability reaction must occur if the human species is to thrive. Brilliant musical scores, life-saving medical discoveries, and record-shattering athletic achievements would never be produced if potential ability did not transform itself by means of individual and collective effort and desire into developed ability.

Each newborn infant is a manifestation of human potential. The tiny creature lying in her mother's arms is the composite of inherited endowments that will be influenced by her environment. She may ultimately become a physicist or the first woman president of the United States. She may inherit her mother's language aptitude or her father's mathematical aptitude. She may abandon her artwork at fifteen, or she may struggle for years to develop her own unique artistic style which may win her fame and fortune.

As children emerge from infancy, they are increasingly defined by their achievements. Will she walk at fourteen months? Will he tie his shoes by the time he's four? Will she read when she is five? When they enter school, children discover that they are judged not by their potential but, rather, by what they do with their potential. In order to transform their potential ability into developed ability, they must acquire the capacity to learn efficiently.

Learning Efficiency

Inefficient learning blocks the process by which potential ability is converted into developed ability. Erik's experiences in school underscored the profound academic and emotional implications of inefficient learning. Although of above-average intelligence, he could not process information properly. Compensating for this deficiency required prodigious effort and intensive, specialized learning assistance.

In order to learn efficiently a child must possess the ability to concentrate, to remember, to think analytically, to decipher written and spoken language, to understand how numbers work, and to express concrete and abstract ideas. Children who fail to develop these abilities are destined to struggle and to underachieve.

Even subtle problems with learning efficiency can cause

inconsistencies between a child's potential ability and his developed ability. Perceptual processing problems such as letter reversals and inaccurate reading can skew classroom performance, achievement test scores, and IQ test scores. (Learning problems are examined in greater depth in Chapter 7.)

Emotional stress can also interfere with learning efficiency and undermine performance. The child who is upset or extremely nervous in class or during a test cannot function at a level commensurate with his potential ability. Under such conditions, it is impossible to assess accurately either the child's potential ability or developed ability. (Emotional problems are examined in Chapter 12.)

Differentiating Potential Ability from Developed Ability

Determining a child's potential and developed ability is far more complicated than simply looking at grades, determining skill level, and measuring IQ. The procedure of making absolute pronouncements about a child's ability is replete with danger. A student may study very hard and receive B's and C's in school. Although her developed ability level is the C to B range, her potential ability may actually be in the A range. Despite her diligence, the student may not know how to study effectively. If she learns a more effective means of studying, she might eventually receive straight A's.* Two serious consequences can result if she does not acquire better study skills. Based upon her performance, her parents and teachers may conclude that her potential academic ability is limited and counsel her to lower her career goals. The student herself may concur and begin to accept mediocre work as the best she can do. If she agrees to lower her expectations, her fate is sealed.

Despite general agreement among educators and school psychologists about standards used for measuring performance and potential, potential ability and developed ability are dif-

---

*See Lawrence J. Greene and Leigh Jones-Bamman, *Getting Smarter: Simple Strategies for Better Grades*. Belmont, Calif.: David S. Lake Publishers, 1985.

ficult to assess in absolute terms. Two types of assessment devices have been created: IQ tests and achievement tests.

IQ tests are designed to measure a child's intellectual endowments and to predict his success in school. In theory, the higher the child's IQ, the better his performance in school. The gifted child with an IQ of 150 would be expected to master academic material with ease. The child with the low average IQ of 90 would be expected to have some difficulty mastering academic material.

Achievement tests are designed to measure a child's developed academic ability. The tests statistically compare a child's performance with that of thousands of children of the same age who take the same exam. In theory, the higher the child's achievement scores, the better his performance in school. The fourth grader who scores at the sixth-grade level in reading skills would be expected to have little difficulty with reading assignments. The fourth grader who scores at the third-grade level in reading would be expected to struggle.

Both IQ tests and achievement tests are fallible, and the data provided by the tests may be inaccurate, misleading, or misinterpreted. It is known that certain children do well on tests but perform poorly in class. Other students do poorly on tests but function well in class. Some children are highly creative, but IQ tests and reading tests do not measure this characteristic. A child who is a brilliant artist may be tested and found to have an average IQ and to be a poor reader. The scores, however, have questionable significance in predicting the child's potential success if she goes to art school and ultimately becomes a professional artist.

In order for children to develop their academic potential, two elements must be added to the ability equation: practice and quality instruction. An English teacher may conclude that one of her students has the potential to become a writer or a journalist, and that another student does not have a great deal of natural writing talent. Were the student with supposedly limited writing talent to work diligently and were he to receive competent instruction, his developed writing ability might exceed that of the student with more natural talent. As a result of effort, desire, practice, and competent instruction, he may be able to transform his potential into developed ability and, ultimately, into high achievement.

Any attempt on the part of parents, teachers, and psychologists to measure a child's potential and developed ability must take into consideration all of the variables that influence achievement. Children who are catalogued on the basis of inflexible or limited criteria are being done a disservice. To suggest that the artistic child who scores in the average range on an IQ test has only average potential is inaccurate and meaningless.

Intelligence

Intelligence is one of the basic building blocks of achievement. Because intelligence is a multi-faceted phenomenon, it assumes many different forms. We describe someone as a brilliant linguist, a math whiz, a creative genius, or a musical prodigy. The following definition of intelligence integrates those features of intelligence that relate to learning and achievement.

> Intelligence is the capacity to perceive similarities and differences, to analyze information, to solve problems, to associate past experiences with current experiences, to learn from mistakes, and to distill complex variables into a comprehensible schema.

The most obvious manifestations of intelligence occur in the areas of creative and analytical problem solving. The following examples illustrate some of the mental processes involved in this problem-solving process.

1. This problem looks like one that I solved yesterday.
2. What are the similarities and differences between this problem and the one that I already solved?
3. How did I get the answer yesterday?
4. This factor has changed. How could this affect the solution to the problem?
5. I have made that mistake before. How can I avoid making it again?

The capacity to think analytically and creatively is to a large extent an inherited trait. This capacity, however, can be developed and refined by means of effort, determination, practice, and quality instruction. Indeed, the primary function of the education process is to train a child's mind and develop his intelligence so that he can solve life's problems and meet life's challenges. A tragic waste of human potential occurs when a child's intelligence remains unfocused and undeveloped.

Aptitude

Aptitude is another basic building block of achievement. The term is applied more specifically than the generic term "intelligence." A person may be described as having good mechanical, scientific, or artistic aptitude. Aptitude may be defined as follows:

> Aptitude is a specialized manifestation of intelligence that is reflected in a specific skill or ability.

Aptitude and intelligence interact in many different ways. Three possibilities are described below.

Specialized aptitude. A person with good mechanical aptitude may be very skillful at taking apart an engine, identifying a problem, correcting the problem, and rebuilding the engine. This same person may not necessarily have a high level of general intelligence. His aptitude in other areas such as art may be limited. The talented artist, on the other hand, may not have mechanical aptitude or may not be proficient at solving math problems.

High intelligence/Low aptitude. A person may have a high degree of general intelligence and have low aptitude in specific areas. The brilliant history scholar may be highly articulate. He may also have a prodigious memory and a highly analytical mind. He may, however, be completely incompetent when he attempts to assemble his child's bicycle.

High aptitude/Average or low intelligence. Some people considered to have average or even low general intelligence may have a high degree of specialized aptitude. For example, a person may have an uncanny ability to use a computer for entering bookkeeping information or processing lists and yet may not be able to solve even the most basic arithmetic problems.

Measuring Intelligence and Aptitude

The means for measuring intelligence and aptitude are, at best, inexact. During the last fifty years several different types of tests have been designed by educators and psychologists to indicate the "quality" or potential of a person's mind.

Although each test's format, specific tasks, and questions differ, all of the tests are designed to evaluate a child's ability to analyze, perceive, associate, and recall. The number of the respondent's "correct" answers is compared with scores attained by others of similar background and age who have taken the test. Statistical norms are established after the test is administered to a broad population of people. (In grading the test, the examiner can use either national or local norms. In theory, the use of local norms reduces cultural bias.) The child's responses to the questions are compared to the norms and a statistically based score is derived. This score theoretically indicates the child's potential level of achievement. The higher the score on the test, the greater the child's potential.

Specific subsections of the test are designed to measure specific aptitudes. Most IQ tests, for example, differentiate verbal aptitude from math aptitude. Certain tests also measure specific abilities such as mechanical aptitude.

Some school districts place more emphasis on these tests than others. A school that offers enriched or accelerated programs for gifted children may make acceptance into such programs contingent upon the student's attaining a certain score on an IQ test. Another school may skip students into a more advanced grade if their scores on IQ tests and achievement tests are very high.

In many school districts, IQ tests are also used to determine eligibility for learning assistance programs. A discrepancy between a child's verbal scores and performance on an IQ test is generally considered by school psychologists to be a primary characteristic of a learning disability. Children in many school districts of California cannot be enrolled in special assistance programs unless there is such a discrepancy on the IQ test.

Despite the relatively widespread use of IQ and aptitude tests as prognostic and diagnostic tools, there are inherent problems with such tests. The scores can be skewed by such factors as cultural deprivation, language deficiencies, emotional problems, perceptual problems, and poor rapport with the examiner. Unfortunately, such potentially flawed scores are often used as the primary criterion for admission to accelerated or enriched programs and clearly discriminate against culturally disadvantaged and language-deficient children.*

To use IQ tests and aptitude tests as exclusive criteria for measuring a child's potential ability is equally unjust. The tests do not assess motivation, nor do they factor into the assessment process the quality of the environment to which a child is exposed. A brilliant child who is raised in an abusive and intellectually repressive environment may never actualize his potential ability. Another brilliant child who has a severe learning problem may conclude that she is dumb and, if she receives no meaningful help in school, she may never develop her potential.

It is a well-known fact that members of organizations limited to those of superior intelligence do not always achieve at a level commensurate with their IQ scores. Brilliant men and women have ended up on skid row or in prison. Other men and women initially deemed by their teachers to be less than brilliant have become presidents of nations, major corporations, and universities. Yet, despite the inherent measurement

---

*A physiological test of intelligence may be possible. Researchers have used lasers to measure the physiological response time of the retina to light. The speed of the response is theorized to correlate with intelligence. Such a test, if proven accurate and reliable, could eliminate cultural bias in testing and could also eliminate the negative influences of emotional stress and perceptual processing deficits.

difficulties and the potential misuse and misinterpretation of scores, intelligence and aptitude do have a significant impact on academic success and must be factored into the achievement equation.

IQ tests can play a helpful role in career selection. Some professions demand high-level comprehension and abstract reasoning skills. Others demand mathematical or artistic aptitude. The child who wants to become a scientist or a physician will be more handicapped by intelligence limitations than the child who seeks a career that demands less developed memory skills or analytical reasoning skills. Students should be encouraged to orient toward those careers in which they have a natural facility or talent, assuming, of course, that the tests which were used to assess their aptitude and talent provided accurate data.

The Achieving Child Model

An achieving child is produced when all of the building blocks of achievement are in place. These building blocks are represented in the figure on the following page.

Smartness and Achievement

Although the elements described in the achieving child model are prerequisites to achievement, these elements alone do not necessarily guarantee achievement. Another vital element must be factored into the model of the achieving child: smartness.

An important distinction must be made between smartness and intelligence. Many brilliant people fail to achieve or succeed because intelligent people are not necessarily smart people. Smartness is the practical application of intelligence. Smart people are typically survivors. They tend to be the ones who calculate the odds and plan strategically. Smart people also have the capacity to bounce back from defeat. They generally define their goals and then figure the most pragmatic means for attaining them. A bright, motivated woman may desire to

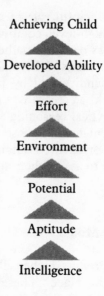

Achieving Child

Developed Ability

Effort

Environment

Potential

Aptitude

Intelligence

become president of a corporation. She may identify a person in the corporation who is intent on blocking her promotion. If she is to achieve her objective, the woman will have to figure out how to bypass, win over, or neutralize the person standing in her way. In order to succeed, she will need to be more than simply intelligent and motivated. She will also have to be calculating and strategic.

In order to understand why some children utilize their potential, develop their abilities, and achieve while others do not, the emotional factors that affect achievement must be examined. This is the subject of the next chapter.

• **PARENTING SUGGESTIONS**

• *Support, acknowledge, and encourage your child.*

The environment that parents create at home plays a vital role in determining whether or not a child's potential will be developed and eventually produce achievement.

• *Be cautious about making or accepting pronouncements about your child's intelligence, aptitude, or potential.*

A child's scores and performance can be affected by many external and internal factors. Anxiety, poor self-esteem, perceptual processing deficits, cultural influences, and poor instruction can affect test scores and classroom performance. Parents must examine all of these factors before accepting professional opinions about their child's supposed intellectual limitations.

4 Self-Image and Achievement

Devon: Punishment Wasn't the Answer

The principal stared at the fourth grader sitting in front of her. This was the third time that Devon had been sent to her office during the last ten days. His misbehavior in class and on the playground had become chronic. Having realized from past experience that she couldn't reason with this child, the principal had been forced to resort to discipline. But discipline had proven equally ineffective. Detention, and even suspension, did not appear to bother Devon.

Devon was the class clown. The nine-year-old would make a face or a noise whenever the teacher turned her back. He seldom completed his assignments, and the work he did hand in was sloppy and inaccurate. His parents were desperate. All their attempts to change his behavior had failed. Seemingly oblivious to punishment, he didn't mind if his bicycle was taken away or if he was grounded. Six "crisis" parent-teacher conferences had produced no tangible results.

Devon attended a private school where the majority of the students were bright, highly motivated, and academically advanced. The school's accelerated curriculum accentuated his relatively subtle learning problems. He had been admitted to the school in kindergarten. He had scored very well on the required IQ test and on the reading readiness test. But by second grade he had begun to struggle and misbehave. Rejected by the other students, he associated exclusively with the one other child in the class who also had behavior problems.

In desperation, the principal had referred Devon's parents to our learning center. My initial diagnostic evaluation indicated that Devon's reading comprehension was at grade level. Unfortunately for Devon, the average fourth grader at his school was reading at the eighth-grade level.

Although I was able to identify some minor learning deficits, I was certain that these deficits were not exclusively responsible for Devon's poor school performance. I suspected that he was intent on sabotaging himself, and I felt that psychological counseling should precede his learning therapy. His parents rejected my recommendation. They insisted that their son's difficulty in school was exclusively attributable to a learning problem and they wanted him to receive only learning assistance.

As anticipated, Devon behaved at our learning center in much the same way he did in his regular classroom. He was a master at baiting teachers and would argue with any adult who attempted to direct or instruct him. He had an uncanny ability to "read" adults and identify their limits. He would push them toward their limits but usually would stop short of a major confrontation. It was clear that he was intent on defeating all our efforts to help him remediate his learning problems.

During a conference in my office, I asked Devon if he wanted to continue attending his private school. He said he did. I then pointed out that all his actions seemed designed to guarantee his expulsion. When I attempted to explore this contradiction with him, he emphatically denied that he was doing anything wrong. He blamed his teachers for being unfair and his parents for being unreasonable.

The situation in school had reached the crisis point. The principal informed me that either Devon's parents would have to withdraw him from the school voluntarily or he would be asked to leave. I suggested voluntary withdrawal. Although disappointed, the parents reluctantly accepted my recommendation.

Realizing that he was not permitted to blow up at his parents or teachers, Devon had developed an alternative means of venting his unhappiness. His solution was to be manipulative and argumentative.

Because children like Devon are usually unconscious of their underlying feelings, they frequently deny that they are angry, unhappy, or upset. Confronting negative emotions can be very threatening to a child, especially when the emotions are entangled in a great deal of pain, fear, anger, and guilt. To avoid this confrontation, children often attempt to disown or camouflage feelings which are perceived as unacceptable or unsafe. Recognizing that they cannot violate the traditional parent/child conventions without suffering the consequences, angry children usually act out their feelings in less extreme forms. They may become sarcastic or physically aggressive, or, as in Devon's case, disruptive in the classroom. The majority would not, however, dare to curse at their parents or throw a rock at their teacher's car.

A child's attempt to avoid, disown, or camouflage his anger is usually futile. Feelings cannot be disowned. They can only be deflected. In time, the negative emotions begin to take charge of the child's life in insidious ways. Devon's behavior exemplified the effects of deflected hostility.

The angry child has two basic choices. He can repress his feelings, or he can find a relatively "safe" way to express them. If the angry feelings are repressed, the child will turn the anger inward where it implodes, causing depression, isolation, self-sabotage, guilt, and, perhaps, recurring nightmares. If the anger is vented, it will probably assume the form of misbehavior, resistance, irresponsibility, or antisocial behavior. Clearly, the angry child is in a no-win situation unless he can be helped to understand and resolve his emotional conflicts.

Devon handled his anger by repressing the blatant hostility and expressing a more sanitized version in carefully controlled doses. Devon, of course, was not consciously aware of the link between his feelings and his behavior. Despite this lack of

conscious awareness, his manipulation of adults was quite calculated. He misbehaved enough to make everyone miserable,
but he usually stopped short of pushing his teacher or his
parents to the point of exploding. The punishment he received
was the price he paid for his "revenge."

A vicious cycle had developed. Devon felt anger and resentment toward his parents and toward adults in general. He
expressed this hostility by pressing their hot buttons. In punishing his parents, he was also punishing himself. Without
intervention, I was certain that this cycle of punishing and
being punished would continue in one form or another
throughout Devon's life. Someday, his boss might be on the
receiving end of Devon's need to punish and be punished, and
he would probably "succeed" in orchestrating his own dismissal. The psychological consequences of permitting his self-
sabotaging behavior to persist could be disastrous.

At my urging, Devon transferred to a public school. The
situation at his private school was not salvagable. Finally willing to accept the reality that their son needed psychological
counseling, Devon's parents agreed to have him evaluated by
a clinical psychologist.

At first, there was not much improvement in Devon's work
and attitude at his new school. He carried with him many of
his negative behaviors, and he got off to a shaky start. As the
counseling process progressed, his resistance to authority and
to school slowly began to abate. He became more communi-
cative and less angry. To our amazement, he actually began to
arrive at the center early so that he could help my secretary.

Six months after beginning therapy, Devon made the honor
roll at his new school. On the day he received his report card,
he came running into my office to show me his grades. He
was proud as a peacock.

Self-Image/Self-Esteem Loop

Self-image and achievement are inextricably linked. With few
exceptions, the more positive the child's self-image, the greater
his achievement. Self-image represents the composite of a child's

conscious and unconscious perceptions about himself. This composite to a large extent reflects the child's experiences in life. Positive life experiences tend to produce children who like and accept themselves. Such children are typically achievement oriented. A self-image/self-esteem loop is created that reflects the child's perceptions of himself. A positive self-image encourages the growth of self-esteem, which in turn encourages positive expectations, which in turn encourage achievement. This loop can be represented graphically. Note that the loop turns in both directions. Achievement stimulates self-esteem, and self-esteem stimulates achievement.

Positive Self-Image

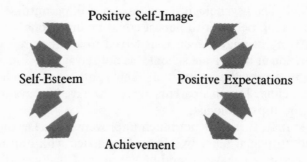

Self-Esteem   Positive Expectations

Achievement

The child who possesses a positive self-image, positive expectations, and self-esteem seeks goals that will enhance the positive feelings he already has about himself. For instance, a girl who aspires to become a world-class swimmer must not only have natural talent, she must also appreciate her talent. She must firmly believe that she can attain her goal. As she trains, she must imagine herself swimming competitively and winning. In her mind's eye, she sees herself pulling ahead of other swimmers in the pool. Then she sees herself at the end of the race with the medal draped around her neck. With each success, her feelings about herself become increasingly positive. Her self-confidence grows and the loop recycles itself.

Three additional elements—self-appreciation, self-acceptance, and self-confidence—must also be added to the list of feelings which comprise a child's sense of self. This amalgam might best be described as the child's self-quotient, or SQ.

The child who has a low SQ will generally have difficulty achieving. His lack of self-esteem, self-appreciation, self-acceptance, and self-confidence will directly impact on his level of expectations. His low expectations will deter him from reaching for the success which could make him feel better about himself. There is an obvious irony here. Achievement might permit the child with a low SQ to feel better about himself, but the child's low SQ functions to inhibit achievement.

In some instances, people with low SQ's manage to achieve success. Everyone has read about talented athletes and movie stars who have attained fame and fortune, yet appear to be profoundly unhappy. For some people, achievement can be a surrogate for things that are lacking in their lives. A playwright may write great plays, but may not be able to sustain a marriage or relate to his children.

Most children with low SQ's function in ways which confirm their already negative sense of themselves. Devon was a classic example of a child caught up in this vicious cycle. His behavior reflected his unhappiness and lack of self-esteem. Seeing himself as a failure, he did everything in his power to guarantee continued failure. Despite his smug "I don't care" exterior, he was a child who desperately wanted and needed attention. He was willing to pay any price necessary to get this attention.

When Devon misbehaved, he reinforced in his own mind and in the minds of others his worthlessness as a person. He expressed his hostility toward the world by antagonizing his parents and his teachers. He expressed his anger toward himself by means of self-sabotage.

Devon could not give himself permission to succeed in school until his SQ improved. For this to happen, he had to extricate himself from the self-defeating cycle that was controlling his life and the lives of those with whom he interacted. Counseling enabled him to do this.

Although much of the foundation of a child's SQ is formed during the first three years of life, this foundation can be repaired, rebuilt, or demolished at any time during the child's life. Life experiences play a major role in the evolution of a child's SQ. A five-year-old, for example, may conclude that sports are fun. He discovers that he has natural athletic ability. As he matures, he develops his athletic skills through practice and effort. His self-image becomes that of a successful athlete. He develops confidence. His achievements and the acknowledgment he receives generate self-esteem. Without any hesitation, he decides to try out for the varsity football team and varsity baseball team, knowing his chances are good.

Another child may also conclude that sports are fun. But if she fails to develop good coordination and consequently never achieves any facility in sports, she will not acquire the self-image of the successful athlete. She may begin to avoid all activities that are sports related. Being chosen last each time her classmates play basketball or volleyball will reinforce her negative perceptions about her athletic ability. By the time she reaches adulthood, she may be convinced that she is an incompetent athlete and assiduously avoid all sports.

A third child may be uncertain about whether he enjoys sports. Although he may not manifest any great athletic ability, he continues to participate in sports. Later, as a young adult, he discovers that he enjoys skiing. He also discovers that if he applies himself, he has the potential to become a good skier. His perceptions about his athletic ability and about himself begin to change. He takes up racquetball and becomes competent at that sport too. Sports now become a relatively important part of his life.

The impact of genetics and life experiences (i.e., environmental influences, achievement, etc.) on the development of a child's self-quotient can be represented graphically:

$$\frac{\text{Genetics}}{\text{Life Experiences}} \rightarrow \text{Self-Quotient}$$

A child who is genetically endowed with special talents may develop a positive SQ because he is exposed to positive environmental influences and experiences success. Conversely, if he is exposed to negative environmental influences and experiences repeated failure or frustration, he will probably develop a negative SQ. Another child with more limited genetic endowments may develop a positive SQ because his life experiences are positive. Encouragement from his parents and teachers may motivate him to compensate for his limitations in natural talent. With their help, he may discover that effort and determination will enable him to achieve success in school or on the playing field. He may also discover that a winning personality or leadership qualities can provide him with alternative avenues to achievement and popularity.

Bradley: Giving Himself Permission to Succeed

The fourth grader resisted eye contact with me. He stared intently at the table while his mother and I talked. Finally, he mustered the courage to look up. When he smiled at me, I felt an immediate and very special connection with this handsome and charming child.

Bradley's mother was a community-college instructor. She and Bradley's father had divorced when Bradley was two years old. Without any help from her husband, she had managed to raise her son while putting herself through graduate school. Limited finances and the absence of a male parental role model had created strains. But these strains, which they had faced together, had created a powerful bond between them. This close bond, however, was also the source of serious problems.

Bradley was doing poorly in school, and his mother was clearly exasperated with him. She felt her son had become lazy and irresponsible. "I constantly have to remind him to do his homework," she complained. "When I get home from work, I always find him planted in front of the TV. His schoolwork is deteriorating, and both the teacher and the resource specialist do not seem to be able to help."

After testing Bradley, I could understand why his schoolwork was suffering. He was reading approximately two years below grade level and was manifesting classic symptoms of a moderately severe learning disability.

When I explained the results of the tests to Bradley's mother, I was surprised that she appeared only slightly mollified. She said that she understood that Bradley had learning problems, but she was primarily concerned about his attitude. I explained that Bradley's attitude reflected the fact that school had become a struggle for him. By avoiding his schoolwork, he was simply protecting himself from frustration.

Bradley's mother asked what I proposed to do to help her son, and I outlined a strategy that focused on correcting his underlying learning deficits. I also emphasized the need to build Bradley's confidence. She expressed satisfaction with the proposal and wanted me to start working with him immediately.

Bradley began each remediation session by being quite cooperative. But he invariably encountered something which proved difficult for him, and he would cave in psychologically. Getting him back on track was all but impossible. Although his instructors made every effort to design academic tasks and challenges that permitted him to succeed, they could not eliminate all of the obstacles, nor could they protect him from occasional setbacks. If he were ultimately to achieve in school, Bradley would have to learn how to prevail over the inevitable upsets and frustrations that all students with learning problems periodically experience.

I held several conferences in my office with Bradley, his mother, and his instructors at the clinic. The tension that existed between the child and his mother greatly disturbed me. It was obvious that they loved each other dearly. Unfortunately, Bradley's mother had slipped into the role of the highly judgmental and supercritical parent.

Bradley idolized his mother, and her constant disapproval of his performance and attitude affected him profoundly. Although he attempted to camouflage the pain that her dissatisfaction caused him, he was clearly suffering.

When Bradley couldn't understand or successfully complete a task, he would "shut down." Each time he stumbled or made a mistake, he was forced to confront the disapproving parent who hovered behind him and continually monitored him. His mother did not even have to be present to make her presence felt. Bradley had integrated her disapproval into his own personality and had become highly intolerant and unforgiving of his own mistakes. Bradley's learning deficits were obviously enmeshed in a complex family system. I knew that the dynamics of this system would have to be realigned if the academic deficits were to be eliminated.

During a private conference, Bradley's mother finally revealed the underlying fear that was causing her to be so critical of her son. "Bradley is black. The world can be a harsh place for a black man who doesn't have a good education."

The door had opened a crack. I could sense the intensity of the mother's fears and concerns about her son's future. Those feelings would persist until she became convinced that her son could survive in a competitive and sometimes harsh world. Only then would she be able to accept and appreciate her son for his many admirable qualities.

To accept and appreciate himself, Bradley required tangible evidence that he was overcoming his learning problems. His mother also required similar evidence before she would be willing to relinqush her fears. The remediation program would have to provide more than simple academic assistance. Repeated opportunities for success, praise, and acknowledgement would have to be carefully orchestrated. Bradley would have to be guided to the realization that he was capable of achieving. I was certain that with sufficient success, his self-confidence would grow and he would become more accepting of himself and more tolerant of his occasional slips.

Bradley's mother also needed to work on some crucial issues. If she wanted Bradley to overcome his learning problems, she would have to become less critical and more supportive. She would have to examine her parenting style and her fears. If she could permit herself to let go of her fears and her unattainable standards, Bradley could in turn let go of his resistance and his resentment. He would then be free of the specter of the disapproving parent.

At my urging, Bradley's mother made a list of all of her

son's qualities that she loved. I asked her to make a conscious effort each day to acknowledge at least one of these qualities.

Bradley began to make significant academic gains. He threw himself into the remediation program and was thrilled with his progress. Within six months he was reading a year above grade level and had received a special award at school for the child who had made the most outstanding improvement. The lowest grade on his final report card of the year was B. We were all very proud.

The Desire to Achieve

Although intelligence, aptitude, potential, developed ability, and a positive SQ are requisite to achievement, these factors alone do not account for the accomplishments of an Einstein or a Beethoven. Another essential element must be added to the equation: desire.

Desire is the fuel which transforms potential into developed ability and achievement. Desire impels men and women to run marathons, climb mountains, discover new medicines, write plays, and build empires.

When social scientists attempt to explain the phenomenon of human desire, they usually focus on the impact of environment on a child's thoughts and actions. Their thesis is persuasive. A child's sense of self is influenced and shaped by the conditions and values to which he was exposed during the formative years of his life. The conditions and values in his home and in his local culture must inevitably color his ambitions and desires.

A child may decide at a very early age that she wants more than anything in the world to become a concert pianist. She is exposed to classical music at home, because her parents value and enjoy such music. At an early age, she too develops a love for classical music. Once she begins taking lessons, she discovers that she has a natural facility for the piano, and she enjoys the thrill of playing beautiful music. She also perceives that her talent pleases her parents and makes them proud of her accomplishments. She is determined to master the instrument. No one has to remind her to practice; she does so voluntarily. In fact, she would rather play the piano than see her friends or watch television.

A second child is forced by his parents to take piano lessons. His father may have always regretted that his parents couldn't afford to provide him with lessons, and he decides that his son should have the opportunity that he lacked. His son, however, intuitively realizes that he has no particular aptitude for music. Unlike the first child, he doesn't enjoy giving up time with his friends in order to practice. He agrees to do so only when his parents insist. Although he tells his parents that he has no interest in learning to play the piano, he is required to continue his lessons. Finally, he begs his parents to allow him to quit. Realizing that he is making little progress, they reluctantly consent.

A third child may want to take piano lessons because her best friend is taking lessons and she wants to do what her friend is doing. She continues to take lessons for several years and becomes fairly competent. In high school, however, she develops other interests and ultimately decides to discontinue her lessons.

Although natural talent is clearly an important component in the achievement equation, it is no guarantee of achievement. Talent unaccompanied by desire is seldom fully actualized.

The interplay of talent and desire is evident in every arena. One need only watch a Sunday football game to appreciate the degree to which intense desire can affect the performance of professional athletes. Those athletes who lack such ambition never fully actualize their potential. Even those with superstar potential risk being demoted or traded if they fail to give their all. Achievement demands intensely focused effort.

History is replete with examples of people who have compensated magnificently for their lack of natural ability with a powerful will to prevail. Many highly motivated athletes, musicians, business people, writers, and teachers with only average genetic endowments have excelled and achieved great success, whereas less motivated superstars with demonstrable natural talent have performed only marginally. It is axiomatic that the more intense the desire, the more likely the objective will be achieved.

The student who intensely desires a career as a pianist, a 4.0 grade point average, or a place on the tennis team must prioritize his goals, direct his energies, and discipline himself. Desire is the catalyst that makes the attainment of these objectives possible. Goals do not have to be monumental in order to activate desire. Even modest goals such as getting a good grade on the next exam or playing well during the next soccer game encourage a child to focus his energies and perform at his best.

Children who hesitate to establish goals and who lack ambition usually suffer from a low SQ. Perceiving themselves as undeserving or incapable of success, they avoid prioritizing, focusing their efforts, and disciplining themselves. Because of insufficient ego development, their resources remain untapped or undeveloped, and achievement becomes highly improbable.

The Ego Factor

Ego affects all aspects of a child's life. It functions as a catalyst in the equation which produces achievement. Without individual and collective ego, human survival and achievement would not be possible.

Ego is the composite of a person's sense of self. On a basic level, ego is comprised of those instinctual forces that impel human beings to satisfy their physical, emotional, and psychological needs. On a higher level, ego is composed of the emotional and intellectual forces that motivate people to establish goals and sustain them through their struggle to attain those goals. Without ego, children would never aspire to become pilots, physicians, scientists, astronauts, football players, ballerinas, Olympic gold medalists, or concert pianists.

Ego, desire, and self-esteem are uniquely human characteristics which distinguish us from other animals. The ebb and flow of these motive forces is controlled by a psychological traffic cop. This symbolic traffic controller can wave them on, slow them down, or pull them over to the side of the road.

(In the Freudian model, the traffic cop is called the superego.)

As a general rule, a healthy ego encourages a child to reach for goals and achieve. An unhealthy ego undermines the child and may discourage or prevent him from achieving. The child who possesses a healthy ego usually focuses his desire on a specific objective that he invests with concrete or symbolic importance. The objective might be a sports car or an A in biology. The goal motivates him, and the attainment of the goal is the payoff for his effort.

The phenomenon of ego development is graphically represented below.

MODEL FOR EGO DEVELOPMENT

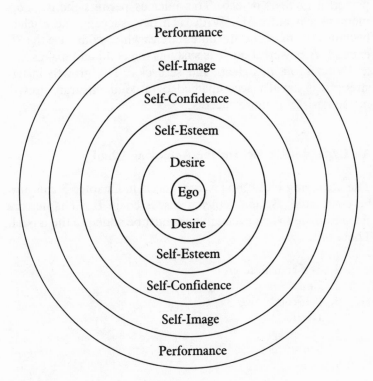

Ego and desire function reciprocally. In order to desire, a child must have ego, and in order to have ego, he must desire. Three other phenomena also interact with ego and desire: self-confidence, self-image, and self-esteem. The model of an atom can be used to represent the interplay of these components. At the center of the atom is the nucleus (ego). Surrounding the nucleus is desire. Because these rings are at the center of the atom, they are difficult for the outside world to perceive.

The next series of concentric circles represent the components of the SQ (self-esteem, self-confidence, self-image). Although not on the surface of the atom, the qualities can generally be sensed by others. One can easily identify the self-confident and self-assured child who likes and respects himself.

The outermost ring represents performance. This ring is the one most evident to the outside world.

Children who have experienced success generally have a powerful nucleus or ego. This nucleus permits the development of a healthy SQ. With each new success, the nucleus becomes stronger and the outer circles which comprise the SQ expand. A powerful nucleus sustains the child and makes him less vulnerable to defeats and setbacks. The growth in ego strength is usually accompanied by a commensurate growth in the desire for more success.

An Expanded Model for the Achieving Child

The achieving child model introduced in Chapter 3 can now be completed. Seven elements discussed in this chapter are also requisite to achievement and must be added to the model. These are:

1. Self-actualization
2. Goals
3. Self-confidence
4. Desire
5. Self-image
6. Self-esteem
7. Ego

ACHIEVING CHILD, EXPANDED MODEL

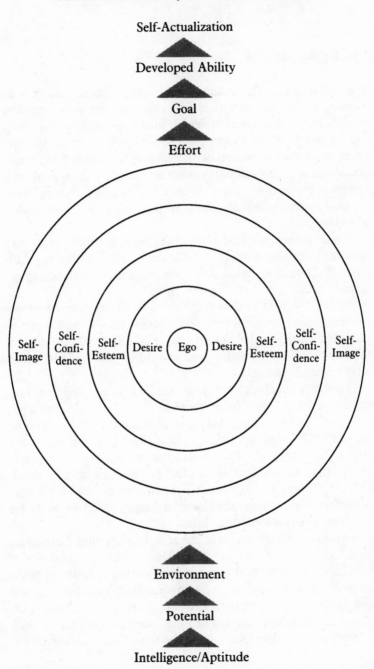

Identifying Jam-ups

The achieving child model is a tool that enables parents to identify those areas in which their child appears to be impeded or deficient. Once these areas are identified, appropriate help can be sought. If, for example, parents were to conclude that their child had a deficit in the area of developed academic ability, they would probably want to have him evaluated by a learning disabilities specialist or by a competent tutor. Specialized learning assistance or tutoring could then be provided if appropriate.

If parents suspect that their child lacks aptitude, they may want to have him tested by a clinical or educational psychologist. This testing could assist the parents in establishing realistic educational goals for the child.

Parents who sense that their child is seriously blocked because of insufficient desire, self-esteem, or ego may want to consult a clinical psychologist, psychiatrist, family counselor, or social worker. The therapist should be able to confirm or allay their suspicions.

If parents conclude that their child's primary deficit is lack of effort, they may decide that the family's communication system or reinforcement/acknowledgment system needs to be improved. Expressing concerns to a child in a nonaccusatory way and purposefully acknowledging even minor accomplishments may be all that is needed to motivate a lazy child. Extrinsic incentives (rewards) and intrinsic incentives (praise) for effort and performance can be highly effective tools for inspiring the unmotivated child.

Any missing component in the achievement model can cause underachievement. It is possible that a teenager who sits at home and vegetates is shutting down because of learning problems which may appear to be insurmountable. His isolation and lack of involvement might also reflect more serious psychological problems. He may be paralyzed by a sense of futility or feelings of unworthiness. Achievement may appear so beyond his reach that he elects to give up and do nothing. (These issues will be examined in depth later in the book.)

The potential for achievement significantly improves when all of the elements in the model are present. In some instances all of the essential elements appear to be in place, yet the child fails to achieve. Such cases can be perplexing and frustrating for parents, children, and educators. A wide range of complex factors is responsible for this paradox. These complex factors must be examined if we are to understand the plight of the underachieving child, and this will be the subject of the next chapter.

● PARENTING SUGGESTIONS

● *Encourage your child to establish goals.*

Goals encourage a child to focus his physical and emotional energies. The attainment of a goal, even if it is a relatively modest goal, provides an opportunity for the child to acquire self-esteem and self-confidence.

● *Encourage the development of desire.*

Desire stimulates creative energy and provides direction. It is the fuel which propels human beings toward their goals. Parents who help their child establish goals and encourage the attainment of these goals are contributing to the development of the child's ego.

● *Identify jam-ups.*

In order to help a child surmount the particular barriers which are impeding achievement, parents must first identify the barriers. Only then can the appropriate support systems be put in place.

Chapter

5 When Children Don't Achieve

Carey: She Wasn't Sure She Wanted to Be Promoted

A dejected eleven-year-old sat staring at the table in my office. While her mother looked on with a pained expression, Carey explained how disappointed she had been with the grades on her most recent report card. "I tried so hard, and C−'s were the best I could do."

Despite her C−'s and her obvious disappointment about the grades, this serious, highly motivated fifth grader had made significant gains in overcoming her learning problems. She was beginning to pick up momentum, and I was certain that her grades would soon reflect her improving academic skills.

Carey's family had recently moved from another part of the state. After the first day at her new school, Carey realized that the academic standards were considerably higher than those at her previous school. Although she had relatively subtle learning problems, she now found herself in a class where most of the other students were reading at the seventh- or eighth-grade level. Their superior academic skills had allowed the teacher to accelerate and enrich the curriculum. Unfortunately for Carey, this accentuated her subtle learning deficiencies.

82

Although Carey understood that her new school had demanding academic standards, she had nevertheless expected better grades. She had worked conscientiously, and she was disillusioned to discover that effort alone did not necessarily guarantee success.

I suspected that Carey's upset over her grades was not the only thing that was bothering her. When I asked her if she felt she was making progress, she hesitated before replying. "Yes, I guess so. But my new school is so much harder than my other school."

Carey informed me that her resource teacher was insisting that she read second- and third-grade material. "I feel so dumb reading those easy little-kid stories. I know I can read better than my teacher thinks I can."

I was frankly surprised at the teacher's remediation strategy. We had recently tested Carey at our center, and she had scored at the middle fifth-grade level in reading comprehension. Carey's mother explained that the resource specialist was concerned primarily about her oral reading. The teacher felt that Carey's reading accuracy and confidence level would improve if she worked on less challenging materials. Before she advanced Carey's reading level, she wanted to be certain she could read without errors.

Carey told me that her regular classroom teacher treated her differently than the staff at our learning center. "At school, my teacher always points out what I can't do. Here, you always point out what I can do."

Six months of academic struggle had taken a heavy emotional toll on Carey. I could sense her apprehension about her ability to keep up with her class. When I asked her whether she felt she would be able to handle sixth grade the following year, she did not respond immediately. Finally, she replied in a defeated tone, "I don't know." I then asked her if she wanted to be promoted. She again hesitated. "I don't know."

The paradox was quite obvious. On a conscious level, Carey wanted to succeed in school. On an unconscious level, she was terrified of succeeding. Despite one hundred percent effort, she was only barely keeping up with her fifth-grade class. If she were to succeed and be promoted, she knew that she would be faced with an even greater challenge in sixth grade. Having no tangible evidence that she could handle a more advanced class, she had begun to believe that her situation was futile and that she was destined never to catch up.

The resource specialist's insistence that Carey read second- and third-grade material had heightened her apprehension and discouragement. She had interpreted being assigned lower-level materials as a confirmation of her inability to progress. Without intending to do so, the resource specialist had undermined Carey's already fragile self-esteem and self-confidence.

Carey was at a crossroads. Unless she became convinced that she was making progress, she would probably conclude that her effort was futile and give up. Once she did, she would shut down emotionally. To avoid psychological damage, we needed to reduce her frustration, provide her with proof of improvement, and create an emotional support system in school and at home.

I suggested to Carey's parents that I meet with both the resource specialist and the classroom teacher. When we did meet the following week, I discovered that both teachers were quite receptive to my suggestions. The resource specialist agreed to raise the level of the reading material that Carey was using, and the classroom teacher agreed to make an effort to acknowledge and praise Carey even when her accomplishments were meager. We also decided that Carey would be given an opportunity to do projects for extra credit.

One week later an ecstatic Carey came into my office to inform me that she was now reading some of the same books that the rest of the children were. "I must be getting better!" she exclaimed. Her face was beaming.

The remedial support soon began to pay off. Carey received all B's on her final report card in fifth grade. Her self-confidence began to surge. By May, she was testing at the beginning seventh-grade level in reading. She had let go of her fears about failing in sixth grade. Had we the temerity to suggest retention, she would have been furious!

Frustration and Underachievement

The frustration produced by underachievement is a double-edged sword. Though frustration can be destructive, cutting away a child's self-confidence and self-esteem, it can also be constructive. Like a machete, it can be used to hack away at the barriers that impede achievement. The way in which the underachieving child uses his frustration will often determine whether or not he ultimately becomes an achiever.

Carey's reactions to her lack of progress illustrated the destructive potential of frustration. Forced to confront her seemingly insoluble academic deficiencies, she became increasingly demoralized. Despite gains in her reading scores, she found herself in a protracted struggle to keep up with her more advanced classmates. During this period, she had no confirmation in school that she was making progress. Her marginal grades and the "demeaning" material she was being asked to read confirmed in her own mind that she was losing the battle. She felt confused and defeated, and frustration cut deeper and deeper into her sense of self.

Once the appropriate academic and emotional support systems were put in place, Carey could begin to mobilize the constructive potential of her frustration. She could become angry at the impediments that were holding her back and could focus her emotional and physical energies on beating down the barriers. Her frustration could then become an ally, which, in tandem with her desire, could permit her to surge ahead.

Unfortunately, the underlying problems of many underachieving children are never identified, and the appropriate academic and emotional support systems are never created. Because they never become convinced that they can succeed, these children do not learn how to mobilize the constructive potential of frustration. They experience only the debilitating effects of frustration—stress, apprehensiveness, insecurity, discouragement, demoralization, fear, ambivalence, poor self-esteem, and poor self-confidence. If the destructive frustration is unchecked, it can ultimately lead to an overwhelming sense of futility.

The child who accepts that his problems are insurmountable and that effort is futile is in serious psychological jeopardy. He is vulnerable to depression, and he is potentially self-destructive. To a despairing child, suicide may appear to be a viable solution to seemingly unresolvable problems.

The frustration a child experiences when he encounters insurmountable obstacles is not to be compared to the healthy frustration which occurs when a child faces a "normal" challenge. Struggling to break out of a batting slump is altogether different from struggling to read a sixth-grade textbook when you are able to read only at the fourth-grade level.

A powerful instinct impels parents to protect their children from pain. Most parents who conclude that their child cannot succeed at something are naturally motivated to discourage him from exposing himself to certain failure. The effect of this well-intentioned attempt to insulate the child from a painful collision with reality may be positive or negative. The appropriateness or inappropriateness of the parents' decision—to protect or not to protect—hinges on two factors: the accuracy of their perceptions about the difficulty inherent in the particular challenge, and the accuracy of their assessment of their child's abilities.

Compelling arguments can be made for discouraging a child from "beating his head against a wall." Equally persuasive arguments can be made for allowing a child the opportunity to determine for himself his own capabilities and limitations. As parents assess each situation, they must consider the potential psychological and emotional risk factor.

In extreme cases, parents have a clear responsibility to deter or even forbid their child from doing something that could damage his physical or emotional health. Parental responsibility and prerogatives, however, are not so clearly defined when the potential for emotional or physical damage is in doubt. Parents are not omniscient, and despite the best of intentions and basically good instincts, they may incorrectly assess a particular situation or incorrectly assess their child's limitations. Challenges that they consider impossible for their child may not be impossible. For example, a shy child who stutters may express a desire to try out for the school play. In an attempt to protect him from possible rejection and embarrassment, his parents may consider discouraging him from trying out. Several scenarios are possible.

1. *The child is deterred from trying out for the play.* In this instance, the child will be spared possible rejection, defeat, and embarrassment. At the same time, he will unconsciously register that he should accept and acquiesce to his limitations, and will adjust his level of expectations accordingly.

2. *The child tries out for the play and is rejected.* In this instance, the child will have to deal with rejection. He might be emotionally crushed by this defeat, or he might surprise his parents and deal with it. If he is crushed, then his parents' worst fears were warranted. It is more likely that the child will suffer pain but he will not be destroyed by it. With parental support and encouragement, he can learn to cope with his feelings. If he can develop the capacity to rebound from setbacks, he will have acquired an invaluable survival skill.

3. *The child tries out for the play and gets a part.* In this instance, the child faces potential emotional benefits and risks. If he stutters during the performance, he might embarrass himself. This experience may prove to be a nightmare, as his parents feared. But with parental support and encouragement the child will probably discover that he can survive his embarrassment. It is also possible that he may surprise his parents and be undaunted by having stuttered. He may conclude that he can prevail over his disability. His speech therapist may teach him relaxation techniques and suggest that he try out for a musical the next time because he probably won't stutter when he is singing. There is yet another possibility. On the night of the performance, the child might say his lines flawlessly. If he does, he would undoubtedly experience elation and pride that could not otherwise be duplicated.

In their attempt to protect their child, the parents in the first scenario unintentionally communicated that stuttering was an insurmountable barrier to achievement. The perceptions of parents can profoundly influence the child's perceptions of himself and his world. Had the child accepted that his speech impediment severely limited his ability to achieve and compete, he might have gone through life fearful of taking risks, reaching for goals, and exposing himself to possible failure.

Although the child in the second scenario was rejected, he had the courage to risk defeat while reaching for his goal. In the process of failing, the child probably discovered that he could survive the setback. Perhaps he even discovered a truth about life that is usually only realized by wizened adults— that the fear of failure can be far worse than the actual failure. With sufficient parental encouragement and motivation, the child with grit will continue to strive for his goals and ultimately prevail.

The child in the third scenario did prevail. Because success tends to feed on itself, achieving children usually continue achieving. His parents' well-intentioned concerns about destructive emotional damage proved unwarranted. Had they been guided by these fears, they would have denied their son a vital opportunity for growth.

Allowing Children to Confront Challenges

As a general rule, reasonable parents provide reasonable protection. Excessively protective parents, on the other hand, are compelled to remove all snags from their child's path. If their daughter doesn't like her fifth-grade teacher, they might arrange a transfer to another class before attempting to help her resolve her personality conflict with the teacher. In their attempt to insulate their child from upset, the parents are discouraging her from confronting and solving her own problems. If they establish a pattern of extricating her from all unpleasant situations, they will create a dependency script that could persist throughout her life. Each time their daughter encounters an obstacle, she will expect to be rescued.

The opportunity to confront and surmount barriers is essential to the development of a child's self-quotient. Parents who permit their child to experience a reasonable number of collisions with the hard facts of life provide the child with an invaluable opportunity to test and develop his resources. For instance, a child who takes karate lessons may be frustrated by his lack of advancement. At some point he must realize that the black belt can only be won by students who are dedicated and conscientious. Another child may want to go to a first-rate college and may be frustrated by the exacting standards of her English teacher. At some point she must realize that A's in English are given only to those students who hand in well-written reports on time and who proofread and edit their work until they have eliminated grammatical and spelling errors.

The child who creates goals, establishes standards of performance, and prevails over challenges acquires faith in himself and a respect for the value of effort. The late Gestalt psychiatrist Fritz Perls wrote:

> In the process of growing up, there are two choices. The child either grows up and learns to overcome frustration, or it is spoiled. It might be spoiled by the parents answering all the questions, rightly or wrongly. It might be spoiled so that as soon as it wants something, it gets it. . . . Without frustration there is no need, no reason to mobilize your resources to discover that you may be able to do something on your own.*

Challenges offer an opportunity for a child to learn how to use frustration constructively. By confronting challenges, he develops a sense of his own power and an appreciation for his own capabilities. He also learns about his strengths and weaknesses, and he discovers an important fact of life: he must work if he is to achieve.

Confronting challenges also helps a child appreciate that frustration is often part of the price that must be paid for achievement. This frustration may not be pleasant, but the ultimate achievement will be all the more satisfying because the child has taken on a challenge and won.

---

* Fritz Perls. *Gestalt Therapy Verbatim*. Lafayette, Calif.: Real People Press, 1969.

Allowing a child to experience a controlled amount of frustration is quite different from allowing him to experience continual frustration and inescapable defeat. Repeated unsuccessful encounters with obstacles inevitably lead to a sense of futility and destroy a child's SQ.

An important differentiation must be made between a child who fails to make the baseball team and one who fails at everything he does. Any child who is defeated or rejected will experience a certain amount of sadness. If the child is successful in other areas of his life, however, he will probably not suffer lasting psychological damage. Children who fail at everything are at risk emotionally because they have no alternative sources for emotional reinforcement. Faced with the prospect of endless obstacles and failure, they become discouraged and demoralized.

When parents, convinced that their child is smashing against emotionally destructive obstacles, attempt to protect the child, they are not being excessively protective. For instance, insisting that a learning-disabled child be provided with remedial assistance is a clear parental mandate.

Excessive protectiveness, however, is not a parental mandate. The overly protected child typically evolves into an adult who lacks independence and emotional survival skills. Such children generally require extensive counseling or psychotherapy before they are able to develop self-sufficiency and emotional maturity.

Seeing a child struggle with frustration can be a heart-wrenching experience for parents. Deciding how much frustration to permit a child to experience can be equally traumatic. At best, the decision is a "judgment call." Parents have no alternative but to rely on their reason, their instincts, and their intuition.

Parental insight and intuition are acquired through a conscious and unconscious distillation of life experiences. Parents who are willing to look at themselves and confront their parenting mistakes generally become more insightful and intuitive parents. They realize that if they are to make proper judgments and reasonable decisions they must learn as much as possible about their child's emotional needs and their own emotional needs.

The following checklist is intended to help parents assess their attitudes on challenges and frustration.

CHECKLIST OF ATTITUDES ON CHALLENGES AND FRUSTRATION

	Yes	No
1. I encourage my child to confront reasonable challenges.		
2. I allow my child to confront difficult challenges.		
3. I discourage my child from confronting unreasonable challenges, but I allow him to do so if he insists and if the challenges do not pose a threat to his mental or physical health.		
4. I actively support my child when he experiences setbacks and help him understand the issues and his emotional responses.		
5. I allow my child to struggle with reasonable frustration and provide as much emotional support as possible.		
6. I evaluate each potential frustration-causing situation carefully and objectively to determine whether or not it can seriously injure my child emotionally or physically.		
7. I try not to be guided unreasonably by my own fears and negative expectations.		

8. I am willing to seek professional help when I perceive that my child's frustration is chronic, counter-productive, or debilitating.   _____ _____

9. I periodically evaluate my parenting style and my emotional responses to my child.   _____ _____

10. I make a sincere effort to examine and understand my child's emotions.   _____ _____

11. I avoid creating emotional dependence.   _____ _____

12. I avoid being excessively protective.   _____ _____

INTERPRETING THE CHECKLIST. Parents who have answered yes to most of the checklist questions can feel confident that they are responding appropriately to the issue of challenges and frustration. Parents who have answered no to most of the questions might benefit from examining their attitudes. Although their intentions may be good, these intentions, if misguided, can impede their child's progress.

Ego Damage

Chronic frustration slices deeply into that part of the underachieving child that is most vulnerable, his ego. The resulting damage can emotionally incapacitate the child.

As stated in Chapter 4, ego is the composite of the elements which constitute a person's sense of self. Its most obvious manifestation is human desire. This desire is requisite to achievement. A ten-year-old might proclaim "I want to be a doctor." The surface meaning of this statement is: "I feel that being a doctor would be neat, and I want to achieve this goal." The psychological meaning of the statement is: "I feel that I have the ability to be a doctor, and I feel that I deserve to be a doctor. I allow myself to reach for this goal." Implicit in the

statement is the child's acceptance of herself, her acknowledgment of her ability, and her willingness to make the necessary commitment and expend the necessary effort required
to achieve the objective. Of course, a ten-year-old does not
consciously understand this psychological process. She has
simply given herself permission on an unconscious level to
desire and to achieve. She does so because she possesses a
strong ego.

It is highly unlikely that a child who has experienced years
of failure and frustration in school would ever declare "I want
to be a doctor." Repeated defeat leaches the nutrients which
sustain a child's ego. Lacking tangible evidence of competence,
the underachieving or nonachieving child unconsciously ad-
justs her goals and expectations to her perception of reality.
For the underachieving child, this reality consists of marginal
success, at best. Aspiring to becoming a doctor would seem
so implausible that even if the idea were to occur to the child,
she would most likely dismiss it.

Children who lack ego strength are the victims of a vicious
cycle. Their lack of success causes them to become frustrated
and discouraged. This frustration and discouragement in turn
undermine their already tenuous egos. The net result of this
vicious cycle is a tragic waste of human potential.

Deserving to Achieve

Careful examination of underachieving, ego-damaged children
reveals several common denominators:

1. Skills deficits
2. Attitudinal deficits
3. Diminished self-quotient
4. Diminished level of expectations
5. Feelings of unworthiness

The life experiences of the achieving child are radically different from those of the underachieving child. The achiever
receives repeated affirmation of his ability, and this affirmation

usually convinces him that he deserves to continue achieving.

A child must like himself in order to feel deserving of success. But in order to like himself, he must experience success. This paradox causes many underachieving children to become academically and emotionally "stuck." The paradox can be represented graphically:

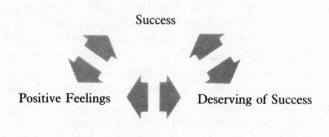

Success

Positive Feelings   Deserving of Success

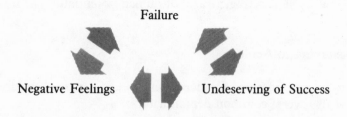

Failure

Negative Feelings   Undeserving of Success

You will note that the arrows in both cycles are pointing in two directions. This underscores the reciprocal relationship that exists between the components. Success produces positive feelings, and positive feelings in turn produce success. For example, a first grader receives A's on his math tests and concludes that he is smart in math. Because he is smart in math, he feels that he deserves to continue getting good grades. He becomes self-confident and desires more success. Each achievement in math confirms his positive feelings about himself and his abilities.

The failure cycle is also reciprocal. Failure produces negative feelings, and negative feelings produce failure. A first grader who does poorly on his math tests concludes that he is "dumb" in math. Because he perceives himself as dumb, he may unconsciously conclude that he deserves to get bad grades in math. He loses his self-confidence, and he acquiesces to his "fate." Each new failure confirms his negative feelings about himself and his abilities.

The elements of "desire" and "deserving" must be added to complete the success and failure cycles. A child must feel deserving of success in order to desire success. If he does not feel deserving of success, he will usually block or sublimate his desire for it. Frustration, anger, and depression often result. Because these emotions are often unconsciously suppressed, they may assume a camouflaged form, such as teasing, chronic shyness, sarcasm, bullying, clowning.

On the following page is a more complete success and failure cycle. The nonachieving or underachieving child who is locked into a failure cycle usually perceives himself as being undeserving. This perception may result in a never-ending loop of poor achievement, negative feelings, and blunted desire. The entire course of the child's life may be dominated by this loop. If they are to avoid this potential tragedy, parents must learn how to help their child break the loop.

Paying the Price for Success

Establishing goals and desiring something intensely is risky business. The specter of failure hovers over one shoulder, and the specter of success hovers over the other.

The prospect of failing can have a paralyzing effect on a

SUCCESS CYCLE

"Deserving" Child

Achievement   Positive Feelings
(success)

Desire

FAILURE CYCLE

"Undeserving" Child

Nonachievement   Negative Feelings
(failure)

No Desire

child whose self-concept is tenuous. Ironically, the prospect of success can have an equally paralyzing effect. Were he to become successful, the child who perceives himself as a failure or a nonachiever might become confused and anxious about his new identity.

Logic would dictate that winning is better than losing and that success is preferable to failure. Emotions, however, seldom conform to the dictates of logic. Just as there is an emotional price to be paid for failing, so too is there an emotional price to be paid for succeeding. The underachieving child realizes consciously or unconsciously that once his teachers and parents discover that he can succeed, their perceptions about him will change. They will begin to expect more from him. The underachiever also probably realizes that if he begins to succeed, his friend's perceptions about him will change. Because children tend to choose friends who are similar to themselves, underachievers typically gravitate toward other underachievers. A child's fear that success would trigger resentment and jealousy in his friends may be quite justified. Fear of social rejection can traumatize a child and can be a powerful deterrent to achievement.

Extreme apprehensions about success can cause a child to become emotionally immobilized. If the child develops an achievement phobia, he may feel compelled to resist doing the very things that could assure success. He may refuse to work diligently, or he may refuse to relinquish entrenched, counterproductive habits such as laziness, irresponsibility, or sloppiness.

It is a commonly held belief that once the underachieving or nonachieving child begins to experience success, he will automatically shed his negative attitudes and develop self-confidence and self-esteem. This assumption may be valid when a child's negative attitudes and low SQ are the direct and exclusive consequence of having experienced little or no success. The assumption, however, is often invalid when applied to children who have underlying emotional or family problems. Profoundly unhappy and conflicted children do not easily give up their negative attitudes, and may actually find the prospect of success highly unsettling because it would require that they alter their self-perceptions. Insecure children, like their adult counterparts, tend to resist change and reject the unknown.

Entrenched habits generally reflect compelling psychological needs, and the reluctance to alter one's self-perception is quite common. The chronically overweight person may diet continually but never permanently lose weight. As he eats, he may unconsciously revert to his childhood. He may associate eating with pleasing his parents and may derive security from eating. To give up the habit would demand a major transformation in his self-perception. Like adults, children tend to cling to their identity and associated behaviors even though the consequences may be painful or destructive.

Achievement brings responsibility and visibility, and this fact often scares underachieving children who have become accustomed to irresponsibility and anonymity. The best hitter on a baseball team is counted on by his teammates and the fans to win the game. The best speller in the class is expected by his teachers and classmates to get an A on every spelling test. Achievers are expected to function consistently at peak performance levels, and their accomplishments and failures are closely monitored. Identified underachievers are exposed to far less exacting standards, expectations, and scrutiny.

Real or imagined envy from those who are less successful can be another potentially painful by-product of success. The child who achieves must be willing to accept that success might place him on a pedestal and set him apart. He must also be willing to accept that he may occasionally fall off the pedestal.

The achievement-oriented child focuses on the positive consequences inherent in attaining success. He is willing to risk defeat and the envy of others. He is also willing to wrestle with major issues and major decisions: "Should I run for class president?" "Should I try out for the volleyball team?" "Do I want to aim for a first-rate college?" "Do I want to go to medical school?" Achievement-oriented children believe that they will make the right choices and, once they make their choices, that they will attain their objectives.

The underachiever does not have the same faith in his instincts or the same conviction that he can and will prevail. He is rarely willing to take the risks and pay the price for success. He becomes habituated to defeat and frustration, and often finds the prospect of letting go of the predictability of continued underachievement frightening. Although painful, this predictability provides the underachiever with a semblance of security and control.

A child acquires confidence in his own power to succeed in stages. Unless there are underlying emotional problems, success usually stimulates the expectation of and the desire for additional success. The high school student who earns good grades in science begins to think about applying for a scholarship to college so that she can study chemistry. Conversely, the high school student who was retained in fourth grade and who has continued to struggle through school may begin to think about dropping out of school and working at a fast-food restaurant.

Wendy: The Lamb Who Became a Lion

The nine-year-old projected the serenity of a nun. As Wendy completed each section of the diagnostic test, she would look up at me meekly to see if I approved of what she was doing. "Did I do it right?" she asked repeatedly.

Wendy worked slowly and almost lethargically. Her work was so methodical and her lack of confidence so extreme that she appeared hypoactive (the antithesis of hyperactive).

The tests revealed that the fourth grader's skills were approximately one and a half years below grade level in all subjects. Her mother informed me that despite her learning deficits, Wendy came home every day after school and immediately sat down to do her homework. She would spend three hours doing assignments that should have taken no more than forty minutes to complete. The child never complained. She seemed resigned to the fact that school would always be difficult for her.

Wendy's teacher terrified her. Her mother explained that her fear was unfounded. The teacher was strict, but she was fair and supportive. Wendy was nevertheless certain that she would never be able to please her teacher.

The diagnostic evaluation convinced me that Wendy's lack of confidence, her tentativeness, and her fear were far more serious barriers to achievement than were her specific learning deficits. The child seemed to have no sense of her own power. Although she was highly responsible about doing her schoolwork, she appeared to have already accepted her "destiny"— that she was inferior and could expect to achieve little in life.

I sensed that Wendy did not have any significant underlying emotional problems. Her fear and insecurity were a direct consequence of her failure and frustration in school. I was convinced that success, praise, and a well-conceived learning assistance program could transform this defeated, self-effacing child into a confident, achievement-oriented child.

A carefully orchestrated learning therapy program was implemented. Wendy was provided with repeated opportunities to excel. We encouraged her to be assertive, and discouraged her passive and meek responses. At the same time, we began to desensitize her to her apprehensions about failing and about displeasing others.

The strategy worked. Within six months Wendy had made dramatic academic improvement. Her classroom teacher moved her from the lowest math and reading groups to the middle groups.

Wendy began to stick up for herself in school and at the clinic. When she felt something was unfair, she would express her feelings. If she were asked to do math problems which she felt were too easy, she would tell us that she wanted harder problems. If another child was bothering her, she would tell him to stop.

At first, Wendy didn't have total control over her new assertiveness. Her mother was quite stunned when one day this previously meek child forcefully contradicted her and insisted that she was right and her mother was wrong. I explained to her mother that Wendy was beginning to develop a sense of her own power. The constraints imposed by her protective hypoactivity were breaking down. Wendy was discovering her ego, and it would take a while before she could establish a

comfortable balance between assertiveness and socially appropriate restraint. I assured her that her daughter would soon
become accustomed to her newfound confidence.

Wendy improved her reading and math skills by three grade
levels within a year. The principal of her school selected her
as the student who had made the most outstanding improvement during the academic year.

Acquired Helplessness

A child's confidence is like a tiny snowball that begins rolling
downhill. As it rolls, it becomes larger and picks up momentum. Although the snowball may brush against obstacles and
be bruised, it quickly acquires sufficient mass and momentum
to bounce away from these impediments. If, however, the
snowball hits a tree soon after it begins rolling, it will lose
momentum and probably become immobilized.

A young child who hits too many major obstacles on his
path through life may also lose momentum and become immobilized. With each new obstacle he becomes increasingly
discouraged. If defeat and frustration wear down his emotional
resilience, he will simply give up. This capitulation may take
many forms. Some frustrated children become rebellious. Others become shy or depressed.

Children with serious learning problems are not the only
ones at risk. Those with subtle or hard-to-define problems are
also psychologically vulnerable. Because underachieving children seldom experience significant success at anything they
undertake, they lack tangible proof of their ability. Although
they may have only subtle problems, they may nevertheless
conclude that they are incapable of success. This negative self-
image can become a permanent part of their personalities.

To protect themselves from having to confront their limitations, underachieving children may develop phobic reactions
to their own desires. If they do not permit themselves to desire,
then they cannot fail. They resign themselves to expecting
very little for themselves and from themselves.

Some children actually acquire a character trait which has

been described by some educators as "acquired or learned helplessness." Perceiving themselves as incompetent, these children integrate this perception into their identity. As they become more and more accustomed and resigned to being incompetent, they not only accept helplessness as their fate in life, they intentionally project their helplessness to the world.

Children who have rendered themselves helpless are not consciously aware of the psychological process that compels them to convince others of their real or imagined inadequacies. Their behavior may range from chronic forgetfulness and sloppiness to appearing dense or even mildly retarded. Having made themselves victims in their own life's drama, they are assured of receiving attention, sympathy, and continuing support. They are also assured that little will be expected of them.

Although children who have learned to be helpless may have significant learning problems, they have an unconscious need to magnify their deficits. Being rescued by their parents becomes one of the major payoffs of their helplessness. An unhealthy symbiotic dependency frequently develops between such children and their parents and teachers. The need for emotional support can become such an integral part of their personalities that they may resist all attempts to help them become more independent.

If they are ultimately to become independent, children must be convinced that they can survive without having to resort to helplessness. Parents and teachers play a vital role in achieving this objective. By purposefully creating contexts in which a child can succeed, parents and teachers help the child restructure his perceptions about himself. Encouraging him to succeed when it is clear that he has the ability to do so can be an essential catalyst in the restructuring process.

Transforming the self-image of the helpless child demands great patience and insight from parents and teachers. They must be able to resist manipulation, and they must be willing to examine their own roles in the emotional drama. This need for self-examination is particularly crucial when parents suspect that they might be contributing to their child's learned helplessness.

Artistry in any creative endeavor, be it parenting or teaching, requires both vision and technical competence. For the teacher, this artistry consists of knowing what is reasonable to expect from the child and then figuring out how to teach him most effectively. Teachers who are fair but demanding can have a profoundly positive influence on the formation of a child's self-concept. Conversely, teachers who accept less than the struggling child is capable of reinforce the child's learned helplessness.

Parenting artistry also demands vision and intuition. Parents must strive to create opportunities for their child to succeed while allowing him to experience occasional defeat. They must discover how to challenge the child without discouraging him. They must nurture, support, and acknowledge while concurrently establishing reasonable expectations and performance standards.

Parents' expectations must be congruent with a realistic assessment of the child's skill and ability. Parents cannot insist that a child with a serious reading problem read without making mistakes. But they can insist that he do his homework and hand in his assignments on time, assuming he is capable of doing the assignments. Parents cannot insist that a child with gross-motor coordination problems make the baseball team, but they can insist, within reasonable limits, that the child with fine-motor coordination problems redo assignments that are illegible or sloppy. The standard for legibility, however, must be relative to the child's abilities.

Aiding the helpless child to perceive himself more positively can involve a long and arduous process. It is a critically important process, and parents must be willing to persevere. In chronic cases of learned helplessness, professional counseling may be required.

Ideally, intervention will occur long before a child learns to become helpless. Early recognition of underachievement is the first step in the process of providing meaningful assistance. This is the subject of the next chapter.

- **PARENTING SUGGESTIONS**

- *Encourage your child to establish goals and prevail over challenges.*

For a child, the thrill of struggling and succeeding at a task perceived as difficult can significantly boost his self-quotient and zest quotient. Children who succeed usually conclude that they deserve more success.

- *Permit your child to experience some frustration and some pain.*

Working through a problem permits a child to develop a sense of his own power and efficacy. The opportunity to overcome an obstacle or prevail over frustration is an important catalyst for growth.

- *Avoid excessive protectiveness.*

When you remove all snags and potential setbacks from your child's path, you may be denying the child the opportunity to develop confidence in his own abilities.

- *Periodically examine your relationship with your child.*

Decide whether you are handling problems adequately. Trust your intuition in making this type of decision. Also determine whether you are giving your child sufficient acknowledgment and praise. Consciously orchestrate situations in which your child can "win."

- *Look at parenting mistakes and attempt to learn from them.*

Decide if you are making the same mistakes over and over. Consider alternative ways of responding to such behaviors as procrastination, laziness, or irresponsibility. (Alternative communication strategies will be examined in Chapter 8.)

- *Identify your child's emotional needs.*

Ask yourself, "What can I do to prepare my child for adulthood?" If your child needs external structure in order to achieve, make a special effort to provide this structure. If he requires extra praise and emotional support, decide how you might best provide these without creating excessive emotional dependence.

- *Protect your child from psychologically damaging collisions with reality by providing appropriate help.*

A child who is unable to function in a particular area should be provided with assistance. No-win situations can quickly destroy a child's self-esteem and self-confidence.

- *Resist permitting a symbiotic relationship to develop between you and your child.*

Taking ownership of all your child's problems impedes the child's emotional development. Overly protective parents are encouraging their child to become dependent on them.

- *Create contexts in which your "helpless" child can succeed.*

Parents must walk a fine line between providing encouragement and emotional support while at the same time insisting on effort and reasonable performance standards. Building the confidence of a child who perceives himself as helpless requires great patience. Parents can improve their child's self-image by orchestrating situations in which the child can succeed. Nothing stimulates the desire for success more than the experience of success.

- *When appropriate, seek professional assistance.*

Don't hesitate to admit you need help in solving a problem that you are not equipped to handle. The therapist or tutor you select is smart enough to go to an electrician or an accountant when needing assistance in areas outside his or her field of competence.

Early Recognition of Underachievement

Seth: A Tragedy Averted

"It was a beautiful day, not quite winter and too late for fall. Nobody in the world felt as exhilarated as I did. I now had a new, perfect, innocent son with whom I could share all the wonders of the world.

"The nurses said I couldn't move because I had had a long labor and there were complications because the baby was born breech. Little did the nurses know that I wanted to dance all around the room with this perfect creature. I was going to be his first teacher. We had to hurry and get out of the hospital. Precious time was flying by, and I needed to show and explain everything out there in the world to my new son.

"I carried my exhilaration home with me. For weeks I was floating on a cloud. Everyone said my baby was the strongest and most beautiful baby they had ever seen. They assured me that his need to feed often and his constant wakefulness were signs of strength and growth.

"At three months I was still operating on exhilaration, but my enthusiasm was beginning to wane. I was exhausted and desperately needed sleep. My pediatrician confirmed that my son was indeed strong and was above average in growth and

106

development. He assured me that he would outgrow his wakefulness. I found it hard to believe that someone so small required less sleep than a grown person like myself. Sometimes in desperation I would shake this three-month-old infant and ask him, 'Why won't you sleep?'

"Everyone was amazed that my son could sit up unassisted at four months of age. We were all even more amazed when Seth began to crawl backward. At nine months he was motoring around the house on his own two feet.

"'No!' to my son only elicited a grin and was interpreted as an invitation to do it some more. I told my neighbors he had a rash on his hand because I was embarrassed to let them know his hand was red from so many slaps. The house was strewn with uprooted potted plants, broken lamps, and broken 'handed down from Grandpa' antique pots.

"We tried going out to dinner as a family, but this 'perfect little innocent boy' would shriek if he couldn't turn over the salt, pepper, and sugar containers. No high chair in the world could contain him for even two minutes. Within seconds, Seth would be over the back of the booth investigating the contents of the woman's purse behind us.

"Once, when Seth was three, I was invited to a baby shower. The hostess thought it would be fun for all the women to bring their toddlers. Fun! My perfect child lasted only fifteen minutes before I heard the now familiar shriek and the outburst of crying. He wanted all the toys. He would only be placated by being allowed to come into the room with the adults. There he managed to spill two cups of tea, to urinate on the hostess's Oriental carpet, and to open five shower gifts. I left fifteen minutes later—embarrassed and in a rage.

"My son could ride a two-wheel bicycle when he was three years old. At four, I would lose him in the grocery store only to find him in the parking lot walking over the hoods of cars.

"At five, Seth's drawings of a person consisted of a very misshapen circle with two dots for eyes. His nursery school teacher thought he was too immature for kindergarten, so I held him out for a year.

"Seth entered kindergarten at five years ten months. On the

second day of school, the teacher called to tell me that Seth was a behavior problem. By the end of kindergarten, he was the only child who didn't know his short vowel sounds.

"In first grade Seth had stomachaches on school mornings and threw temper tantrums during the day. He began to hate school. Most of his classmates were reading at or above grade level, but Seth was struggling with the basic primers.

"Seth's first-grade teacher told me that my son had dyslexia.* She explained that he couldn't remember his letters, was highly distractible, and was a behavior problem. One of the administrators at the school informed me that my son had an incurable learning problem and that he would have it for the rest of his life. Seth was somehow able to function near grade level, however, and he did not qualify for any special program. My 'perfect little boy'—I cried for two days.

"In third and fourth grade Seth began to fall further and further behind academically. He had no self-esteem. He was trying desperately to survive in school, but he was using all of the wrong techniques. My son had become bossy, demanding, overly sensitive, and blaming. Still, the school authorities did not suggest any special program. Because I had been a teacher, I did not insist that Seth be given remedial assistance. I was confident that I could help him myself.

"Despite his obvious learning problems, everyone was impressed with my son's intelligence and ability to verbalize. Seth's teachers, his pediatrician, and other parents assured me that he was bright. But my son had become convinced that he was dumb. Because of his misbehavior and the resulting reprimands, he also began to see himself as bad.

"By fifth grade the situation in school had deteriorated even further. I happened to read in a newspaper that a learning disabilities specialist was offering a course for parents at a local community college. Could he possibly help my son? I wondered.

---

*Dyslexia refers to a learning problem characterized by inaccurate reading. Typically children will read or write letters or words backward. The term is sometimes inappropriately used to describe any learning or reading problem.

"The class was comprised of teachers and parents. As we shared experiences, I discovered that other parents were going through the same ordeal that I was. Their children were also encountering daily frustration and heart-wrenching failure.

"The instructor answered our questions about why our children were struggling, and he demonstrated methods for correcting their problems. He did experiments with the class which helped us to experience what it is like not to be able to understand or remember information. He also had us experience activities specifically designed to correct the perceptual processing deficits that were causing our children to hate school. For the first time, I could fully appreciate how demoralizing it was for Seth to go to school!

"I knew that I had found what I was seeking. I enrolled Seth in an intensive learning disabilities program that utilized the instructor's methods. Seth learned how to concentrate and he began to learn more efficiently.

"As Seth began to succeed in school, his self-concept improved. He no longer misbehaved. He was also less hyperactive and distractible. By chance I had stumbled onto the solution to my son's problems. This 'accident' changed both of our lives.

"Seth is now nineteen years old. He graduated last spring from a highly academic high school with a B+ average. In junior high school, he was a straight-A student (with the exception of one semester when he received a D in band because he forgot to bring his uniform to a performance). While attending high school, he not only held a twenty-hour-per-week part-time job at a car wash, but he was also an outstanding athlete who played on several varsity teams.

"My son is currently attending an excellent college where he is taking eighteen units per semester. Seth is responsible and highly successful at everything he does. He is a leader and is very popular with his peers. His goal is to become a millionaire. I know that he will achieve this goal."*

---

*This anecdote was written by a woman who later became a member of my staff.

Figuring Out What's Wrong

The ultimate resolution of Seth's learning problems hinged on two factors: competent diagnosis and appropriate treatment. Seth was fortunate. His problems were ultimately identified and treated. Despite the fact that no one was able to pinpoint the problem, Seth's mother remained adamant in her conviction that her child needed help. She simply refused to give up.

Seth was not dyslexic, nor was he incurably learning-disabled. Specific perceptual processing deficits were responsible for his distractibility, his hyperactivity, and his reading difficulties. Once these deficits were identified, they could be remediated. A specific teaching protocol was designed which trained Seth to concentrate, to attend to tasks, and to read.

Seth's story had a happy ending. Many stories do not. Although each year hundreds of thousands of nonachieving and underachieving children in the United States receive quality learning assistance in their local schools, there are hundreds of thousands of children with learning problems who receive little or no meaningful assistance.

The explanation for why many children like Seth do not receive appropriate help is complex. Inadequate funding for special education has forced many school districts to reduce or eliminate important services. Other explanations include inadequate teacher training, lack of local and national commitment to providing superior programs for the learning disabled, and a general decline in academic standards.

When publicly funded programs are unavailable or inadequate, parents may be forced to take an alternative active role in procuring help. Before they can do so, parents must first have adequate information about not only the symptoms but also the source of their child's problem. The starting point in the identification and solution-finding process is intuition.

Parental Intuition

Intuition is one of the highest manifestations of human intelligence. Although we use intuition every day, we often take it for granted or discount its validity. We trust a salesman because we like his smile or we sense that he is honest. We avoid a dark alleyway because we sense that there may be danger. Our intuitive response reflects much of the cumulative wisdom that we have acquired in the process of living. Intuition is thus a distillation of countless experiences in life.

In a millisecond our intuition can evaluate the conditions and weigh the variables inherent in a particular situation. Some situations, of course, demand a more consciously calculated assessment process. But even the businessman preparing an earnings forecast and the scientist designing an experiment—with all their access to extensive data, statistics, computers, and formulas—frequently factor intuition into their decision-making process.

A person may appear to be responding instinctively as she wrestles with whether or not to go down a dark alleyway or whether or not to trust the smile of a salesman. In actuality, the data she derives from her senses are being processed, analyzed, and evaluated by a sophisticated mental computer. The brain instantaneously compares the new situation with all past associations with alleyways and smiles which are stored in her memory. "Danger" or "Trust" flash on the screen, and she decides to walk down the alleyway or avoid it, or to trust or distrust the salesman.

The analytical or empirical person may dismiss intuition as nothing more than a feeling. The feeling, however, is actually the end product of a highly analytical process. Under appropriate conditions, intuition can be as valid a guide for our actions and reactions as the most methodical, rational decision-making process.

Intuition is one of a parent's most valuable resources. The resource is there, waiting to be used. Parents must learn to trust it. When something appears to be wrong with a child, something probably is wrong.

Early Identification—The First Step

Why does a seemingly normal infant develop into a child who must struggle desperately to survive in school? Although there is no simple answer to this question, it is clear that many learning-disabled children are affected by a complex mix of genetic, metabolic, environmental, and emotional factors.

A universal thought crosses every mother's mind when her new infant is first handed to her: Is my child healthy? As she holds the infant in her arms, relief mingles with exhilaration and joy. He is healthy and, in the eyes of his mother and father, he is beautiful and perfect! The mother's realization that this defenseless and innocent infant is totally dependent upon her enhances the natural bonding process.

In reality, of course, no human being is perfect. Each of us is endowed with positive and negative genetic traits. To new parents, this fact is irrelevant. They are preoccupied with the thrill of parenthood and the pride of having created a new life.

The transition from euphoria to reality occurs quickly. The infant's many needs must be met. Although the mother is still exhilarated, she must now deal with feeding cycles, fatigue, and the realization that life for her and her husband has radically changed.

Providing for the needs of an infant can be one of life's most challenging assignments, yet parents of children with typical needs generally become "pros" very quickly. Within a few weeks, most new parents seem like battle-wizened veterans.

The parents of an infant with atypical needs face greater challenges. A colicky child or a child with congenital problems can severely test the emotional and physical resources of any parent.

Although the baby born with serious genetic defects or health problems is quickly targeted for treatment, the child with subtle developmental or organic problems is seldom detected. Subtle problems, or those not evident at birth, often escape early recognition. Even if such problems are identified, they may not be treatable during the early stages of a child's life.

Examples of relatively minor organic problems which do not manifest themselves initially include farsightedness, nearsightedness, and certain allergies. Even more serious organic problems such as impaired vision or hearing loss may not be detected in the infant. Subtle-to-moderate mental retardation or emotional illness may also escape detection until the child enters school.

Other, non-organically based problems may not be apparent until the child is five or six years of age. These include learning disabilities, language deficits, and subtle coordination deficits. (A problem is considered organic when it involves a defect which can be measured physiologically. Hearing loss, poor eyesight, or brain damage are considered organic problems. Learning problems that do not involve brain damage or mental retardation are considered to be nonorganic.)

Many new mothers sense intuitively that their child has a problem, but they may not be able to pinpoint it. Other problems may be so subtle that even the most perceptive of parents may not recognize the nature of the problem.

Convincing others of an intuitive suspicion can be a real test of the strength of a parent's convictions. This is especially true when the symptoms are hard to define or are intermittent. Within a few months of her son's birth, Seth's mother recognized that something was wrong, but no one believed her.

A mother of a six-year-old may sense that her child is abnormally distractible or impulsive. She expresses her concerns to her pediatrician, but on the day of her visit to the physician's office, her child does not act distractible. Based upon observations in the office, the pediatrician may discount the mother's concern: "Don't worry. Distractibility is common in six-year-olds. Your daughter appears to be perfectly normal. Bring her back in if the distractibility seems to be getting worse."*
The doctor's assurances might appear reasonable, and in fact,

---

*Some physicians overreact to parents' concerns about distractibility or overactivity. These physicians may prescribe medication whenever there are indications of overactivity or learning problems. Although I am not a phy-

may be what the mother wants to hear at the time. Temporarily placated, she leaves the office and returns home. But the distractibility persists, and the mother becomes increasingly convinced that her child has a problem. She is now faced with the dilemma of deciding whether or not to trust her intuition or to trust the pediatrician's advice. Should she risk appearing as an overly concerned parent? Should she try to convince the pediatrician of her concerns? Should she seek another opinion?

The challenge of convincing others of an intuitive suspicion is even greater when the child is a firstborn and the mother has no frame of reference for comparison. In insisting that her child needed help even though no one else agreed, Seth's mother ran the risk of being considered overly protective, fearful, and even neurotic.

Parental reactions to a child's learning problems vary significantly, ranging from nonchalance to excessive concern. Three general parenting styles can be identified.

INTUITIVE PARENTS Because intuitive parents trust their instincts, they seek a professional opinion when they suspect that something is wrong. This opinion may either confirm or contradict their intuitive suspicions. If they feel the professional assessment is well grounded, they will accept it. Otherwise, they will most likely seek another professional opinion.

EXCESSIVELY CONCERNED PARENTS Excessively concerned parents have a compulsive need for their child to be the "best." They often look for problems when none exist. Although the child may be working efficiently and receiving B's in school, his parents feel that he should be receiving A's. Convinced that their child is either lazy or disabled in some way, they tend to seek out someone who will confirm that something is wrong.

---

sician, I recommend that parents be very cautious about the use of amphetamines. I consider medication to be a last resort that should be prescribed only in extreme cases of hyperactivity or when all alternative educational protocols have failed. It has been my experience that most distractible children with subtle-to-moderate problems can be trained to concentrate and to overcome their learning problems without the use of medication.

Parents who seek out a professional opinion when they are concerned about their child's learning progress are not necessarily being overly concerned. If there is a possibility of an underlying problem, it is preferable that parents err on the side of too much concern than too little. Parents who insist, however, that their child is an underachiever or learning-disabled simply because he functions below their expectations may need to examine their expectations, realistically and objectively. Those parents who remain convinced that their child is functioning below his potential should seek an independent professional opinion. At the same time, parents must recognize that if their own psychological needs compel them to make their child "perfect," they risk causing resentment, stress, confusion, and neurosis.

DENIAL-ORIENTED PARENTS Denial-oriented parents are at the opposite end of the concern spectrum. They refuse to accept evidence that clearly indicates that their child has a problem. This refusal may stem from a compulsion to deny any suggestion that their child is less than perfect. Such parents may persist in denying that their child has a problem in the face of overwhelming evidence that the child is in desperate need of help.

Parents who choose to disregard or deny a blatant problem generally do so because they identify too strongly with their child. Because of their own psychological conflicts, these parents become emotionally threatened when forced to confront their child's problems. Some denial-oriented parents unconsciously fear that the child's imperfections will reflect their own imperfections. Others fear that they are in some way responsible for their child's problem. By refusing to confront the child's problem, they avoid guilt and emotional turmoil. (It has been my experience that fathers are more likely than mothers to respond this way.)

Parents who attempt to categorize themselves based upon the descriptions above may throw their hands up in despair. If they follow their intuition and insist that their child has a problem, they run the risk of being overly concerned. If they resist being overly concerned, they run the risk of being irresponsible.

The line between justifiable concern and excessive concern can be very clear in some instances, and very obscure in others. Parents who are having difficulty making this distinction will benefit greatly from the objective assessment of a competent professional.

Persistence and Perseverance

One of the most frustrating experiences that parents face occurs when a problem is identified but there are no practical solutions. Seth's mother struggled for years with a lack of professional responsiveness to her son's learning problems. She recognized Seth's hyperactivity when he was a toddler. The physician discounted her observations. But even if the physician had concurred, he would have had limited medical options available for treating a hyperactive one-year-old.

The classroom teacher also recognized that Seth had a problem. She described him as "immature" and recommended the traditional solution to academic problems: retention. Unfortunately, she misdiagnosed Seth's problem. He was not immature. In fact, relatively few children who struggle in school are actually physiologically immature. Most who are so labeled have specific learning deficits and would be far better served if their deficits were identified and treated. Retention, which should be considered only when a child manifests unequivocal symptoms of developmental or physiological delay or when there are no other available educational alternatives, would not have resolved Seth's hyperactivity and distractibility. Fortunately, his mother's persistence and perseverance prevailed and Seth received the help he required.

Nineteen years later, parents are still dealing with the frustration of trying to find appropriate diagnosis and treatment for their struggling children. As a general rule, the protocols available for diagnosing and treating severe developmental problems are more extensive and more widely available than those for diagnosing and treating less extreme problems. This can be very frustrating for the parents of an underachieving or moderately learning-disabled child.

When professionals are faced with tangible, definable deficits, they can draw upon proven diagnostic and treatment methodologies. A child who suffers from arthritis can often be treated with a drug and/or physical therapy program that can control the disease. No analogous medical protocol exists, to my knowledge, for treating the child who manifests symptoms of moderate hyperactivity and distractibility during the first three years of life.

Parents who sense that something is wrong with their child must have the courage to trust their intuition, even if it means appearing "neurotic." If their pediatrician or other professionals can convince them that their concern is unwarranted, then so be it. But if the parents remain unconvinced by this opinion, then they have a responsibility to persist in seeking out a professional whose counsel they trust. Too many parents have been told "he'll outgrow it" only to discover later that their child did not in fact "outgrow" his problem. Too many children have suffered unnecessary emotional damage because their parents accepted advice which contradicted their intuition.

In some instances the symptoms of a learning problem may go into temporary remission. Although the problem may appear to be resolved, it may reappear in either the same form or a different form later in the child's life. A hyperactive, chronically distractible first grader, for instance, may outgrow his hyperactivity by the time he reaches adolescence, but in the process of outgrowing the problem he may never have learned to read properly. He may no longer be hyperactive when he is fifteen, but he may by then be a functional illiterate or a juvenile delinquent.

A word of caution must be interjected. Some professionals may confirm a parent's concerns even though these concerns are unwarranted or excessive. Although these professionals may be sincere and well intentioned, they may misdiagnose the child's problem because of their own limitations as a diagnostician or because they have been provided with flawed or biased information by the child's parents.

Other professionals may confirm a parent's unwarranted concerns or plant seeds of doubt in the parent's mind because they want to make money. A common ploy of the unscrupulous professional is to predict all sorts of dire consequences if the child is not immediately enrolled in a particular program. Parents who are concerned about their child are emotionally vulnerable. Their intense desire to help the child may cause them to become susceptible to unscrupulous salesmanship.

Parents should check out the reputation of the service organization or the private practitioner before having their child evaluated or treated. Selecting a professional on the basis of a recommendation from their pediatrician, a respected teacher, or a trusted friend reduces the risk of being exploited.

Critical Questions and Critical Choices

The parents of underachieving and nonachieving children are faced with complex issues and heart-wrenching decisions, such as:

> Does my child have a learning problem?
> Is the special help she is receiving in school adequate?
> Is he hyperactive?
> Should I allow the doctor to prescribe medication to help
>   him concentrate?
> Why does she hate school?
> Should I get my child a tutor?
> Should we help him write his book report?
> How do I deal with his procrastination?
> How can I help him feel better about himself?
> How can I get her to be more responsible?
> Why is she sabotaging herself?

The answers to these questions can have a vital impact upon whether or not the struggling child ultimately achieves success in school, at home, and with friends. Before parents can make appropriate responses to these questions, they must answer an even more basic question: What is responsible for my child's difficulties in school? This is the subject of the next chapter.

• PARENTING SUGGESTIONS

● *Take an active role in the process of identifying and finding solutions to your child's problems.*

Do not be deterred by the fact that you may not have professional credentials. Creating a context in which your child can achieve and succeed is one of parenting's most important responsibilities.

● *Learn to trust your intuition.*

Your instincts about your child's potential and performance are probably on target. It is preferable to err on the side of overconcern than on the side of inadequate concern.

● *Seek competent professional confirmation if you feel that your child is an underachiever or has a learning problem.*

Asking someone you trust to help you evaluate your child is the first step in the process of identifying the source of an actual or potential problem.

● *Be persistent and persevere if you are not satisfied with the advice you receive from a professional.*

Do not be deterred if the school or a private practitioner discounts your concerns. If you are skeptical about their assessment or recommendations, seek another opinion.

● *Verify the credentials and professional reputation of the individual or organization evaluating and/or treating your child.*

The best source of referral for an objective professional assessment of your child or for a treatment program is your family physician or pediatrician. A trusted friend whose child has been helped by a particular therapist or organization is another excellent referral source. If you live near a university or teachers college, request that a professor in the learning disabilities or reading department refer you to a reputable agency.

The Underachiever with Learning Problems

Benjamin: He Lived under a Microscope

Benjamin smiled when I showed him the math test. "That's easy!" the eight-year-old exclaimed. With a big smile and great enthusiasm, he began solving the problems.

I explained to the second grader that the test was used with children in first through third grades and that the problems would become more difficult as he progressed. I told him to stop when the problems became too hard.

Benjamin completed the first page without difficulty. By the second page, his smile and his enthusiasm disappeared. He began to struggle.

I could see that not knowing the answers greatly upset him. His face mirrored his increasing frustration. From time to time he would glance at his mother forlornly and apologetically. Her own facial expression offered little comfort. She watched him intently as he worked, and she appeared both concerned and, at the same time, disapproving. Finally, Benjamin asked her to help him, and to my amazement she began to show him how to solve the problems. I diplomatically explained that she would invalidate the test if she assisted him. My request that she desist appeared to anger her.

When I asked Benjamin to read for me, I noted that his

reading was quite labored and inaccurate. He had difficulty deciphering phonetic and nonphonetic words. As he struggled, I could see the look of desperation return to his face. I was about to ask him to stop, when he once again looked to his mother for help. She proceeded to help him sound out the word with which he was having difficulty.

I had evaluated thousands of children with their parents present, but I had never encountered a parent who interfered so blatantly in the testing procedure. Having parents present during portions of the test is, of course, risky. Although their presence creates the potential for interference and for self-consciousness on the part of the student, it also provides important potential benefits. The parents have an excellent opportunity to gain firsthand insight into their child's specific learning strengths and weaknesses, and the discussion about the test results is all the more meaningful.

It was clear that my normal testing procedure was not working. I asked Benjamin's mother to wait in the outer office while I completed the assessment. She consented to do so with great reluctance. Benjamin's subsequent responses and reactions concerned me. I asked him to complete a self-evaluation form. On a scale from 1 to 10 (10 = extremely happy), Benjamin rated his happiness in school at 2. He rated his happiness at home at 3. When asked to rate how smart he was in comparison to his classmates, he gave himself a 3.

I had Benjamin complete the remaining academic sections of the test in a colleague's office, and I invited his mother back into my office. As soon as she sat down, she began to make excuses for her son. She explained that Benjamin had not read or worked on math during the entire summer vacation. She contended that his skills had regressed because of three months of academic inactivity.

I was surprised when she informed me that Benjamin had scored at least one year above grade level in all subject areas on the standardized test that had been administered at his parochial school. Despite these test scores, Benjamin was struggling to keep up with his class. Although I did not know his IQ, I was certain from my conversation with him that he was of superior intelligence. His mother confirmed this. He had scored 136 on the Stanford-Binet IQ test.

Benjamin's mother expressed grave concern about his learning problems. She informed me that he had recently been evaluated comprehensively by an educational psychologist. The tests had revealed some subtle perceptual learning deficits, but there were no indications of a profound learning problem. She had decided to bring Benjamin to me for a confirmation of the psychologist's assessment.

The family pediatrician had also examined Benjamin. Her evaluation had failed to uncover any neurological problems. Nevertheless, Benjamin's mother was considering asking the pediatrician to refer her to a neurologist so that her son could be given an EEG (electroencephalogram) to determine if he had minimal brain damage. Another option she was considering was asking the pediatrician to put Benjamin on medication to control his "hyperactivity." (I was fairly certain that the pediatrician would refuse this request.) After completing my evaluation, I concluded that Benjamin's reading and math deficiencies were in the subtle-to-moderate range. There were indications of distractibility, perceptual processing deficits, and anxiety, but I found nothing that suggested an organic problem such as minimal brain damage, nor did I observe symptoms of hyperactivity. I could only assume that the discrepancy between Benjamin's poor oral reading skills and his high scores on the reading test was attributable to his superior intelligence. Although he had undoubtedly struggled while reading the material on the test, he must have made intelligent guesses on the multiple-choice questions.

As I discussed the results of the test with Benjamin's mother, I was struck by the contradictory positions she took. She seemed compelled to uncover serious learning problems in her son and, at the same time, to make excuses for his learning deficits. When I began to explore this contradiction with her, she became quite agitated. She told me that her own mother had been extremely demanding and critical. As a child, she was always being compared to her gifted older brother. Her mother had never been satisfied with her school performance. If she received an A −, her mother would ask her why she hadn't received an A. When she did receive an A, her mother would suggest that she was taking easy courses. Although she was convinced she could never please her mother, she had always felt a compelling need to justify herself. She still felt inadequate despite the fact that she now had a master's degree in English literature and was teaching at a community college.

Benjamin had been drawn into a drama whose script had been written twenty-five years before his birth. His mother was driven to identify and ferret out his "imperfections" because she unconsciously construed these flaws as symbols of her own imperfections. If she could make her son more perfect, she could then make herself more perfect. Her mother had died ten years previously, but she was still driven to seek her acceptance and approval. This compulsive need dominated her life and Benjamin's life. Continually subjected to the relentless scrutiny of an obsessed mother, the eight-year-old was defenseless. His father could offer little protection. He was divorced from Benjamin's mother and had remarried. He lived in another state and saw his son only at Christmas and for one month during the summer.

Benjamin had been placed under a cruel microscope. Because his mother was so entangled in her own emotional drama, she failed to perceive that she was psychologically abusing her son. Ironically, she had put Benjamin in the same emotionally destructive no-win situation that she herself had experienced as a child.

Benjamin's emotional vulnerability concerned me far more than his learning deficiencies. In self-defense, he had managed to adjust to the stress. Although I had seen him fold under his mother's intense scrutiny, I felt that he was still relatively intact emotionally. Red flags, however, were waving. I was certain that he would soon begin to suffer serious and permanent psychological damage if his mother persisted in subjecting him to her constant criticism.

Learning assistance alone would not solve Benjamin's problems. I had no illusions about his mother relinquishing her obsessions. Her need for perfection was too deeply entrenched in her personality. She would require psychotherapy, and I had to help her accept this. In the interim, my responsibility was to do whatever I could to assist her son.

The Problematic Diagnosis

Diagnosing a child's learning problem can be a relatively simple procedure when the symptoms conform to accepted diagnostic criteria. Making an accurate diagnosis is infinitely more challenging when the symptoms are unclear, intermittent, nonspecific, or enigmatic. Every diagnostician loves to confront "standard" problems, which lend themselves to standard solutions. Diagnosticians are on shakier ground when the problem is atypical or is compounded by other factors with which they are not totally familiar. Under such conditions, the diagnosis can be tentative, and there is a risk that the problem may be misunderstood, misinterpreted, or overlooked.

The complex mix of academic and psychological factors which compounded Benjamin's learning difficulties defied a simple diagnosis. He was obviously struggling in school, but his struggle was only partially attributable to reading and math deficits. Emotional stress and excessive criticism played a far more significant role.

Although the support of a resource specialist would have undoubtedly helped Benjamin with his reading, it would not have eliminated his most pressing problem. He was in danger of being destroyed by a neurotic mother. Resolving his learning problems would require more than tutoring. The entire family dynamics needed to be realigned. To treat the learning problem without addressing the psychological issues would be the equivalent of covering a seriously infected wound with a Band-Aid.

Underachievers in the Gray Area

At any given time during the school year as many as ten million American children are struggling in school. Some are struggling desperately to survive academically. Others have given up the fight because they have become demoralized or profess not to care.

Only a fraction of the children who have problems in school are ever officially diagnosed as having specific learning disabilities. Many of those not identified also have learning deficiencies, but their deficits either do not conform to the standard identification criteria or are considered insufficiently severe to warrant learning assistance, or even a diagnostic assessment. These children with marginal learning problems generally fall into a gray area in our education system.

Benjamin's situation illustrated the plight of the underachieving child in the gray area. He had obvious learning deficits and family problems. Despite these problems, he would have probably been disqualified in many public school districts from receiving special learning assistance because of his high test scores.

Underachievers in the gray area rarely elicit as much attention as the more blatantly learning-disabled children. Like slightly wounded soldiers in battle, children with subtle problems are sent back to the front lines because their injuries are deemed insufficient to warrant treatment. If left untreated, however, these "minor" wounds can fester and ultimately become as debilitating as major wounds.

A wide spectrum of symptoms characterizes underachievers in the gray area. Although their symptoms may be less extreme and harder to identify than those found in the classically learning-disabled student, the symptoms nevertheless interfere with learning efficiency and impede academic achievement.

The diverse characteristics of underachievers in the gray area are represented by the graph on the following page.

You will note that the underachieving child's motivation level can vary from poor to highly conscientious. His standardized test score performance may range from grade level to significantly above grade level. On exams and report cards his grades may vary from below average to slightly above average. His specific learning disabilities may extend from subtle to moderate. His self-quotient and zest quotient may range from extremely poor to above average. The range of his IQ may extend from slightly below average to gifted.

UNDERACHIEVERS IN THE GRAY AREA

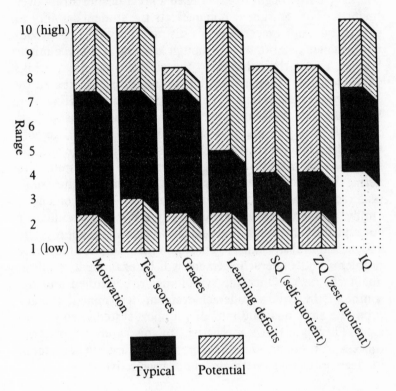

Because underachievement has so many diverse symptoms and assumes so many different forms, precise identification can be challenging. The bright student who studies diligently and receives B's is as much an underachiever as the student of average intelligence who studies diligently and receives C's.

The specific sources of underachievement may also be difficult to identify because a child's problems in school may reflect several overlapping causal factors. Each individual factor may be quite subtle, but the combined effect may be debilitating. For example, a child may have a slight tendency to be distractible and disorganized. Despite these problems, he does relatively well in school. But then his father loses his job, and his parents begin to experience a great deal of stress over finances. This tension at home affects the student's ability to concentrate and exacerbates his distractibility. His classroom performance deteriorates. Although learning assistance might help, it is not the solution to the child's problem. A child whose learning problems are being caused or exacerbated by stress would benefit far more from short-term counseling than he would from tutoring.

The first step in the process of providing appropriate help for underachievers in the gray area is to identify the specific symptoms of their problems. The next step is to attempt to define the source of these symptoms. Determining if the child's underachievement is the result of an emotional problem, a family problem, a learning disability, poor study skills, or cultural influences is a prerequisite to providing appropriate and meaningful assistance. (These potential sources of learning problems and underachievement will be examined in subsequent chapters.) Once the symptoms are identified and the source of the child's underachievement determined, the appropriate emotional and remedial support systems can be created. There are three alternatives to this careful, sequential process of problem identification: do nothing, do something ineffective, or do something counterproductive.

Slipping Through the Diagnostic Screen

Standardized achievement tests, IQ tests, diagnostic testing procedures for learning disabilities, and classroom performance generally do an excellent job of identifying the learning-disabled child. These tests, however, if not properly utilized and interpreted, can present an incomplete picture of the underachieving child.

The scores on standardized (nationally normed) achievement tests generally provide the first objective indication of academic deficiencies. The tests are designed to yield a very precise indication of a child's performance level relative to other children of the same age. The tests, however, are not designed to indicate why a child is struggling.

Achievement tests have another serious limitation. Although they may offer a comprehensive profile of a student's academic strengths and weaknesses, the tests do not indicate whether or not a child is achieving at a level commensurate with his ability. A very bright child, for instance, may score one year above grade level in reading and may still not be achieving at a level consistent with his potential ability. If the child has an IQ of 140, he should be expected to test at least two years above grade level.

Comparing a child's IQ scores with his achievement scores can provide the diagnostician with valuable insight. Although the results of IQ tests and achievement tests can be skewed by emotional and perceptual problems, these results can be important instruments for diagnosing underachievement and learning problems. Inconsistencies in the scores should alert parents to a potential problem. If the results on a child's IQ test, for instance, indicate above-average intelligence and the results of his achievement tests indicate below-average skills, this discrepancy suggests underachievement. Another child's IQ scores and achievement scores may be high but his classroom performance may be average or below average; this pattern also suggests underachievement.

Diagnostic tests for learning disabilities are quite precise and very effective in detecting specific learning deficits. There are, however, conditions which can jeopardize the accuracy of these tests. For instance, a child who is sensitive to sugar may become hyperactive and distractible after eating sweets. The accuracy of any test administered to the child after he has consumed sugar would be highly suspect. Another child may be experiencing emotional stress at home, and his test results would also be highly suspect.

The validity of any diagnostic or achievement test hinges on the skills and the perceptiveness of the person administering and interpreting the test. The diagnostician must look at the entire picture. The child's scores constitute only one piece in the mosaic. Family, emotional, cultural, and attitudinal factors must be factored into the diagnosis, and the potential for specious test results must be considered. To overlook or discount these factors is to increase the risk of a flawed diagnosis.

Educational Testing and Treatment Priorities

The underachieving child with nonspecific or subtle deficits who is functioning near grade level can easily slip through the cracks in most school diagnostic screening procedures. In some school districts in California, for instance, only those children with blatant problems are targeted for an assessment by the school psychologist. Those who are tested must usually score at least two years below grade level in reading or math and/or manifest a significant discrepancy between their scores on the verbal section and the performance sections on an IQ test in order to qualify for help.

Even if he is tested, the underachiever may be misdiagnosed or disqualified from receiving help because his symptoms are not deemed sufficiently severe. Limited financial and personnel resources have forced many schools to prioritize who receives time with the resource specialist. The energies of the special education personnel are usually reserved for the more seriously academically handicapped students. Underachieving children who are more or less able to keep up with their class are generally low on the learning assistance priority list.

Underachieving children who have learning problems which involve complex educational and psychological components are particularly at risk. Few schools have the financial or personnel resources to deal with complex, multifaceted problems. Many districts have been forced to cut back on the support systems they provide. Social workers and even school counselors are being eliminated in the more financially troubled districts. Unless there is evidence of physical, psychological, or sexual abuse, school administrators generally do not intervene in family problems. Although children in need of counseling may be referred to other agencies, these agencies may not fully appreciate the educational ramifications of the child's problems.

Because of limitations in school testing programs, the responsibility for identifying the less seriously learning-disabled underachiever now generally falls on the shoulders of concerned classroom teachers and parents. But before parents or teachers can hope to make a difference, they must recognize and understand the underlying problems.

Defining a Learning Disability

The wide spectrum of symptoms and types of learning disabilities makes it difficult to find an all-encompassing definition for the term. The first step is to differentiate between subtle learning disabilities and severe learning disabilities.

The symptoms of a severe learning disability are substantive, specific, and relatively easy to identify. Letter and word reversals, for example, can usually be recognized by alert parents and teachers. Disorganized problem-solving skills, occasional difficulty following oral or written instructions, and intermittent inattentiveness are characteristics of a potential learning disability. But these latter, more diffuse characteristics may be more difficult for even perceptive parents and teachers to pinpoint.

Despite the wide range of symptoms and different types of learning disabilities, there is a common denominator: most children with learning disabilities have difficulty processing sensory information efficiently. The ability to decipher written and spoken sensory data is a prerequisite to learning. Words and numbers must be computed. Instructions must be followed. Facts must be remembered. The brain must be able to integrate and associate this input within a millisecond. If the brain cannot perform these functions efficiently, it cannot learn effectively.*

The following definition of a learning disability underscores the function of efficient perceptual processing skills in the learning process.

---

* See Lawrence J. Greene, *Kids Who Hate School*, revised edition, Atlanta: Humanics, Ltd., 1984, for a comprehensive treatment of the different types of learning problems.

Learning disability: A pattern of academic responses which is inefficient. This inefficiency interferes with the student's ability to understand, remember, apply, or integrate the material being taught.

The processing or decoding of sensory data by the brain is called perception. The child who reads inaccurately, forgets what he sees or hears, or fails to pay attention in class probably has perceptual processing deficiencies. The condition may be called a perceptual dysfunction, minimal brain dysfunction (MBD), or attention deficit disorder (ADD).

One child with visual perception deficiencies may have difficulty remembering the written symbols which are used to communicate information. Words or numbers may not compute properly in his brain because his brain does not utilize visual information efficiently. Another child with visual perception problems may have difficulty reading words accurately. If he has difficulty with visual discrimination and tracking he may see the word "bad" and say "dad," or he may see the word "was" and say "saw." When writing, he may copy the number "99" when "66" has been written on the blackboard. Another child with visual tracking problems may lose his place when reading or omit syllables or word endings. (This type of reading problem is often referred to as dyslexia.)

The child with auditory processing deficits may forget information or become confused when instructions are given. He may not be able to discriminate the difference between sounds. For instance, the teacher may say "bad" and he might write the word "bed."

Perceptual processing deficits can impair a child's performance in some or all academic subject areas. Each child can be affected differently. Some children will have difficulty exclusively with reading. Others may have problems in math. Still others may have difficulty with spelling or writing. Some children with serious perceptual dysfunction will have deficiencies in all academic areas. The child who intends to write a "b" and instead writes a "d" could be the same child who has difficulty remembering his teacher's instructions in class.

In addition to the symptoms described above, there are other common manifestations of a perceptual dysfunction, such as inattentiveness, impulsivity, hyperactivity, distractibility, poor handwriting, and poor coordination. A child need not manifest all these characteristics in order to be diagnosed as having a perceptual learning disability.

Early Indications

The inability to master basic academic skills is the primary indication of a learning disability. Because the identification of a learning disability is directly linked to academic skill mastery, the identification of such problems in younger children who have not yet been exposed to basic academic skills can be very difficult. In the absence of evidence of neurological impairment, delay in motor development, chronic distractibility, hyperactivity, or maturational lag, parents and professionals may have difficulty recognizing a potential learning problem in preschool children.

A key component in the process of identifying potential learning problems in young children is the correlation of skill mastery to highly predictable developmental stages that children normally experience. As a child progresses through these stages, he acquires specific learning capabilities. At each level of his development, he is expected to be able to master certain skills. No one would be particularly concerned if a one-and-a-half-year-old cannot speak in complete sentences. A three-year-old, however, who has not developed the necessary language skills to be able to communicate in simple sentences would elicit concern. Although a four-year-old would not be expected to catch a ball, a seven-year-old who has not developed the requisite eye-hand coordination to do so may be signaling motor-development delay. When evaluating children, preschool teachers, educational psychologists, and pediatricians look for indications that a child is not able to perform age-appropriate developmental tasks. Such indications suggest developmental delay and increase the possibility that the child may develop subsequent learning disabilities.

Some children, of course, are late in developing motor, language, social, and preacademic skills. Many of these initially delayed children may subsequently catch up without special help. This natural ability to catch up makes the job of determining which preschool children need special assistance and which do not quite challenging. Excessively slow motor development, chronic inattentiveness, hyperactivity, and delayed academic readiness skills in preschool and kindergarten are warning signals which parents and teachers cannot afford to disregard.

The identification process is somewhat easier in the case of school-age children. The quality of the child's work in the classroom is the litmus test for determining if he is underachieving or has a learning problem. Any deficits should alert parents and teachers to a potential problem. If the teacher is the first to see the red flag, he or she must warn the child's parents. Conversely, if the parents are the first to see the flag, they must alert the teacher.

A few words of caution are necessary. Certain symptoms of learning disabilities, such as distractibility or letter reversals, are quite common among children in preschool and kindergarten. These characteristics do not necessarily mean that a child is dyslexic or destined to be learning-disabled. If, however, the child is chronically distractible and if he persists in reversing letters and numbers in first grade, he should be evaluated by the school psychologist.

Preschool teachers who are concerned about a child should be especially diplomatic when they present their concerns to the parents. Such statements as "Your daughter is developmentally delayed" can alarm parents. A simple statement such as "Becky is having a difficult time paying attention, and her motor skill development seems somewhat slow" should be followed by a recommendation that the parents consult with their pediatrician.

Impediments to Early Identification

Ideally, the identification of a learning problem should occur in kindergarten. There are, however, several significant barriers to making such an early identification.

The symptoms of learning problems may be difficult to identify. The diagnosis of a blatant learning problem in school-age children can be as straightforward as the diagnosis of a blatant medical problem. Letter reversals, inaccurate reading, illegible handwriting, and memory problems are easily recognized deficits. Once identified, the problem can then be treated with appropriate remediation procedures. Less definitive problems, however, such as inconsistent classroom performance, fluctuating test scores, intermittent lapses of memory, and episodic problems with concentration, are more challenging to understand, diagnose, and treat.

Symptoms of different problems may overlap. Identifying and delineating complex learning problems involving emotional, family, or cultural components can be difficult. Symptoms can be misleading and/or misdiagnosed by even highly conscientious parents and professionals.

Preschool teachers and pediatricians may misinterpret the symptoms. Symptoms which might indicate a learning problem or underachievement are seldom as definitive in the case of younger children as are the symptoms of a blatant physical problem. Because these symptoms may be obscure, the opportunity for an early diagnosis may be missed. Parents are frequently told that the child will "outgrow it" or that the child is "immature."

Early intervention can significantly reduce the risk that a child's early developmental deficits will ultimately become full-blown learning problems. Ideally, the child who demonstrates atypical developmental patterns in either preschool or kindergarten will be closely monitored. If he continues to manifest deficits in first grade, he should be targeted for a workup by the school psychologist or learning disabilities specialist. Parents must assume the responsibility for monitoring their child should it become apparent that the preschool or elementary school monitoring system is inadequate.

The mandated training requirements for preschool teachers vary from state to state. These requirements are often insufficient to ensure early recognition of developmental deficits and potential learning problems. In states that have not established rigorous requirements for the licensing of preschools and for the training and certification of preschool personnel, the risk of a child with developmental deficits slipping through the diagnostic screen is considerably greater.

Because of these licensing and training inadequacies, far too many high-risk four-year-olds and five-year-olds are not being identified by the very people who are in the best position to recognize potential problems. These children carry their problems into elementary school and beyond, with often tragic consequences.

Acquiring Essential Information

The parents of elementary school children have access to extensive information about their children. Parents who listen to their child read will be able to hear if he is reading inaccurately and struggling. Parents who watch their child do her math homework will be able to see if she has problems with math computations, or perhaps with comprehending math concepts.

Report cards, parent-teacher conferences, test grades, and homework assignments also provide invaluable input. Parent-teacher conferences can alert parents to problems with letter and number reversals, distractibility, difficulty following instructions, sloppy work, and incomplete assignments. Report cards will indicate whether a child is having difficulty with handwriting, spelling, reading comprehension, math, or language arts. Written homework will reveal problems with sloppiness, illegible writing, spelling, and verbal expression.

Recognizing less specific deficits such as difficulty understanding concepts, difficulty drawing inferences, disorganization, and poor planning skills can be more problematical.

Parents may have to ask the teacher specific questions about these potential problem areas. Although the teacher may not have the answers, expressing these concerns will alert the teacher to the need to monitor the child more closely.

If untreated, subtle or moderate learning problems can ultimately cause as much emotional havoc as severe learning problems. Deficits which appear relatively minor during the first or second grade may become significant impediments to learning as the child progresses through school. The child may respond to increasing academic demands by becoming frustrated and discouraged. Serious self-concept damage may result.

Some learning problems are atypical. A student may do very well during the first few years of elementary school and then suddenly begin to have difficulty in fourth grade. Or a student may do well in class and on standardized achievement tests but do poorly on the tests that the teacher designs. Children with enigmatic or unusual learning patterns such as these may never be properly diagnosed and treated.

The skills and resources of diagnosticians and parents may be severely challenged by the atypical learner. Parents may suspect that their child is struggling, but the school authorities may not be able to identify any specific deficits and may recommend retention as a solution to the child's academic "immaturity." Or parents may observe a deterioration in their child's self-esteem and attitude about school. When they broach the subject with the teacher or the psychologist, they may be told that the child is manipulative. Although the parents may feel dissatisfied with such explanation, they may feel stymied and insecure about how to proceed.

Parents who lack confidence in their own perceptions are often reluctant to make waves. They may feel insufficiently qualified to insist that their child be evaluated or provided with learning assistance. Under such conditions, feelings of frustration, desperation, and powerlessness are quite common.

Parents who do not find concurrence or support are faced with a serious dilemma. Should they trust their own intuition, or should they simply accept the assessments and recommendations of professionals and discount their own feelings?

The following Learning Problems Checklist is designed to help parents who suspect that their child has a learning problem to pinpoint the specific learning deficits. Those parents who are already convinced that their child has a learning problem may elect to skip this evaluation process. The checklist, however, may still be of value because it can help them identify deficits with greater precision.

To evaluate your child properly, you will need to consult the child's teacher for information about classroom performance.

LEARNING PROBLEMS CHECKLIST

	Yes	No
Academic		
Poor reading comprehension		
Difficulty with phonics		
Letter and number reversals		
Inaccurate reading		
Difficulty with math computation skills (addition, etc.)		
Poor handwriting		
Inaccurate copying (from blackboard or at desk)		
Difficulty understanding math concepts		
Difficulty working independently		
Sloppy work habits		
Difficulty with spelling		
Difficulty with written language arts (grammar, syntax, etc.)		
Poor organizational skills		

Poor planning skills   ———— ————

Incomplete projects   ———— ————

Difficulty following oral instructions   ———— ————

Difficulty following written instructions   ———— ————

Behavior
Short attention span   ———— ————

Difficulty following directions   ———— ————

Overactive   ———— ————

Impulsive   ———— ————

Fidgety   ———— ————

Distractible   ———— ————

Accident-prone   ———— ————

Forgetful   ———— ————

Daydreams   ———— ————

Slow in completing tasks   ———— ————

Excitable   ———— ————

Unpredictable   ———— ————

Disturbs other students   ———— ————

Chronic procrastination   ———— ————

Chronic irresponsibility   ———— ————

Coordination
Gross-motor coordination deficits (sports,
etc.)   ———— ————

Fine-motor coordination deficits (drawing,
handwriting, etc.)   ———— ————

Clumsy   ———— ————

Awkward   ———— ————

Poor balance   ———— ————

Right/left confusion   _____ _____

Fear of physical activities (climbing, sports,
etc.)   _____ _____

INTERPRETING THE CHECKLIST. A pattern of "yes" answers to
the statements on the checklist probably indicates that your
child has a moderate-to-severe learning disability. Occasional
"yes" answers probably indicates a subtle-to-moderate learning
problem. A preponderance of "no" answers probably indicates
that your child does not have a learning disability. It is important
to note that your child may not have an identifiable learning
disability and yet may still be an underachiever.

If after completing the checklist you suspect that your child
does have a learning problem, do not hesitate to discuss your
concerns with the teacher. Show the teacher the list and ask
if he or she concurs with your assessment. If the teacher agrees
with your evaluation, request that your child be evaluated by
the school psychologist or a learning disabilities/resource
specialist. In the event the teacher does not concur with your
concerns, seek an independent professional opinion. If your
child does not qualify for testing or for learning assistance,
you may need to have him evaluated by a private agency.
(Procedures for seeking out and evaluating private agencies
will be discussed in Chapter 10.)

It bears reemphasizing that many children who are
performing below their potential in school may not fit the
classic textbook profile of the learning-disabled child.* These
underachieving children may have few or no identifiable
deficits.

Any learning problem, even one that is subtle or intermittent,
can have profound consequences for both the child and his

---

* For a more complete discussion of the symptoms and behaviors described
in the Learning Problems Checklist, see my book *Kids Who Hate School*,
revised edition, Atlanta: Humanics, Ltd., 1984.

family. For this reason all learning problems should be remediated, irrespective of their severity or frequency.

When learning problems begin to interfere with academic performance, some form of intervention is crucial. In order to intervene effectively, parents must be able to make intelligent, strategic decisions about their child's needs. Accurate information about the child's learning deficits is essential to making such decisions. The primary sources of this vital information are the pediatrician, the classroom teacher, the school psychologist, and the resource specialist. Parents should not hesitate to request the information they need from them. If they have doubts about what they are being told, then they must seek a second and sometimes even a third opinion.

● PARENTING SUGGESTIONS

● *Do not accept educational platitudes or simplistic solutions.*

The source of subtle learning problems and underachievement can be difficult to identify. This should not deter you. Subtle problems can have as devastating a psychological effect on a child's self-concept as severe problems. Do not accept stock statements such as "He's immature," or "Be patient," or "I'm sure she'll outgrow her learning problem."

● *If you suspect that your child has an underlying learning problem, actively, and if necessary, aggressively seek an accurate diagnosis.*

Standardized achievement tests do not provide all of the information that parents of struggling children need in order to make critical decisions about their children's education. These tests indicate only a child's level of performance. The tests do not suggest the source of the problem. If a child does not qualify for a diagnostic workup by the school psychologist or the learning disabilities specialist, he should be privately evaluated.

- *Strive for early identification of the symptoms of under-achievement and learning problems.*

Monitor your child's performance in preschool and kindergarten. If atypical developmental or learning patterns appear, check with the teacher. If you feel the teacher is not sufficiently trained to identify the potential problem, consult your pediatrician. In the event that you are still dissatisfied, continue to seek professional advice until you are convinced that the advice is accurate and appropriate. Trust your intuition!

- *Do not impose your own drama on your child.*

Examine your concerns as they relate to your own emotional process. Excessive concern can be as destructive as inadequate concern. A parent who imposes his or her fears and insecurities on a child and who looks for problems when none exist can cause the child to become equally fearful and insecure. Periodic introspection is an important requisite of responsible parenting.

8 Underachievers with Poor Study Skills

Marci: "I Can't Figure Out What the Teacher Wants Me to Know"

"Well, I did it again. Straight C's." The fifteen-year-old's face mirrored her disappointment. "It could be worse, I suppose. I could have gotten D's or F's. But I was certain I would do better this semester. I studied so hard."

Marci's mother explained that her daughter had always been extremely conscientious about her schoolwork, but her diligence had never borne fruit. Although Marci might occasionally receive a B– on an exam, she invariably received C's on her report card. In elementary school, Marci had spent between two and three hours each evening on her homework. Now that she was a sophomore in high school she would sometimes study as much as five hours each evening. Despite this prodigious effort, she was just barely passing. As I talked with Marci, I could sense her pain and discouragement.

MARCI: Sometimes I wonder if it's all worth it. My friends sure have a lot more fun than I do. They go to parties and to the beach. All I do is study. When I graduate, I know that I could get a job on a production line in the electronics industry and earn nine dollars an hour. Maybe I'm crazy to think I could go to college.

LJG: Tell me why school is so difficult for you, Marci.

MARCI: I can't remember things. Most of the time I can't figure out what the teacher wants me to know. I take the exam, but it's as if I studied from the wrong textbook.

LJG: Do you feel that you understand the material?

MARCI: Sometimes. Other times, though, when I don't understand the material, I just try to memorize the facts. But then I get confused by the questions on the exam, or I forget the facts.

Marci had been tested in fourth grade for a learning disability because her teacher had become concerned about how hard she was struggling to keep up with the class. The tests had not revealed any significant problems. Her reading comprehension was slightly above grade level, and her IQ was in the high-average range. Marci's mother recalled that the school psychologist had noted some subtle deficiencies in auditory and visual memory, but the deficits were not considered sufficient to warrant special assistance. Subsequent achievement tests had repeatedly confirmed that Marci's reading and math skills were in the average to above-average range.

The first step in the process of identifying the source of Marci's academic problems was to verify that she did not currently have a learning disability. It was possible that the auditory and visual deficits detected by the school psychologist in fourth grade had become more pronounced.

My diagnostic evaluation indicated that she still had subtle memory deficits, but I found no other symptoms of a learning disability. Her comprehension skills and inferential reasoning skills were in the average range, as were her math skills and written expression skills. Although she was discouraged, she did not appear to have any significant emotional or family problems.

I was certain that Marci's memory deficits were not exclusively responsible for the discrepancy between her effort and her grades. For some as yet unexplained reason her above-average intelligence and her diligence had not allowed her to compensate for her subtle memory deficiencies. The process of elimination pointed in the direction of inadequate study skills. A subsequent study skills assessment confirmed my suspicions. The test revealed that Marci (1) had poor organizational skills; (2) did not know how to budget her time; (3) did not know how to prioritize; (4) did not know how to take effective notes; (5) did not know how to outline; (6) did not know how to identify important information when reading material from her textbooks; and (7) had not developed an effective system for remembering data.

Marci was spending long hours each evening going through the motions of studying. Although she was not learning-disabled according to the traditional criteria, she nevertheless had a serious learning problem which required remediation. Her above-grade-level reading comprehension scores were misleading. Marci did not understand what she was studying, and she attempted to compensate for her lack of comprehension with extra effort. To have tutored her in a specific subject would have been a waste of time. Marci needed to be taught *how* to study.

As we discussed the results of the study skills assessment, I could sense that Marci was experiencing mixed emotions. She felt relieved now that she finally understood why she was struggling in school and, at the same time, she felt apprehensive about whether the problem could be resolved.

LJG: I sense that you are a bit discouraged by the results of the test.

MARCI: Yeah, a little.

LJG: You feel that the problems are unsolvable.

MARCI: I don't know what more I can do.

LJG: Would you be willing to commit ap-

	proximately thirty hours of your time to an intensive study skills program?
MARCI:	I guess so.
LJG:	Marci, I am confident you can resolve these problems. You're bright, and your academic skills are above average. You simply need to learn how to study effectively. If you are willing to work, you have the potential to become a solid B student. It wouldn't surprise me at all if you became an A student.
MARCI:	Really?
LJG:	Really. Marci, I need more than an "I guess so." I want a commitment. I know that if you make the commitment, you'll give one hundred percent. You've proven over the last ten years just how conscientious you are.
MARCI:	O.K. I'll make the commitment.
LJG:	Great! Let's talk about when the class will meet.

I knew Marci wasn't totally convinced, but I also knew she would become more enthusiastic once she began the class. And so it was. Six months later almost all her grades were in the B range. There was one exception: she received an A in history.

The Implications of Poor Study Skills

Children who do not know how to study play a unique type of Russian roulette every time they take a test. If the child's "hammer" strikes a cylinder which contains information, he may pass or even do moderately well. If the hammer strikes an empty cylinder, he will either do poorly or fail. Because underachievers rarely know how to load their "revolvers" properly, the cylinders are typically empty.

The student who enters junior high school not knowing how

to study properly is being set up to fail. Parents and educators should not be surprised if the student develops behavior and attitude problems.

Poor study skills go hand in hand with underachievement and nonachievement. The student with chronically poor study skills often perceives his inability to achieve as a confirmation of his inferiority. Like his learning-disabled counterpart, the student generally suffers from low self-esteem, has tenuous emotional resiliency, and constructs elaborate defense mechanisms. If his study skills problem remains unresolved, it will cause him to become increasingly discouraged and defensive. Once he acquiesces to his limitations and accepts that he is incapable of doing well in school, he has four basic options:

1. He can shut down and refuse to study.
2. He can lower his standards and expectations.
3. He can go through the motions of studying.
4. He can continue to study conscientiously with little tangible reward.

Most children will select options one, two, or three. For reasons that are difficult to explain, some, like Marci, will select option four. Endowed with extraordinary grit and determination, they refuse to give up. Grit and determination, however, do not guarantee academic success. Without help, the student with poor study skills will probably never experience the joy and pride of receiving an A in a course. His reward for three or four hours of studying may be at best a B and at worst a D or even an F.

As a general rule, students who have the most significant study skills problems are the most resistant to studying. This resistance is quite understandable. Convinced that they can't get the job done, they attempt to protect themselves psychologically. To a struggling student, irresponsibility, procrastination, and resistance offer an attractive illusion of protection. Not trying can easily be equated with not failing.

Although Marci's diligence was exceptional, it had the same effect as a tire spinning on ice. There was no traction and little movement. Had she not received assistance, it is likely that she would have resigned herself to marginal grades and ultimately to a career that would have dissatisfied her.

Few students with chronic study skills problems remain as conscientious as Marci. By the time they enter junior high school, most underachievers with chronically poor study skills have already given up.

How the Good Student Differs from the Poor Student

Intelligence and motivation are, of course, two of the primary factors which distinguish good students from poor students, but these two qualities alone do not necessarily guarantee good grades. Two other vital characteristics are requisite to academic success: the ability to learn and the ability to study.

Most good students somehow discover how to learn and study by means of a mysterious educational osmosis process. At a relatively early age they develop their own individualized system for identifying, comprehending, and remembering important information. Whether they are assigned thirty spelling words to learn or a science chapter to prepare, they figure out how to get the job done effectively.

Teachers and parents who equate the capacity to study effectively with intelligence assume that the capable child will naturally and effortlessly acquire good study skills. Consciously or unconsciously, these teachers and parents subscribe to the belief that "the cream always rises to the top."

The inefficient learner cannot rise to the top because he does not undergo the same educational osmosis process as the efficient learner. He may be as intelligent as his more successful classmates, and he may have been exposed to the same educational experiences, but he seems unable to figure out how to utilize his intelligence and capitalize on his experience. Unlike cream, he will, if left to his own devices, settle to the middle or the bottom.

ACTIVE THINKING The efficient learner with good study skills does more than simply read his assignments or review for an exam. As he studies, he thinks about what he is studying. He attempts to understand the material. He seeks relevance. He relates what is currently being studied to what he has already learned. This process of active thinking and active participation enhances the comprehension and retention of information.

A high school student, for example, may be assigned to read a section in her textbook about the American Revolution. If she participates actively in preparing the assignment, she will ask herself questions as she reads. She will examine the underlying issues that influenced the British and Colonial positions. She will ponder why General Washington selected a particular battle plan. Because she is most likely goal oriented and thinks strategically, she will attempt to identify information that her teacher might consider important. As she delves below the surface, she makes the material more meaningful, more relevant, more comprehensible, and more memorable.

PASSIVE THINKING One of the primary concerns of the passive learner is to complete his assignments as quickly as possible. Passive learners often delude themselves that they are studying when they are simply turning the pages of their textbooks. They typically read material without examining the underlying issues, and attempt to memorize facts without understanding their importance. Because they do not actively involve themselves in what they are studying, passive learners are usually shocked when they discover at exam time that they have neither understood nor remembered what they have ostensibly prepared.

A passive learner, for example, might be given a history assignment to study one of the Federalist Papers. If he is a typical passive learner, he will read the paper without considering its significance to American history. It is also doubtful that he would question why the author wrote the essay or examine the role that the Founding Fathers played in the American War of Independence.

Some passive students do poorly in school simply because they are unmotivated. These students do the least possible amount of work. Assignments that are attempted are often shoddy and incomplete.

Some passive learners are actually highly conscientious. Although they may spend hours on their homework, they have not figured out how to comprehend what they are studying. Because of inadequately developed analytical thinking and strategic planning skills, their efforts are diffuse and scattered.

The student who participates passively in his education uses only a fraction of his potential mental powers. In time passive learners tend to become intellectually anesthetized. Like unused muscles, the unstimulated and unused mind soon atrophies.

GOOD STUDY SKILLS VERSUS POOR STUDY SKILLS In addition to their active involvement, other specific characteristics distinguish efficient learners with good study skills from passive, inefficient learners with poor study skills.

Goals. Students with good study skills usually establish short-term goals and long-term goals. For example, the student's short-term goal may be to raise her Spanish grade on her next report card from a B − to a B +. Her long-term goal may be to become an attorney.

In contrast, students with poor study skills are seldom goal oriented. They devote little thought to how they can apply or utilize what they are studying to the pursuit of a defined objective. Such students seldom perceive the value in what they are attempting to learn and may consider school to be a burden that is unfairly imposed on them by their parents and teachers.

Organizational skills. Students with good study skills tend to be well organized. They are generally meticulous about recording their assignments and deadlines in their notebooks. They know when their book reports are due and when the next biology exam will be given. Because they are able to budget their time and to prioritize, they plan ahead and allow sufficient time to complete their assignments.

In contrast, students with poor study skills are typically disorganized. They rarely develop an effective system for recording their assignments and deadlines. They do not know how to budget time and plan ahead, and reports and studying are usually left until the last minute. Important materials needed to complete an assignment may be left at home or in a school locker.

Notetaking and outlining skills. Students with good study skills usually develop an effective system for taking notes from their textbooks and during lectures. They know how to identify important information. They also know how to outline and can effectively use their notes and outlines while studying to reinforce their comprehension and recall.

In contrast, students with poor study skills rarely develop a workable system for recording vital information. They often do not know how to distinguish important facts from less important information. The majority do not know how to outline properly. Because they do not keep good notes, they are usually at a severe disadvantage when reviewing for tests and exams.

Memory skills. Students with good study skills have figured out a system for remembering information. As they study, they may visualize the dates of a battle or the definitions of vocabulary words. Or they may use written or oral repetition to help them recall. Some children associate new information with a formula or an acronym. For example, a student in a basic geometry course might use the following formula to help him remember vital information: SohCahToa (Sine = opposite over hypotenuse/Cosine = adjacent over hypotenuse/Tangent = opposite over adjacent). Efficient learners use the memory techniques that best correspond to the way in which they access and represent information.*

In contrast, students with poor study skills seldom develop an effective system for remembering important data. They often become locked into one method, and they may persist in using this method despite the fact that it has proven ineffective.

Environmental factors. Students with good study skills usu-

---

*See Lawrence J. Greene and Leigh Jones-Bamman, *Getting Smarter: Simple Strategies for Better Grades,* Belmont, Calif.: David S. Lake Publishers, 1984, for specific methods that will help the student master the skills mentioned in this chapter.

ally control their study environment so that they are not distracted. Most serious students recognize that loud music, TV, or constant interruptions interfere with learning efficiency. Although they might study occasionally under such conditions, when appropriate they will make the necessary sacrifices to get the job done properly.

In contrast, students with poor study skills often work under the worst possible conditions. They may insist that they can concentrate with loud music blaring in the background or with the TV on. They also tend to allow frequent interruptions while they are studying. They may attempt to study while in bed or on a crowded lawn at school without acknowledging that sleepiness or distractions will diminish their learning efficiency.

Trying to convince the inefficient learner that environment can play a significant role in his ability to concentrate can severely test a parent's patience, creativity, and communication skills. Children in our society have grown up with loud music. They may argue that they can function as well or better with this noise as they can without it. Suggesting otherwise may meet with a great deal of resistance. The issue might best be broached as an experiment. A parent might say: "I'd like to propose an experiment. For the next week I suggest that you study without any music or TV. The following week you can study with all the music and TV you want. Let's then get together and compare the results." Such an approach may defuse the common reactionary response when teenagers are convinced that they are being oppressed.

Identifying the Student with Poor Study Skills

The student with poor study skills must first be identified before he can be helped. Many inefficient learners require only limited assistance in order to improve their school performance. They may simply need to learn some study skills "tricks." Such tricks include memory techniques, organizational methods, strategic planning skills, and note-taking skills.

The following Study Skills Checklist has been designed to help parents identify their child's specific study skills deficits.

STUDY SKILLS CHECKLIST

	Yes	*No*
1. My child is well organized.	_____	_____
2. My child establishes specific short-term goals (an A on the next biology exam).	_____	_____
3. My child establishes long-term goals (college or a particular vocation).	_____	_____
4. My child establishes priorities.	_____	_____
5. My child knows what his or her assignments are each evening.	_____	_____
6. My child plans ahead (does not leave studying to the last minute).	_____	_____
7. My child can identify the important information when studying.	_____	_____
8. My child can remember important information.	_____	_____
9. My child usually is able to understand what is being studied.	_____	_____
10. My child takes effective and useful notes in class.	_____	_____
11. My child makes effective and useful notes when studying.	_____	_____
12. My child knows how to outline.	_____	_____
13. My child can usually figure out what the teacher expects the students to know on an exam.	_____	_____

14. My child can concentrate when
    studying.   _____ _____

15. My child is able to study for thirty
    minutes without becoming distracted
    (fourth grade and above).   _____ _____

16. My child reviews before exams.   _____ _____

17. My child goes over his or her
    assignments to find errors.   _____ _____

18. My child has confidence in his or her
    academic skills.   _____ _____

INTERPRETING THE CHECKLIST. A pattern of "yes" answers to the statements on the checklist suggests that your child probably has good study skills. A pattern of "no" answers should be interpreted as a danger signal. Parents who uncover such a pattern are advised to request that their child be enrolled in a study skills methods program.

Until recently, study skills have received very little emphasis in American schools. Fortunately, this situation is now changing. More and more school districts are acknowledging the value of teaching study skills and are beginning to integrate study skills programs into their curricula.

In the event that a program is not available at the child's school, parents should consider buying a study skills book which their child might work on independently. Parents who feel that their child cannot use such a book without help should consider either hiring a qualified tutor to work with the child or seeking a private agency which offers an effective program.

Learning Styles

Deficient study skills are not the only factor which can impact on a child's ability to learn efficiently. The child's particular learning style must also be understood. There are many learning styles, including:

Auditory learning. The auditory learner has facility at understanding and remembering what he hears. He will probably have little difficulty remembering the details of a long story or recalling jokes. A student who can recall much of what he hears in a lecture is most likely an auditory learner. If he recognizes his auditory facility, he will most likely attempt to remember information by repeating it aloud or to himself. Auditory learners provide an unconscious clue to their learning style (the way in which they access and represent information) when they use such expressions as "I *hear* what you are saying," or "It *sounds* like you're saying..."

Visual learning. Visual learners have facility at accessing, representing, and remembering information that they see. They generally have less difficulty mastering textbook material than material presented in a lecture. Typically, such students rely heavily on their notes to help them remember the information. They will probably attempt to reinforce their memory by writing information repetitively. Visual learners often signal their learning style by using such expressions as "I *see* what you mean" or "It *looks* easy."

Kinesthetic learning. The kinesthetic learner responds best to "hands-on" experience. A child who is struggling with math may be able to understand math concepts if he is shown how to use concrete materials to represent number units. By manipulating blocks of wood of different sizes, the child can begin to appreciate the relationship between numbers. With sufficient practice, he should begin to develop the ability to do the math computations without having to use the blocks. The kinesthetic modality serves as a vehicle by which the child can comprehend basic math concepts and reinforce basic math operational skills.

Many adults also learn best kinesthetically. An automobile mechanic who accesses information kinesthetically may learn to disassemble and assemble an engine through hands-on experience. He may be able to "feel" how parts fit together and may never need to look at a manual. It is actually possible for a competent mechanic with highly developed kinesthetic ability to be illiterate or even blind.

Informational learning. Some children assimilate material easily and are able to retrieve the stored information without much effort. Although they may not be consciously aware of their learning style, most children recognize their facility to grasp and retrieve information. Students who learn sequentially and who can assimilate information generally do well in courses that stress quantitative learning. Examples of subjects that emphasize the memorization of data, symbols, facts, and dates include biology, chemistry, and history.

Conceptual learning. Ironically, there are very bright children who have difficulty in school because they learn conceptually. These children may see the overview, the main themes, the common denominators. Although they are able to distill and analyze, they may not be able to remember detailed information which does not appear to be particularly relevant to them. Dates of battles may elude them, but they may be able to expound at length about the issues involved in the Civil War. Conceptual learners may remember the important issues of what they have studied long after the sequential learner has forgotten the facts he has memorized.

Multimodality learning. Some children have facility at accessing, representing, and recalling information both auditorily and visually. These children may be as comfortable dealing with concepts as they are with hard data. Such students, of course, have a distinct advantage because they have many options and can choose the best learning mode or combination of modes for mastering what they are studying.

Adjusting to the System

Primary and secondary education programs in America are strongly information oriented. Children are expected to memorize multiplication tables, non-phonetically spelled words, irregularly conjugated Spanish or French verbs, chemical formulas, and historical dates. Although some teachers emphasize conceptual learning, many do not.

Each teacher determines his or her teaching emphasis and criteria for measuring a student's performance. The criteria may be quantitative (how much information the child remembers) or qualitative (how well the child understands and remembers). In either case, the ability to recall information is an essential part of any measurement of skill mastery.

In an information-oriented system, students with good memory skills have a distinct advantage. The conceptual learner who can distill and extrapolate information can also achieve success in an information-oriented system, assuming he can retain the information. The student who learns conceptually, however, may have to make some adjustments when he encounters teachers who strongly stress data. In virtually any system, the multimodality learner has the greatest potential advantage because he has the greatest number of learning options.

Parents and teachers who identify and understand a child's learning style can help the child learn how to utilize his strengths and compensate for his limitations. The auditory learner, for instance, must somehow acquire and remember information that he reads in his textbooks. Concerned parents and teachers may be able to help the child devise methods for transforming the written word into the spoken word. The student may discover that he can recall written data if he puts the information into a script and then pretends that he is a teacher giving a lecture. By verbally recounting the information to his "students," he will be accessing and representing the written data auditorily, and thus be utilizing his own most effective learning mode.

The reality of thirty children in the classroom prevents most teachers from catering to a child's particular learning style. For this reason, the child must devise a strategy to accommodate himself to the teacher's style. Creativity is an important part of the accommodation process. The child needs to identify (with help from either his parents or a professional) how he learns best. He then needs to learn how he can best capitalize on his particular facilities. Finally, he needs to identify what his teacher expects the students in the class to learn and what the teacher's learning orientation is.

A "smart" student figures out how to identify the specific academic challenges that he faces, and how to compensate, when appropriate, for his weaknesses. For instance, an informational learner who memorizes easily may find himself in the classroom of a teacher who wants her students to understand concepts. He may also discover that she employs essay exams to gauge her students' understanding. If he is to succeed in her class, he will have to reorient his natural learning style. He will not only have to discipline himself to seek out concepts, but also develop his ability to communicate his understanding of these concepts.

The conceptual learner, on the other hand, may discover that her teacher stresses facts and dates and utilizes multiple-choice and yes/no questions to assess achievement. She may need to use flash cards or a tape recorder to help remember the information. The ability to adapt is essential to survival not only in the jungle, but also in the classroom.

Helping the Inefficient Learner

The student with severe study skills problems will probably have to be deprogrammed of his inefficient habits and then reprogrammed with more efficient habits before he can begin to succeed in school. The deprogramming and reprogramming process is best performed by someone who is not emotionally involved with the student. Children often resist their parents' attempt to play the role of schoolteacher.

Parents who can successfully communicate with their child may be able to help the child develop beneficial study habits by providing guidance on the budgeting of time, the recording of assignments, the prioritizing of responsibilities, and the organizing of materials.

BUDGETING TIME Children, like adults, have a finite amount of time to complete a seemingly infinite number of tasks. Helping children develop a time schedule can be an invaluable contribution. A method for acquiring information from the child so that he can budget his time is suggested below.

> QUESTION: How much time do you need to complete your assignments on a typical night?

QUESTION: How much time do you want to spend on each study segment before you take a break? Twenty-five minutes? Thirty minutes? Forty minutes?

QUESTION: When do you want to start studying? Right after school? At four o'clock?

QUESTION: How long do you want your breaks to be?

QUESTION: How much time do you want to set aside for talking with your friends on the telephone?

QUESTION: How much time would you like to set aside for TV or listening to music?

QUESTION: What time do you need to be in bed?

STATEMENT: Let's see if we can make up a chart that will help you budget your time. You can try it as an experiment. As you go along you'll probably have to make some adjustments. We'll plot your grades over the next month and see if the time chart works for you.

RECORDING ASSIGNMENTS Many students with poor study skills do not write down the vital information they need to do their work properly. They do not record the dates of exams or when reports are due. Nor do they record the conditions that the teacher has imposed. For example, the teacher might say: "I want your preliminary draft on the research paper double-spaced. If you are not using a typewriter, I want you to skip one line between each written line. I also want a one-half-inch margin on the right side of the paper. The draft is due on November 12 at 3:00 PM." The student with poor study skills would probably fail to write down these essential details.

Parents might want to purchase or design an assignment notebook to add some order to the child's life. They can then spend some time helping the child learn how to record information in the notebook, and diplomatically monitor him until they are certain he understands how to use the notebook.

ESTABLISHING PRIORITIES Helping a child learn how to prioritize can significantly improve the child's studying efficiency. An effective question-and-answer method for achieving this is suggested below. (Parents should *listen* to their child's answers before proceeding to the next question. Bombarding a child with questions will only trigger defensiveness.)

QUESTION:	Let's take a look at what has to be done in school this week. What is your most important assignment?
QUESTION:	How do you want to work on it? Every day for the next week? Or do you want to start studying three days before the history midterm?
QUESTION:	How much time do you think you should spend each evening studying for the midterm?
QUESTION:	When do you want to begin your research for the biology report?
QUESTION:	How much time do you want to set aside for doing research and writing your note cards?
STATEMENT:	Let's see if we can make a list of the priorities in the order of how you propose to work on them. At the same time, we'll budget the time you need to get each job done.

DEFINING PROBLEMS Many children with poor study skills seem oblivious to the fact that they have deficient study habits. Helping them identify the deficits is the first vital step in resolving their problems. A method for helping children identify problems is outlined below.

QUESTION: What's happening in your history class?

QUESTION: Do you understand the material?

QUESTION: Do you see any solutions to your problem?

QUESTION: Do you feel you can catch up without help?

QUESTION: Have you spoken with your teacher about the problem?

QUESTION: How can your mother and I help you?

STATEMENT: It's my understanding that you will budget extra time for catching up. If you run into too many problems, let me know and we will find a tutor for you.

ESTABLISHING GOALS Goals can help children solve problems. This is especially true in the case of students with deficient study skills. By helping their child focus on goals and objectives, parents provide the child with a means for confronting and overcoming the obstacles in his path.

QUESTION: What grade are you aiming for in chemistry?

QUESTION: What do you need to do between now and the end of the semester to achieve this goal?

QUESTION: Will you need any support from your mother and me in order to attain your objective?

STATEMENT: It's my understanding that you're aiming for a B+ or perhaps an A− in chemistry. You feel that everything's under control and that you have a workable plan for achieving your objective.

CAUTION: When asking questions of a child, be sure to hear his responses. Resist being judgmental. If the child's responses do not appear to be in sync with reality, attempt to explore this with him in a nonaccusatory way. Also, do not give your child the third degree when exploring these issues. Diplomacy and sensitivity are essential. Try to interject humor if appropriate. If your child perceives you as the Grand Inquisitor, he will resist your efforts to help.

Effort Without Reward

The student with good study skills is not necessarily more intelligent than the other students in the class. Rather, he has discovered important tools that significantly improve his chances for success in school and in life. These tools permit him to use the intelligence with which he has been genetically endowed.

A prolonged pattern of inefficient learning and underachievement usually produces two results: poor attitude and deficient effort. With the appropriate instruction and encouragement, virtually every child can be taught how to use his mind more effectively. Parents who conclude that their child's school does not provide this instruction must assume the responsibility for finding alternative resources.

Resolving learning problems and underachievement requires strategic planning. Specific solutions for learning problems and underachievement are examined in the next chapter.

● PARENTING SUGGESTIONS

● *Determine if your child knows how to study properly.*

If you conclude that your child has study skills deficits, request that he or she be enrolled in a studies skills program at school. If such programs are not offered at the school, investigate the availability of private programs that may exist in your community.

● *Encourage your child to participate actively in what is being studied.*

The student who learns to think and question will understand and retain more about what he is studying. Active participation and active thinking are the catalysts that link efficient learning and good study skills.

● *Help your child determine his or her learning style.*

Once the child understands how he learns, he can begin to develop a learning strategy that utilizes his particular strengths. He can also begin to make the requisite strategic accommodations to the particular teacher's teaching emphasis.

● *Help your child learn how to budget time, record assignments, prioritize, define problems, and establish goals.*

Parents who can help their child develop organizational skills are providing him with an important resource. Once the child with poor study skills becomes better organized, he can begin to focus his energies on overcoming his study skills problems.

9 Strategies for Resolving Learning Problems

Craig: Putting the Pieces Back Together

I was stunned by the psychological deterioration that had occurred during the five years since I had last seen Craig. The despondent thirteen-year-old sat staring at his hands, which were drumming nervously on the table.

Because I had already comprehensively tested Craig, I did not feel it necessary to do another complete diagnostic workup. The results of an abbreviated assessment of Craig's academic skills proved shocking. The ninth grader's reading, writing, and math skills were all at the second-grade level. Craig was unable to express even the most basic ideas in writing, and he had no understanding of the rules of grammar or syntax.

Craig's learning problems had initially manifested themselves in first grade. On the teacher's recommendation, he was retained. By the end of the school year, his mother realized that repeating the year had not resolved Craig's learning problems. She made an appointment for me to test her son. The evaluation revealed that this seven-year-old had severe learning disabilities. He manifested a classic, textbook profile of symptoms: inaccurate reading, letter reversals, comprehension deficits, illegible handwriting, distractibility, and poor memory skills. His mother agreed with my recommendation that Craig be enrolled at our center in an intensive learning assistance program.

Craig remained in the remedial program for approximately one year and attended a special class two hours a week. Although he made progress, the progress was slow. Difficulty in concentrating and perceptually based reading deficits compounded the challenge of helping him master basic academic skills.

Against our recommendation, Craig's mother decided to discontinue the learning assistance. She felt that her son had reached the point where he could make it on his own with the help of the resource specialist at school. She would not be dissuaded, and Craig was withdrawn from our program.

The effects of his mother's decision were now apparent. Craig had made virtually no academic progress during the ensuing five years. He was demoralized, depressed, and uncommunicative. His behavior was that of an immature seven-year-old.

Craig was refusing to do any work in school. He had been placed in a self-contained learning-handicapped class in junior high school. Now in high school, he was still in a self-contained class. His teachers reported that he was resisting all efforts to help him. Craig had shut down both emotionally and intellectually, and he made no attempt to hide the fact that he hated school.

Craig refused to discuss his feelings with me. His reaction to all questions consisted of a silly giggle and "I don't know." Before responding, he constantly looked over at his mother to gauge her reactions. His behavior evidenced his insecurity and the terrible emotional toll that his learning problems, a doting mother, and years of academic frustration had taken. Convinced he was stupid, Craig had decided that effort was fruitless.

Craig was extremely resistant to the idea of receiving learning assistance. Terrified by the prospect of risking another failure, he would agree only on the condition that he be allowed to discontinue after a trial period of three months.

I assigned Craig to a remarkable learning therapist. I had seen her work successfully with hundreds of hard-to-reach children, and I felt that if anyone could "salvage" Craig, she was the person to do it.

With infinite patience, Robbie began to cajole, praise, prod, and threaten Craig into working. She was totally committed to helping him break out of the cycle of failure. At first, he actively resisted all of her efforts. He would refuse to work in class or do the assigned homework. He came to class unkempt and dirty. To get attention, he would make strange noises and act silly. His inappropriate behavior appeared expressly designed to try the teacher's patience and to goad the other students into making fun of him.

Conditioned to the inevitability of defeat, Craig devised behavior to deflect attention from his inadequacies and vulnerability. He was, of course, deluding himself. His behavior simply called attention to his inadequacies.

Despite his resistance, his overwhelming academic deficits, and innumerable setbacks, Craig slowly began to make progress. A remarkable transformation had occurred. Within a year, the thirteen-year-old had mastered many of the basic academic skills he needed to survive in school. His personal hygiene began to improve. He became less silly and resistant.

At first, Craig's efforts were tentative. Having perceived himself as a failure for so many years, he had become accustomed and resigned to failure. The prospect of acquiring a new identity was unsettling, and he relinquished his negative perceptions of himself grudgingly.

As his skills improved, Craig started to take risks. He no longer needed to be coerced into attempting a difficult math problem or deciphering a difficult word. His progress accelerated, and he stopped his attention-getting antics in the classroom. He actually began to enjoy the thrill of achievement.

Another transformation occurred. This previously obnoxious teenager began to develop charm. As his self-esteem improved, his physical appearance also improved. Craig actually became more handsome! In fact, one of the girls in the class developed a crush on him, and she asked him to go to the junior prom with her.

Craig is now a junior in high school. He is no longer segregated in an educationally handicapped class at his high school, but has been "mainstreamed" into the general population of students. Although he still has some difficulty mastering new material, he is able to keep up in all of his classes.

Craig's story is not a fairy tale. Because of residual learning problems, he continues to receive two hours per week of academic support at our center. He is currently functioning approximately one year below grade level in math and reading. His vocabulary, writing skills, and study skills are still deficient. He has mastered basic math computational skills, but he still finds newly introduced concepts difficult to grasp. Nevertheless, Craig has improved more than seven grade levels in both subjects in less than two years.

Craig has recently become interested in computers. He is fascinated with how they work, and his goal is to enter a technical school and become a computer technician.

Remediation Options

A learning-disabled child is in some respects like an automobile that needs repair. If the problem is disregarded or inadequately fixed, it will ultimately cause the car to break down. If, however, the problem is addressed, it can usually be corrected and more serious damage avoided. When Craig was brought to our center for the second time, he was on the verge of an educational breakdown. Had his mother waited any longer before seeking help, the damage might have become irreversible.

The parents of underachieving, nonachieving, and learning-disabled children have four basic options:

1. They can do nothing and hope the problem corrects itself.
2. They can find help within the school system.
3. They can seek outside assistance as an alternative or as a supplement to the help provided in school.
4. They can retain their child in the hope that greater maturity and an opportunity to reexperience the academic material will resolve the problem.

Craig's mother availed herself of the last three options. She sought help within the school system. She sought outside help and brought her child to our center. She also permitted him to be retained in the hope that this extra time in first grade would allow him to mature, and would reduce the academic pressure. She also did something that might be considered an additional option. Against our recommendation, she withdrew her son from his clinical remediation program before he had resolved his learning problems. She did so because she hoped that Craig's remaining learning problems would go away of their own accord.

Determining the most appropriate course of action in treating a learning problem can be an emotionally wrenching experience for parents. The choices that parents make can have profound implications. Recognition of this fact can cause the decision-making process to be all the more traumatic. Flawed decisions by even well-meaning parents can negatively influence the subsequent course of a child's life.

Hoping the Learning Problem Will Go Away

Some learning-disabled or underachieving children discover how to overcome their problems without adult assistance. They intuitively perceive what they must do to compensate for their academic deficiencies. For example, a high school student who has difficulty taking notes during a lecture may discover that he can do well on exams if he borrows a friend's lecture notes each evening and copies them. Another student who has trouble remembering information that he reads in his textbooks may discover that recording the essential facts on a cassette tape and replaying the tape will help him to remember the information. These are logical, productive compensatory mechanisms.

To hope that a problem will go away of its own accord is quite natural. But sometimes the reluctance to seek a professional opinion can have disastrous implications. Needed assistance may not be provided, and, through neglect, the problem may become much more serious.

The majority of learning-disabled children require assistance. Their problems will not go away of their own accord, and the longer help is postponed, the more entrenched the learning problems will become. Relatively few struggling children have the requisite insight, resolve, and strategic planning skills to prevail over a learning problem without adult guidance and help.

The struggling child will signal his distress in various ways. Specific academic deficiencies are, of course, the most blatant signals. The child's behavior is another potential red flag. The underachieving or learning-disabled child may compensate for his deficiencies by becoming unmotivated or lazy. Or he may act out in class or at home. Some children signal their difficulties by becoming emotionally or socially isolated. Some become frustrated and angry. Others choose to develop skills in a specific area of their lives, such as sports, and completely neglect their schoolwork.

Parents may not recognize, or may choose not to recognize, the danger signals. The reasons for this denial of reality are diverse. Parents who avoid confronting their child's learning problem may do so because they feel powerless. Or they may convince themselves that the problem will go away of its own accord. They may seize upon a minor improvement in behavior, attitude, or skills as a confirmation that there is nothing to be concerned about. This can be a serious mistake, especially if desperately needed remediation is postponed or neglected.

The profile of a child's learning deficits may change as he progresses through school. With the advent of puberty, the inattentiveness and distractibility of the overactive child may become less apparent or may even disappear. Although the child may appear to have overcome his primary problem, he may still have difficulty understanding or following written or oral directions. In high school he may find that he has difficulty studying for exams. The blatant symptoms of his learning problems may have changed somewhat, but the basic underlying problem with attention and concentration still remains.

Even reading problems which appear to have been remediated sometimes have a disturbing tendency to reappear if the underlying deficiencies have not been completely resolved. The reading skills of a child with visual decoding or visual tracking deficits (symptoms: letter reversals and reading inaccuracies) may improve even without formal learning assistance. This improvement, however, may be temporary or illusory. The child whose oral reading problems have been resolved in third grade may discover in ninth grade that he cannot understand the contents of his textbooks.

Determining definitely whether or not an underlying learning problem has been resolved can be difficult not only for parents but also for professional educators. Achievement tests and even diagnostic testing procedures do not provide an absolute guarantee that a child's learning problem has been completely eliminated. This is especially true in the case of nonspecific and/or intermittent learning problems. The only means for determining if a learning problem has been resolved is for parents to continue monitoring their child's classroom and test performance.

Despite highly competent learning assistance, three disturbing events may occur after a learning problem has been supposedly remediated:

1. The "resolved" learning deficiency may reappear.
2. A new learning deficit may subsequently manifest itself.
3. A child who has been making academic progress may begin to regress.

Although the prospect of having to deal once again with a seemingly resolved issue can be very discouraging, the issue must be confronted. Parents and children must renew their resolve and determination, and they must persevere. Unfortunately, the time required to remediate a learning problem cannot be predicted with any certainty. Some problems can be corrected relatively quickly, and others may persist in spite of intensive remediation. In some cases, children with serious or resistant learning problems may require remedial assistance for an indeterminate amount of time.

A distractible third grader with reading or math problems

who receives little or no remedial assistance in elementary school stands an excellent chance of becoming a discouraged, academically incapacitated teenager. Craig clearly illustrated the implications of allowing a learning problem to remain unresolved. Although his mother made an attempt to provide him with assistance, she did not persist. Her unilateral decision to discontinue remedial help after one year had disastrous consequences. His problems persisted, and his early gains were quickly wiped out.

Some learning problems are particularly resistant. Although it is possible for a learning deficit to disappear without intervention, it is more probable that the deficit will become increasingly debilitating if the child is left to his own devices. This risk factor is a compelling justification for procuring help for the struggling child.

Programs Within the School System

The procedures for procuring help within a school district vary from state to state and from district to district. The qualifying criteria for special assistance also vary.

Usually, the classroom teacher is the first to identify the struggling child. The teacher will probably alert the student's parents and request their permission to have the child evaluated by the school psychologist or psychomotrist. Sometimes parents recognize the symptoms of a potential learning problem before the teacher does. They may observe chronic distractibility or hyperactivity at home. Or they may become alarmed by their child's lack of academic progress or sloppy work.

In theory, once a child is tested and identified as having learning problems, he should be provided with specialized learning assistance. In reality, this assistance is not always available to all children who would benefit from it.

The spectrum of special assistance programs offered by school districts ranges from self-contained classes for students with serious learning problems to resource programs that provide tutorial assistance for those with less severe problems. Less severely learning-disabled children are often "mainstreamed" (integrated) into regular classes for the major portion of the day.

The quality, efficacy, and entrance requirements of learning assistance programs can vary greatly from state to state, from district to district, and even from school to school within the same district. The qualifications, skills, and dedication of teachers also vary. Parents can play a key role in determining the quality of the special education programs offered at their child's school. When they are involved, informed, and supportive, they serve notice on the teachers and administration that they expect a quality program.

Parents whose children are enrolled in special programs cannot assume that their child's educational needs are being met simply because the child has been placed in a special program. They must continue to monitor closely their child's progress in the learning assistance program.

Parents must also be reasonable. Adequate time must be allowed for the learning assistance program to make inroads into a child's problem. Serious learning problems do not generally disappear in six months or even a year. If, however, parents do not see progress after a reasonable period of time, they should request a conference with the resource specialist or the special education teacher. During this conference, they should feel justified in asking penetrating questions about the objectives of the remediation program, the methodology being used, and the effectiveness of the teaching strategy.

It is important that the tone of parent-teacher meetings be positive and nonaccusatory. The purpose of the meeting is not to find fault or to attack the teacher. Rather, the purpose is to gather information and to discuss remediation strategies and objectives. The child's lack of progress may have nothing to do with the teacher's competence. The teacher may be very talented and may have a well-conceived program, but the child may continue to struggle. Chronic distractibility and hyperactivity, for instance, are difficult to treat in the classroom, and the distractible child may require a great deal of time and effort on the teacher's part before he makes significant academic progress. The primary issues explored in the conference should include the correct identification of the child's underlying problem and the strategy (or strategies) for resolving the problem. If an alternative approach or supplemental assistance is advisable, these options can be examined and evaluated.*

The attitude of parents in dealing with their child's teacher can play a pivotal role in the ultimate efficacy of the remediation program. Parents who are insensitive, unreasonable, aggressive, intolerant, arrogant, or hostile will probably elicit a defensive reaction from the teacher. Conversely, parents who approach these exploratory conferences with an inquisitive but open mind will probably discover that the teacher is more than willing to do his or her best in helping the child. The objective of the conference is to create a spirit of cooperation and a willingness to work as a team to achieve a common goal. In this sense the respective roles of parents and teacher overlap. Everyone must work together if the remediation process is to be successful.

Resource programs which help the child to complete his assignments may serve a pragmatic and important function, but this type of support is generally less effective in the long run than programs which address the source of a child's learning problem. For example, a reading problem that is caused by visual perception deficiencies (inaccurate reading, letter reversals, omissions) is most effectively treated by remediating the underlying source of the problem. The same principle applies to math deficiencies. If a child's math computational difficulties are caused by an inadequate understanding of math concepts, he must be helped to understand the concepts. Insisting that the child memorize multiplication tables will not help him understand math. Although he will ultimately need to memorize that $5 \times 5 = 25$, he must also understand how numbers "work" together to form a system. A child who understands math concepts is far less likely to have problems

---

*See my book *Kids Who Hate School*, revised edition, Atlanta: Humanics, Ltd., 1984, for a more complete discussion of methods for evaluating and developing effective remediation strategies.

with computations or with more advanced math courses.

The following Effective Remediation Checklist is intended to help you evaluate your child's remediation program.

EFFECTIVE REMEDIATION CHECKLIST

	Yes	No
1. I feel that my child has been adequately evaluated.		
2. The nature of my child's problem has been clearly explained to me.		
3. I understand the goals of the remediation program.		
4. My child appears to be placed in the appropriate program.		
5. I have confidence in the professionals who are responsible for providing for my child's learning needs.		
6. My child appears to be making satisfactory progress in overcoming his learning deficits.		
7. The learning assistance strategy appears to be well organized and effectively implemented.		
8. I am confident that my child will ultimately overcome, compensate for, or in the case of more severe learning handicaps, make the most progress possible in resolving his disability.		
9. I receive periodic updates on my child's progress.		
10. The special education teacher is willing to confer with me when appropriate.		

11. The teacher is not defensive when we discuss my child's progress.   _____ _____

12. I am satisfied with the quality of communication between myself and the professionals at my child's school.   _____ _____

13. My child's self-esteem appears to be improving.   _____ _____

14. My child's attitude about the remedial program is basically positive.   _____ _____

15. I support and respect professionals who are working with my child.   _____ _____

INTERPRETING THE CHECKLIST. A pattern of "yes" responses to the statements on the checklist should allay any concerns that parents might have about their child's learning assistance program. Conversely, a pattern of "no" answers should elicit concern, and parents are advised to discuss their perceptions with the appropriate school personnel.

If parents are not satisfied with the programs offered by their local school, they may be forced to seek outside private assistance. A variety of remediation resources are available in most communities, and parents are advised to examine each of these resources closely.

Private Programs

Parents who conclude that their child's learning needs are not being adequately addressed in school will probably consider one of the following learning assistance options: (1) tutoring, (2) a reading center, (3) a full-time private school that offers learning assistance, or (4) a clinical learning assistance program.

TUTORING Tutoring is usually the most readily available resource for helping children who are struggling in school. In almost every community, parents can find currently employed or retired teachers who supplement their income by offering private tutoring services. Graduate students, college students, and even high school students also frequently offer their services as tutors.

The quality of private tutoring can vary widely. Three primary factors will determine the effectiveness of the tutoring program: (1) the qualifications of the tutor, (2) the teaching skills of the tutor, and (3) the nature of the child's problems.

Children who have significant learning problems will probably require specially trained tutors. Although a retired classroom teacher may have been extremely effective in the classroom, he or she may not know how to help the child who has specific auditory perception, visual perception, visual tracking, or math concept deficiencies. These deficiencies may manifest themselves as reading inaccuracies involving letter or word reversals, transpositions, or omissions. Or they may manifest themselves as an inability to remember the multiplication tables or to understand fractions. A college student majoring in mathematics may have excellent math skills and the best of intentions, but he or she may not know how to help a third grader understand basic math concepts.

In some communities, private tutoring may be the only resource available to parents. This is especially true in the case of families living in small towns or rural areas. In fairness, it should be pointed out that many nonspecialists are extremely competent. Although they may have received little or no formal training in the field of learning disabilities, these tutors may possess natural teaching instincts. The teacher with natural talent can often sense intuitively what needs to be done to help a child overcome or compensate for his learning deficits.

Parents who hire tutors should monitor their child's progress closely. They should maintain close communication with both the tutor and the classroom teacher. If the child bogs down, a meeting should be held at the school to discuss alternative strategies. Ideally, the tutor should participate in this meeting.

READING CENTERS Reading centers can now be found in many towns and cities. There are several different types of reading centers. Some of these facilities are connected with teachers colleges or universities. Learning-disabled children are often assigned to graduate students who must gain clinical experience to fulfill degree or credential requirements. Students in graduate reading and learning-disabilities programs are usually closely supervised during their training, and the services they provide will generally range from competent to excellent.

The majority of reading centers are not affiliated with universities. They are private enterprises, and the programs offered are in many respects similar to tutoring. Most centers administer a pre-enrollment battery of standardized achievement tests to determine the child's reading and vocabulary levels. For instance, a child whose reading score on the tests is 4.9 has answered a certain number of reading comprehension questions correctly, indicating a fourth-grade, ninth-month reading level. Grade level is determined by statistically comparing a child's scores with those of thousands of other children of the same age who have taken the test.

Typically, children enrolled at a reading center will be periodically retested so that their pre- and post-test scores can be compared. If the student's score improves and if he tests at or above grade level, he is usually considered to have successfully completed the program.

In theory, the tutors at reading centers are credentialed or certified by the state and have classroom experience. And in theory they have had extensive experience working with children who have special learning needs, and have been specially trained either at the clinic or in graduate school. Unfortunately, the tutors in many private reading clinics actually receive very little formal, specialized training.

Reading centers can be distinguished from private tutoring in one important respect. Most reading clinics are committed to a particular teaching methodology. This methodology may be proprietary; that is, it was developed exclusively for use at the center, or it may be the same methodology used at the child's regular school.

Any program which offers a sound remediation program implemented by well-trained and committed instructors can be highly effective. It should be noted that many reading clinics rely on improvement in their students' achievement scores as the primary test for verifying the effectiveness of their program. When parents are told that they can expect dramatic gains in reading levels and significant improvement in classroom performance, they should carefully scrutinize the claims. To avoid disillusionment, parents are advised to ask the director of the program several key questions before enrolling their child:

1. What tests are used to determine reading level?
2. Do these tests correspond to the tests administered in school?
3. Is the test form administered before the child begins the program the same as the one administered after he completes the program? (A child taking the same test twice may score better the second time because he is familiar with the test questions. Ideally, a different form of the test should be administered.)
4. How do students who complete the program perform in school? (Parents should ask for several references.)
5. Is the same teaching methodology used with all the children enrolled at the center?
6. What are the criteria for determining whether this methodology is appropriate for my child?
7. What is the background and training required of your staff?
8. Does the staff maintain communication with the classroom teacher and the resource specialist?
9. What are the criteria used to determine when a child has completed the program?

As parents evaluate the director's answers to these questions, they should keep in mind that a child's score on a reading test does not necessarily correlate with his performance in class. The child may test higher than he is able to function in class, or he may test lower than his in-class reading level. The litmus test for evaluating the efficacy of any remediation program is whether or not the skills being taught transfer to the classroom.

Perhaps the most significant failing of many reading centers is that they do not test children to determine if they have learning disabilities. As a result, underlying problems may not be identified. In many instances, a reading problem represents only one facet of a more complex problem. A student who has difficulty reading may also be distractible and inattentive, or he may have problems following oral or written directions. As a result of personalized assistance, the child's reading performance may improve considerably. Although he may concentrate and work well at the center where the ratio of students to tutors is low, he may continue to have difficulty functioning efficiently in his regular classroom. If the child's underlying learning problems are not resolved, he will probably continue to struggle in school irrespective of his reading improvement.

Private reading centers are businesses. This reality does not detract from the quality of the service provided, nor does it necessarily create a conflict of interest. Physicians, dentists, accountants, and attorneys are highly trained professionals who sell their services. The fact that a reading center or a physician generates income and ideally makes a profit actually increases the probability that quality service is being offered. The marketplace is governed by a basic axiom: organizations that offer poor service to the public are destined ultimately to fail.

Children enrolled in reading centers typically receive several hours per week of group or private instruction. Some centers utilize proprietary teaching materials developed exclusively for use at the center. Other centers utilize the same materials as those of most public schools. Because of a high teacher-to-children ratio, students generally receive more direct assistance from the tutor at the center than they would normally receive from their classroom teachers. This extra assistance can greatly accelerate skill mastery.

Before parents decide to enroll their child at a private reading center, they are advised to check out the program's reputation. As an extra precaution, they should inquire if any of their friends have had direct experience with the center. They should also ask the family pediatrician and their child's teacher if they have heard of the program. Requesting that the center provide the names of satisfied clients may also serve to allay concerns. If parents still have doubts, they should investigate whether there have been any complaints lodged against the center with consumer protection agencies.

The final safeguard is parental intuition. Parents must ask themselves some basic questions:

1. Does the program "feel" right for our child?
2. Do we have confidence and faith in the director?
3. Are we impressed with the skills of the teachers?

These questions are the basis for an analytical and intuitive process that should enable parents to make the appropriate decision.

PRIVATE SCHOOLS Some private schools work exclusively with students who have learning disabilities. These special schools have boarding programs and/or day programs which are usually designed for students who have more severe learning problems.

Traditional private schools may also offer special programs for students who have subtle-to-moderate academic deficiencies. Because these schools do not work exclusively with learning-disabled students, they have a diversified student population and offer the learning-disabled child an opportunity to interact with a broad spectrum of children. At the same time, this type of exposure may pose a potential disadvantage because the child may not be as protected as he might be at a specialized school. Another potential disadvantage of a diversified school is that the learning assistance programs may not be highly developed or focused.

Schools that specialize in teaching a specific population of students have a powerful incentive to develop a good remediation program—the school's reputation hangs in the balance. Private schools offering programs for learning-disabled students generally provide small classes, individualized curricula, tutorial services, and specially trained staff. Unfortunately, most of these schools are quite expensive. In California the fees can range from four thousand to eleven thousand dollars a year for a day program. Boarding programs are usually even more expensive.

Private day schools providing learning assistance are generally located in or near urban areas. Boarding schools are frequently located in non-urban areas. For families living in rural areas and desiring a full-time program, a boarding school may be the only option.

Some parents elect to enroll their struggling children in private schools which do not specialize in providing learning assistance because they feel that the educational programs offered at private schools are superior to public schools. These parents are convinced that smaller classes and better trained, more dedicated teachers will increase the probability that their child receives a superior education.

Although many private schools do offer smaller classes, some actually have classes which are as large as or larger than public school classes. This is especially true in the case of the parish parochial school.

As in public schools, the teaching quality in private schools can vary considerably. Some private schools have excellent teachers; others do not. The fact that a school is private does not guarantee that the teaching standards will be higher than in a public school.

Parents of underachieving children who enroll their child in a nonspecialized private school in the expectation that the child will flourish in such an environment may be disillusioned with the results. Although small classes and dedicated teachers can increase the chances that the struggling child will show improvement, these factors do not ensure achievement.

In many instances learning-disabled children can benefit far more from a quality special education program in a public school than they would from a nonspecialized program in a private school. The training, personality, and energy level of the particular teacher will have far more impact on the outcome than will the type of school. Talented, qualified, and dedicated teachers are as likely to be found in public school classrooms as in private school classrooms.

One of the primary features distinguishing public schools

from private schools involves the issue of accountability. Over the last two decades the power of the public school principal has been circumscribed. Although principals have the option to terminate or reassign an incompetent tenured teacher, they may, for both political and labor relations reasons, have difficulty exercising this option. Headmasters and headmistresses at most private schools, on the other hand, still maintain relatively autocratic authority in overseeing the quality of the educational programs offered at their schools. The headmaster has total control over the educational standards and admissions requirements, and his direct supervision can increase the probability of a quality program. If a teacher does not conform to the headmaster's standards, the teacher is subject to dismissal.

One of the most compelling reasons for enrolling a struggling child in a specialized private school is that the school may be able to insulate the child from some of the social and emotional stress associated with a learning problem. Children who are having academic difficulty generally recognize that they are "different" from the other children in the school. Unfortunately, students placed in segregated learning-handicapped classes in public schools are sometimes subject to ridicule by other children. When such conditions exist at a school, they reflect incompetence or insensitivity on the part of the school administration. It is the principal's responsibility to help the children in his or her school develop sensitivity to the feelings of students who have special educational, physical, or emotional needs. The teasing of students with special needs should not be tolerated.

Mainstreaming the learning-disabled child into the general school population also poses some potential risks. If the child has significant learning deficits, he may feel inadequate and self-conscious. The child may conclude that he is abnormal, and may begin to act abnormal.

As they wrestle with their options, parents will undoubtedly discover that there are trade-offs. The primary issue that parents should examine is not the advantages and disadvantages of public education versus private education but, rather, the pluses and minuses of a particular school program, be it public or private.

CLINICAL LEARNING ASSISTANCE PROGRAMS Clinical learning assistance programs are generally found in urban areas which have a sufficient population base to support them. Such programs may be independent, or they may be affiliated with hospitals, universities, teachers colleges, or medical schools. Most clinical programs offer extensive diagnostic services and diversified remediation options. Usually, a broad spectrum of specialized professional services is available. It is not uncommon for university-affiliated clinical programs to be staffed with educational psychologists, learning disabilities specialists, speech therapists, art therapists, and occupational therapists. Some clinics also have pediatricians, clinical psychologists, social workers, family therapists, neurologists, and psychiatrists on staff or on call.

Many university-affiliated clinical programs also offer the advantages of consultation between professionals representing different areas of specialization. Generally, the staff at a learning disabilities clinic is carefully selected. Because the fees for the services offered are often quite high, there is usually a commensurately high level of competence and accountability. Clinics which charge high fees and offer an inadequate program will not survive.

There are both advantages and disadvantages to clinical programs. Many clinics require extensive diagnostic testing. Although diagnostic testing is vital to designing a remediation strategy, testing "overkill" can sometimes be a very expensive and unnecessary indulgence. Many clear-cut learning problems can be quickly identified, and the money that might be spent on extensive testing could be better spent on remediation.

It is not uncommon for some clinical programs to charge fees ranging from one thousand to two thousand dollars for a complete multidiscipline workup which may include an evaluation by a pediatrician, a psychiatrist, a neurologist, an educational psychologist, a clinical psychologist, a social worker, and a learning therapist. Although such extensive workups may be justified when a child is suspected of having a complex, enigmatic, or hard-to-treat learning disability or an organic problem, the workup may be far more comprehensive than is required to design a remediation program for the typical learning-disabled child. Another potential disadvantage of a clinical program is that the staff at the particular center may be so committed to their philosophy or teaching methodology that they may refuse to consider alternative approaches which might prove to be more effective in treating the learning problem.

Parents should monitor private assistance programs every bit as carefully as they monitor public school programs. They must, however, have realistic expectations. They must allow a reasonable period of time to elapse before they become critical of the program. Some learning problems respond quickly to treatment. Other problems may take longer to resolve. The remediation timetable will vary from child to child and will be influenced not only by the quality of the remediation program but also by the nature and severity of the child's problem and by the commitment of the family to the remediation process.

Parents who become discouraged with their child's lack of progress should discuss their feelings with the professional who is assisting the child. They should not hesitate to inquire diplomatically about goals, timetables, and progress. A simple statement can be used to initiate the discussion: "I think my daughter is still struggling in school. Could I have an update on her progress?" A qualified and emotionally secure professional should be able to examine the parents' concerns objectively and analytically. If parents perceive that the professional is becoming defensive or resentful about this "interference," they should consider seeking another specialist.

Retention

Retention may appear to be a viable option for helping the struggling child who seems incapable of keeping up with his class. In the case of the learning-disabled or underachieving child, however, this option is at best a stopgap measure that should be utilized cautiously.

A vital distinction must be made between children who are developmentally, physiologically, or emotionally immature and those who are learning-disabled or underachievers. The parents and teacher of a five-year-old who barely met the age requirement for admission to kindergarten may agree, after having observed the child's classroom performance over a nine-month period, that the child has not acquired sufficient reading-readiness skills and maturity to handle first grade. They may conclude that by retaining the child three important objectives would be accomplished: the pressure on the child would be reduced, the risk of self-concept damage would be lowered, and the probability of academic success would be increased. In view of the careful consideration given the decision, the judgment of parents and teacher in this instance would be reasonable and appropriate.

Unfortunately, the term "immature" has been so overused by elementary school teachers that it has lost credibility. Teachers and other professionals who cannot figure out why a student is having difficulty keeping up with his class have a tendency to call such a child immature. In most instances, the academic difficulties of the struggling child have nothing to do with physiological or emotional immaturity. Most children who are labeled immature have specific, undiagnosed learning problems.

Although retention would undoubtedly reduce the academic pressure and stress that the learning-disabled or underachieving child often experiences, the reduction of pressure will not resolve an underlying learning problem. Before the struggling child can succeed academically, his specific deficiencies must be identified and treated. Retention may keep the child from foundering, but it simply places the learning problem on hold and buys time. Initially, the child may do better if he is retained because he is covering material for the second time. A false sense of euphoria may result. But underlying deficits which are not remediated have a disturbing tendency to reappear. By the end of the school year, it is likely that the retained child will once again be struggling to keep up with his class.

Retention is a rather drastic recourse, and there are grave psychological risks inherent in the decision to retain a child.

Before parents make the decision, they must carefully weigh the potential negative emotional ramifications against the potential academic advantages.

The most common rationale for retention is that it will protect the child from unnecessary frustration and self-esteem damage. Although this may be true in the case of the child who is struggling and who is not receiving assistance, the converse may actually be more accurate. The self-esteem of most learning-disabled and underachieving children is at best tenuous. Retention may actually be perceived by the struggling child as an ultimate failure and a confirmation of his inadequacies.

The potential for psychological damage is very high when children are retained in the upper grades of elementary school or in junior high school. The later the retention occurs, the greater the potential psychological risk. Most older children are extremely sensitive to the reactions of their friends, and the prospect of being teased or socially rejected can be devastating.

The danger of self-esteem damage is reduced when children are retained in preschool or kindergarten. Parents who are advised by the teacher or school psychologist to retain the preschool or kindergarten child should feel comfortable with the recommendation before accepting it. Each child being considered for retention should be carefully assessed. The child's classroom performance should be compared with specific criteria that the school district considers to be requisites for promotion to the next grade. Well-researched standards for retention such as "Light's Retention Scale" (H. Wayne Light, Academic Therapy Publications, 1984) should be consulted. Parents should also consult with their child's pediatrician. If they still have reservations, they should have their child independently evaluated.

Immaturity and specific learning problems must be differentiated. The conditions are not equivalent and to treat them as such would be a serious mistake. Specific learning deficits require specialized remedial assistance. If retention is recommended for the learning-disabled or underachieving child, it should be considered only in conjunction with a comprehensive and competent learning assistance program.

● PARENTING SUGGESTIONS

● *Learn to identify the behaviors in your child that are symptoms of academic or emotional stress.*

Parents who attempt to deny the reality of a problem may be postponing desperately needed academic remediation or counseling. Unresolved learning problems and emotional problems seldom disappear of their own accord.

● *Monitor your child's progress if he or she is enrolled in a special program.*

You cannot assume that your child's learning assistance needs are being adequately met. Be reasonable and supportive of the specialist who is working with your child. If you conclude that your child is not making progress or is "stuck," do not hesitate to discuss your concerns with the child's instructor.

● *Be diplomatic.*

If you have reservations about the program in which your child is enrolled or are critical of the specialist working with your child, do not "attack" or denigrate the professional or the program. Far more can be accomplished when the issues are examined in a nonthreatening and non-emotionally charged context. Children make the most significant gains when their parents and instructors work together as a team.

● *Carefully examine the available remediation options.*

Each remediation option has potential advantages and disadvantages. Try to find a specialist or a program which can best meet your child's particular needs. In order to do so, you must first identify your child's specific deficits. Involve the professional in the identification and decision-making process. This will afford you insight into his or her skills.

If you feel intuitively that the specialist is on target and understands your child's problem, permit the person to work with your child.

- *Carefully examine the potential advantages and disadvantages of retention before making a decision.*

The option of retention should be considered when children are clearly developmentally delayed or immature. Retention of the learning-disabled child should be considered only if the child cannot possibly keep up with his class and there are no alternative remediation options available. If parents do elect to retain their child, they should insist that specialized learning assistance also be provided.

- *Be cautious about accepting that your child is immature.*

Very few children are actually developmentally immature. Teachers who describe children as immature often use the term because they have not been trained to recognize the symptoms of learning problems and cannot differentiate between learning problems and actual physiological or emotional immaturity.

10 Communicating with the Underachieving Child

Michelle: It Was More Than Laziness

The thirteen-year-old entering my office looked depressed and apprehensive. She sat down, drew her knees up to her chest, rested her feet on the seat of the chair, and wrapped her arms tightly around her legs. Her face was set in a tight frown, and her eyes stared down at the table.

Michelle's grim-faced father sat next to her. With barely contained anger, he explained that he had requested the meeting because he was at his wit's end. Michelle had become totally irresponsible about her schoolwork, and the grades on her last report card had been terrible. He attributed her poor grades to chronic laziness. As he expressed his exasperation and disappointment, he seemed oblivious to his daughter's distress. Michelle responded to his criticism by clenching her jaw and tightening her arms around her drawn-up legs.

In an attempt to get father and daughter to communicate directly with each other, I asked him to tell Michelle precisely what she was doing that upset him. The following is an approximate recounting of the dialogue that ensued.

FATHER: I knew you would get a D on that book report. You kept putting off reading the

189

	book until the last minute. And you didn't begin to write the report until the night before it was due.
MICHELLE:	I hate reading, and I hate writing book reports.
FATHER:	If you weren't so lazy you could get decent grades.
MICHELLE:	I try. I just can't seem to write the way the teacher wants.
FATHER:	Spending more time on your homework might help. And not talking on the phone for two hours every evening with your friends might also help. I sure hope you get your act together because I want you to know, young lady, that I'm not prepared to support you throughout your life.
MICHELLE:	I hate my teacher, and I hate English! Why are you always on my back?
FATHER:	Because I love you, and I don't want you to fail.
MICHELLE:	All you do is worry about me and complain about me.

I was certain that the drama unfolding in my office had played many times before. The father's role was that of the critical, disillusioned parent. Michelle was the oppressed victim. The more he pushed, the more she resisted. I interjected at this point:

LJG:	Do you think Michelle is avoiding her work because she finds the work difficult?
FATHER:	When I find something difficult, I grit my teeth and force myself to do it. Overcoming a problem says a lot about a person's character.
LJG:	I sense that you feel confident that you

	can conquer most things if you set your mind to it.
FATHER:	Yes, I do!
LJG:	You've probably proven this to yourself many times.
FATHER:	Yes. That's what success is all about. I've worked very hard and I've achieved most of the goals I've set.
LJG:	You indicated that you are an engineer. Let me ask what might appear to be a silly question. Do you feel that you could write an effective jingle for a laundry detergent?
FATHER:	No. I was never particularly good at creative things like writing. I also can't read or write music.
LJG:	Do you think that if you had to, you could do it?
FATHER:	No. I'm not creative in that way.
LJG:	Michelle, do you feel that you are a good reader?
MICHELLE:	I get confused and I can't explain things.
LJG:	How does that make you feel?
MICHELLE:	Horrible.
LJG:	Dumb?
MICHELLE:	Yes.
LJG:	Do you think your daughter might be less lazy and irresponsible if she felt confident she could do the work?
FATHER:	I suppose so.
LJG:	There are parallels between Michelle's lack of confidence in English and yours in writing jingles.
FATHER:	I see the point you're making. But Michelle can't go through life avoiding everything that's difficult.
LJG:	That's true. But let's get back to why she's neglecting her work. Would you

	agree that her lack of confidence is at the root of it?
FATHER:	Yes.
LJG:	Michelle avoids having to deal with material that requires skills she is convinced she doesn't possess. She has not had any real success in school. It's difficult to feel confident about something when you've never experienced success. Although you are a confident person, you've admitted that in some areas you are not confident. Do you think that you might procrastinate if your boss assigned you the job of writing a jingle for your company's advertising promotion?
FATHER:	Yes.
LJG:	Michelle, tell me—what does your dad mean when he says that you procrastinate?
MICHELLE:	I put things off.
LJG:	Do you?
MICHELLE:	Yes.
LJG:	You procrastinate about doing your schoolwork because . . . ?
MICHELLE:	I can't do the work. I feel terrible trying to do something and knowing I can't do it.
LJG:	I think your dad understands that now. But there is an important fact that you have to face, Michelle. Your dad doesn't have to write jingles, but you have to do your schoolwork. It may seem unfair, but that's life. I'm sure your dad has to do things on his job that he doesn't enjoy.
FATHER:	I hate writing reports.
LJG:	Michelle, we all tend to avoid things that are difficult for us. I have two important questions to ask you. One, do

MICHELLE: you want to acquire the skills you need to succeed in school?

MICHELLE: Yes.

LJG: Two, are you willing to work? Before you answer, let me emphasize that you won't be able to master these skills without making a great deal of effort.

MICHELLE: I'd be willing.

LJG: Good. Let's talk about setting up a program to help you.

Michelle's parents were divorced. Her mother lived in another state and rarely saw her daughter. As a single parent, Michelle's father faced the difficult challenge of raising his adolescent daughter alone. He ran his family in the same way he ran his division at work—autocratically. He possessed a powerful personality and strong opinions, and he expected his daughter to conform to his value system. Convinced that Michelle would fail miserably if left to her own devices, he had assumed the role of policeman and judge.

Frustration, resentment, and anger dominated the relationship between father and daughter. He made no attempt to hide his disappointment in her. Michelle's only recourse for expressing her own anger and resentment was to resist.

My diagnostic evaluation confirmed that Michelle lacked basic academic skills. Having concluded that she couldn't do the work, she had chosen the path of least resistance. She had shut down. Frustration had led to a sense of futility. Repeated failure had destroyed her self-confidence. To protect the vestiges of her self-esteem, Michelle had retreated behind a defensive wall comprised of irresponsibility and avoidance behavior. She deluded herself into thinking that by not trying she could hide her inadequacies and reduce her vulnerability. Until she became convinced that she no longer needed to protect herself from her father and her learning problems, she would remain behind the wall.

Her father's continual criticism and Michelle's defensiveness compounded the challenge of resolving the learning problem. The father was so caught up in his role as the disciplinarian that he failed to realize that his attitude was causing Michelle's irresponsibility and laziness to become more entrenched.

Michelle and her father had stopped listening to each other. Each was preoccupied with his or her own position and perceptions. The father was fixated on his concern and his disapproval. Michelle was fixated on her resentment, resistance, and pain.

Before the stand-off could end, the negative feelings and energy would have to be syphoned off. The alternative was continued poor school performance, anger, and stress. If Michelle and her father did not quickly resolve their communication problems, they would soon become irreconcilably alienated from each other.

My proposal that we take over the responsibility of monitoring Michelle's academic performance was greeted with grave reservations. As an engineer, Michelle's father was reluctant to place his trust in a methodology that he considered to be "nonscientific."

I felt strongly that the family needed counseling, but I was certain that he would not agree to see a family counselor. He had indicated that he didn't believe in psychology and that he had come to us because he felt we wouldn't try to analyze him. I feared that if I pushed therapy, Michelle's father would reject all help. I decided to propose learning therapy for Michelle. The issue of counseling could be examined once I established credibility with him.

After explaining Michelle's specific learning deficits, I outlined a remediation strategy. We would work with Michelle on eliminating the underlying learning problems, and we also would provide crisis-intervention tutorial assistance so that she could complete her assignments and pass her courses.

Michelle's father was ambivalent about my proposal that he disengage from his monitoring role. Although he was relieved by the prospect of relinquishing his role as the "heavy," he was apprehensive that Michelle would fail without his supervision.

Michelle was equally ambivalent and apprehensive. Like so many struggling children, she had developed an aversion to work, and the aversion had become a habit. She realized that the remediation program I was proposing would demand a great deal of effort and commitment. She was being asked to take some major risks, and she was frightened.

Michelle decided to take the risks. At first her effort was tentative, but as she began to make progress she became increasingly conscientious. Within eight months her basic reading comprehension skills improved by three grade levels. Michelle's father ultimately did agree to see a family therapist. He and Michelle spent twelve sessions with her, and the quality of their relationship improved dramatically.

Today Michelle is in her second year of college and is maintaining a B average. Her goal is to become a teacher.

The Function of Parent-Child Communication

The challenge of establishing an effective communication system with an unhappy, struggling, and resistant child can seem as overwhelming as the challenge of running a telephone wire across the Himalayas. During the ascent, parents will encounter conditions which may severely test their resolve. But if they persist and establish the communication system, they will then no longer need to climb the mountain each time they have something to discuss with their child.

Establishing the communication network represents only one facet of the challenge. Once parents string the line across the mountain, they must continually monitor the line to make sure that it remains open. Despite their vigilance, however, parents must accept the fact of life that even the best communication system can go down during a storm. In this event, they have no alternative but to climb the mountain once again, find the problem, and repair it.

The quality of communication is one of the litmus tests of the health and strength of the family. When the members of a family are unable or unwilling to share their feelings, perceptions, and ideas, they are signaling their estrangement from each other.

The desire and ability to talk and listen serves another important function. It provides pleasure. A child may express to her mother her enthusiasm about something she has learned in her science class. By sharing her joy, the child is reaching out to her mother. Her mother might respond in several different ways. She might exclaim, "Lisa, that seems really exciting! I can tell how enthusiastic you are about what you are learning in science class." By reacting in this way, the mother is communicating to her daughter that she shares her enthusiasm. Her response is an affirmation of her child and encourages continued communication and enthusiasm. Contrast that response with the following reaction: "Well, Lisa, I hope that now that you are so enthusiastic about school, you will be prepared to study a bit more conscientiously." The mother's criticism negates her child's enthusiasm and discourages her from expressing her feelings. With justification, the child may be very reluctant to share ever again this type of experience with her mother. In fact, she may be reluctant to share any emotional experience with her mother.

The quality of the communication between parents and children can either support or inhibit achievement. A child might exclaim, "I just made the junior varsity wrestling team." The parent's response to this news might be: "Great! I'm really proud of you because I know how hard you worked to make the team." Or the parent might respond: "One more thing to take you away from your studies." The parent who reacts in a negative or derogatory manner should not be surprised if the child becomes increasingly reluctant to share events in his life. The parent's reaction may also have an even more dire consequence: the child may become reluctant to establish and attain goals.

Quality parent-child communication is also essential to problem solving. A child might summon up the courage to tell his father, "My Spanish teacher thinks that I'm lazy." The parent might react by saying, "It sounds as though you're having difficulty keeping up." Such a reaction would encourage the child to provide more information about the situation, and father and child could begin the process of identifying, examining, and resolving the problem. Contrast the previous statement with the following: "Well, she's right. You are lazy, and I've told you so many times. I don't blame her for being upset with you." The child who elicits disapproval when he attempts to explore a problem with a parent might find flunking the course preferable to his parent's criticism or disdain.

When parents denigrate their child, they not only undermine the child's faith in himself, they also undermine his faith in their fairness as parents. Michelle's father was a classic example of a parent who had unwittingly fallen into the disapproval trap. He violated virtually every rule of effective communication. He failed to differentiate the symptoms of his daughter's problem from the source. He construed Michelle's resistance and avoidance behavior as a personal rejection of his value system, and he showed no empathy for her pain. By continually communicating his negative expectations, he was inviting his daughter's resentment and resistance. Her tenuous self-esteem could not deal with the onslaught of criticism. Rather than struggle with her learning problem, it was easier for Michelle to give up and simply fulfill her father's negative expectations.

During the formative years of a child's life, parents have virtually all of the power. If they are fair in exercising this power, they elicit trust and encourage intimacy. If they exercise their power unfairly, they court distrust and defensiveness. The defensive child may turn his emotions inward and resist communication with his parents, or he may gravitate toward an alternative support system which might be centered on peers, sports, or even drugs. Rather than express his feelings and emotions, the child learns to repress them. Resentment, hostility, estrangement, antisocial behavior, and/or depression usually result.

Barriers to Communication

Six conditions significantly increase the probability of a communication breakdown between parent and child:

1. The child and/or his parents become preoccupied with asserting or defending their respective positions.
2. The parents convey a highly critical or judgmental attitude.
3. The child and/or the parents are not in touch with their underlying feelings.
4. The child and/or the parents become so caught up in their own emotions that they lack sensitivity for the feelings of the other person.
5. The emotions expressed (anger, resentment, disillusionment, etc.) are so intense that they undermine reasoning and problem-solving abilities.
6. Manipulative behavior (guilt, deception, etc.) is used to control the actions of the other person.

It would be unrealistic to expect that a child who is struggling to survive in school would not be profoundly affected by this experience. It would be equally unreasonable to expect that the child's parents would not also be profoundly affected by this struggle. In order to cope with stress, children and parents usually develop their own systems for protecting themselves emotionally. For children, this system might consist of defensiveness, denial, irresponsibility, poor motivation, and avoidance behavior. For parents, the system may involve overprotectiveness, denial, criticism, sympathy, frustration, irritation, or anger. These defense systems can function as impenetrable barriers to communication. The impasse that prevented Michelle from communicating with her father clearly illustrated this phenomenon.

When parents and children communicate, the children take many more risks than do the parents. Each time a child talks with his father or mother, he faces the possibility of having his feelings or ideas dismissed or discounted by the two most important people in his life. If the child concludes from experience that communication with his parents is synonymous with rejection or disparagement of his perceptions, he has a powerful incentive for avoiding or resisting communication.

Children can generally accept criticism and even punishment if they feel that their parents are fair. Disparagement is far more traumatic. An eight-year-old may be convinced that he is old enough to take the bus alone to an amusement park, and he confidently states his position to his parents. They do not concur, and they are faced with the challenge of rejecting the child's idea without having the child feel rejected or demeaned. One possible response might be: "Son, we know that you are growing up. Mom and I realize that you have become very responsible, and we are proud of you. However, we think that you are still too young to take the bus alone. You need a couple more years under your belt before we would feel comfortable letting you go to the amusement park alone. Believe me, you'll get your chance to take the bus by yourself!" The parent might have also responded: "That's ridiculous. Your mother and I aren't going to allow an eight-year-old to take a bus by himself to an amusement park. You could get lost or be kidnapped." Although the parents' reasoning may be sound, the manner in which they respond demeans the child. The response almost brutally rejects the child's need for confirmation that he is growing up and deserves greater freedom and responsibility.

Because struggling, underachieving children are usually less emotionally secure than children who achieve, they are particularly vulnerable to parental responses which may be perceived as confirming their inadequacies. For this reason, parents have a special responsibility to monitor how they express their criticism, anger, and disapproval. Parents who desire to communicate with an emotionally vulnerable child should provide an extra measure of love, support, encouragement, sensitivity, and empathy.

Communicating with Younger Children

Contrary to popular belief, young children have the capacity to comprehend many complex issues which impact on their lives. Unfortunately, parents often deny their children the opportunity to examine these issues. Some parents, for instance, assume that a six-year-old child lacks the necessary maturity and reasoning ability to understand why he is being retained in first grade. In the absence of an explanation, the child may have no recourse but to conclude that he must repeat first grade because he is bad or because he is dumb.

Clarity and age-appropriate language are the keys to helping a young child understand complex issues. Although the child may not fully comprehend everything that is explained and may periodically require a review of the issues, he deserves the opportunity to learn why and how certain decisions about him are made. Parents, of course, need not share every decision, but when they do communicate with their child about issues which affect him they are helping him learn how to reason, think, and communicate.

There are several requisites to communicating successfully with all children and particularly young children:

1. Parents must use language the child can understand.
2. Parents must strive to appreciate their child's perspective.
3. Parents must be sensitive to their child's fears and anxieties.
4. Parents must gear the content level of their communication to their child's level of maturity.
5. Parents must be willing to listen to their child.
6. Parents must be sensitive to the messages and feelings that are often hidden behind their child's words.

For example, the child who is going to be retained is facing an experience which could have serious emotional implications. The child may not show or even be in touch with his feelings, but he will undoubtedly be affected on some level by the retention. He may actually feel relieved because the academic pressure will be reduced, or he may perceive the retention as a profound defeat. He may be upset by the prospect of having to make new friends, or he may feel confident that he can easily make new friends. He may be confused about how to interact with old friends who have been promoted, or he may be unconcerned about what his friends will think.

The manner in which parents broach the subject of retention is critical. Six-year-olds are already sensitive to failure and to ridicule from their peers. For this reason, the retention must be presented as positively as possible. Two approaches are suggested below. In the first example, the unilateral approach, the parents have already made the decision to retain their child and are presenting it to him as a *fait accompli*:

> PARENT: Tommy, your teacher thinks you will find school much easier if you repeat the first grade. Mom and I agree with her. We want you to repeat first grade so that you can become one of the best students in your class. How do you feel about this idea?

Some parents prefer making major decisions without involving younger children in the decision-making process. They are more comfortable consulting with each other and with the appropriate school personnel, weighing the issues carefully, arriving at a decision, and presenting their decision to the child. This unilateral approach with younger children is appropriate, with the proviso that the parents encourage the child to express any feelings, misgivings, or fears he might have. These emotions should be examined with sensitivity and compassion. Parents should not insist that the child immediately concur with the decision. They may need to allow him time to mull over the issues and adjust to the decision.

Children who are retained are usually most concerned about how their friends will react: "Will my friends still be my friends?" "What will the kids in school say?" "Will the kids think I'm stupid?" "Will I have to make all new friends?" Parents should initiate a discussion of these issues if the child himself doesn't bring them up. Children, like their adult counterparts, may have a difficult time expressing their fears. Silence on the child's part does not necessarily mean that he isn't concerned or experiencing turmoil.

A parent might open the discussion by asking: "Are you worried about what your friends might think?" If the child responds "no," the parent might ask how he would feel if a friend were held back in school. If the parent observes that the child is reticent, he or she might suggest some possible reactions to encourage the discussion. For example, "Do you think that you might feel sorry for your friend? Do you think your friend would be sad?" If the child admits that the prospect of retention is scary or makes him feel that he is stupid, he should be encouraged to talk about these fears. Parents might begin the conversation by discussing famous historical figures who had learning problems and prevailed over them (for example, Thomas Edison, Nelson Rockefeller, Bruce Jenner and Albert Einstein).

The following dialogue models an alternative means of presenting the prospect of retention. The child in the hypothetical dialogue is a third grader. It should be noted that this problem-solving approach can also be used successfully with children as young as five, assuming the presentation is geared to their level of maturity:

PARENT:	It's really important that your friends like you, isn't it?
CHILD:	Yeah.
PARENT:	Do you think your friends might not like you or want to play with you if you had to repeat third grade?
CHILD:	I'd have to make all new friends. And my old friends would make fun of me.
PARENT:	Would you make fun of a friend if he had to repeat third grade?
CHILD:	No.
PARENT:	Why do you think you have to repeat?
CHILD:	'Cause I am not doing well. I'm dumb.
PARENT:	If you did well, would you be dumb?
CHILD:	No.
PARENT:	If you do well next year, would you still consider yourself dumb?
CHILD:	No.
PARENT:	Mom and I think that you should repeat third grade because we feel that an extra year would help you to catch up. If you

have a good year in school and get good
grades, do you think you might consider
yourself smart?

CHILD: Yeah.

PARENT: I agree! Let's figure out what you need
to do well next year. Repeating will take
the pressure off of you. But maybe
something else is also needed to make
sure you catch up. Do you think some
extra help from a tutor might help?

CHILD: O.K.

PARENT: Now, I wonder what you could tell your
friends.

CHILD: I don't know.

PARENT: Could you tell them that you are repeating the year because you want to be
one of the best readers in the class?

CHILD: Yeah.

PARENT: Do you think that your old friends might
not want to play with you?

CHILD: Maybe.

PARENT: What about making new friends, if necessary?

CHILD: I'm good at making new friends.

PARENT: That's certainly true. Now I am going
to ask you to do Mom and me a favor.
Before you make any decisions about
how smart or how dumb you are, wait
and see how well you do next year. First
thing we have to do is get you a good
tutor so that you can be one of the best
readers in your class. Are you willing to
wait for a year before you decide if you're
dumb?

CHILD: Yeah!

The preceding dialogue models a technique for helping a
child understand the rationale for making an important de-

cision which directly affects him. Although his parents have already decided to retain him, they nevertheless encourage him to participate actively in the reasoning process which led to the decision. The father carefully avoids exaggerating how smart the child is, but does strongly imply that he will do very well in school if he repeats the year and receives learning assistance. The father anticipates and addresses the child's probable anxieties about social rejection and helps him perceive the situation positively. Although he suggests strategies for dealing with his friends, he resists the temptation to take ownership of his child's problem.

There are two common traps that parents fall into when they try to help their children deal with problems: (1) they attempt to give advice (which is usually rejected); and (2) they attempt to solve their child's problem (which inhibits the child from learning how to solve his own problems). A way to avoid these traps is for parents to perceive themselves as facilitators for solving problems. The role of the facilitator is to help the child identify and find solutions to his own problems.

Although the parent in the dialogue might have used a similar communication strategy to involve the child in the actual decision-making process, his primary objective was to help his child understand the decision already made and help him deal with possible repercussions. The parent asked questions which encouraged the child to express his fears about retention, and suggested strategies for handling these concerns.

Parents walk a fine line. They must provide support and encouragement without creating excessive emotional dependence. They must nurture without smothering. They must illuminate without denying their child an opportunity to gain his own insights.

As parents attempt to communicate with struggling children, they must recognize that children who have been damaged by their experiences in life are usually terrified of exposing themselves to situations which might lead to additional frustration, ridicule, and failure. Because of their insecurities, many vulnerable children prefer to remain behind their defensive walls and may aggressively or passively resist their parents' attempts to help them or communicate with them. To an insecure child, the prospect of discussing his problems and feelings can be very threatening. Parents must remind themselves that the insecure child uses his defensive and resistant behaviors to protect himself from pain and feelings of inadequacy. To assault this line of defense will succeed only in triggering more defensiveness. The protective wall must be dismantled slowly. In cases of chronic defensiveness, resistance, and uncommunicativeness, professional counseling will probably be necessary.

Sometimes the most appropriate strategy for dealing with a resistant child is to go around the protective wall. Head-on confrontations with a child's defenses rarely lead to the resolution of problems. If parents conclude, for example, that the issue of homework invariably triggers resistance and stress, they might consider offering an incentive to the child for completing his assignments without having to be reminded. The child could be awarded points each time the homework is completed before bedtime. The points could be used for acquiring skates, a bike, or spending money. The efficacy of this behavior-modification strategy is, of course, predicated on the assumption that the child is capable of doing the homework.

Communicating with Adolescents

The transitional years from childhood to adolescence can be painful not only for teenagers but also for their parents. Reasoning with someone who is no longer a child but not quite an adult can severely test a parent's emotional and creative resources.

Adolescents tend to be somewhat myopic. They generally see only what is up close and have difficulty understanding the long-term consequences and implications of their actions. Because of their limited perspective, teenagers generally fail to see the overview.

Because adolescents have had limited life experiences, their perceptions are quite different from those of their parents.

Most teenagers are unwilling to view the world through the same lens that their parents use to view the world. Their insistence on their own perspective is quite normal. Although they are affected by their parents' perceptions and values, children need to discover their own truths.

Despite the maturing child's desire for increased independence, he still requires the protection and guidance of his parents. Wanting to test himself, a thirteen-year-old may insist that he can ride his skateboard down a dangerous hill or swim across a cold lake. With misgiving, his parents may allow him to do so. But they may also say no, and the child must accept that his parents have a responsibility to establish reasonable guidelines for his behavior.

If experience is the material which grinds the lens through which human beings view life, then knowledge and wisdom are the materials which polish the lens. The grinding process is slow and laborious, and the patina of knowledge and wisdom is acquired slowly. Parents, of course, know this. Teenagers generally do not. The teenager's insistence on using his own unfinished lens to view the world makes some distortions of reality inevitable. These distortions sometimes produce errors in judgment. The greater the distortions, the more serious and more frequent the errors.

An adolescent's unwillingness to accept his parents' perception of reality can be very frustrating. There is a natural tendency for frustrated parents to become highly critical. Reciprocal resentment and counterproductive behavior typically result. The teenager will become angered by his parents' insistence that "things be done their way," and the parents will, in turn, become angered by their child's unwillingness to conform. Under such conditions there is a high risk that an adversarial relationship will evolve between parent and teenager. Such a relationship can quickly destroy the potential for communication.

During the formative years, a child's perspective is shaped by four major influences: parental values, school, life experiences, and peers. Parents who desire to communicate effectively with their children—and particularly teenage children —must be willing to acknowledge that other values besides their own can affect their child's attitudes. The more parents understand about these other influences, the better they will understand their child. Although loud, throbbing music or attention-getting clothing and hair styles may be offensive to parents, these styles may appeal to their children. Parents who insist that their child subscribe only to their values are being unrealistic. Those who demean their child's values will elicit resistance and resentment. Although parents may find their patience and emotional resources sorely tested by their child's addiction to current fads, they must remind themselves that the child's priorities, attitudes, and values will evolve as he matures. The adolescent who insists on surrounding himself with ear-shattering music may one day prefer to spend a quiet evening at home playing bridge with his wife and neighbors.

By the age of thirteen most adolescents have acquired exposure to many of the realities of life. The typical teenager has probably experienced the death of a relative, an acquaintance, or a family friend. He has probably also experienced fear, sickness, defeat, disappointment, disillusionment, and rejection. Despite this exposure to many aspects of reality, the teenager's view of the world and his understanding of cause and effect are still incomplete. Most teenagers, for instance, have far less regard for physical danger than do most adults. Death is something that happens only to old people and seems far removed from an adolescent's world. Because teenagers unconsciously believe that they are invincible, they tend to take more risks with their lives. This tendency is reflected in the grim auto fatality statistics compiled by this age group.

The communication guidelines which apply to younger children also apply to teenagers. If they wish to communicate with their adolescent child, parents must acknowledge his perspective. They must be particularly sensitive to the feelings of the teenager who has experienced a great deal of frustration or defeat. They must attempt to understand his defense mechanisms, and seek to understand the reasons for distortions in his perspective. They must listen to their child's words, and they must listen for hidden messages. Before reacting, they must differentiate the symptoms of the problem from the source of the problem. Whenever possible, they must allow their child to solve his own problems. And finally, if they conclude that they cannot deal adequately with a problem, they must seek professional assistance.

Parents cannot reasonably expect their child to accept all of their truths and wisdom. Parents may know that their daughter will continue to do poorly in school unless she begins to study consistently, but telling her this each day will probably have little effect. In fact, it will probably cause resentment, and the child may express her resentment by becoming even less consistent. The parents' only means for effecting changes in their daughter's behavior are to help her to understand the cause-and-effect relationship between conscientious effort and performance or to offer her a meaningful incentive for changing her behavior.

The attitude of parents plays a vital role in determining the quality of communication. The following Effective Communications Checklist is designed to help parents assess their attitudes about communication.

EFFECTIVE COMMUNICATIONS CHECKLIST

	Yes	No
1. I attempt to get information before I give advice.	____	____
2. I attempt to distinguish between the symptoms and the source of a problem.	____	____
3. I establish trust with my child.	____	____
4. I listen to what my child has to say.	____	____
5. I express my feelings without attacking or bullying.	____	____
6. I create a safe context where my child can express his or her feelings.	____	____
7. I permit my child to express negative feelings.	____	____

8. I am sensitive to my child's feelings.   _____ _____

9. I make every effort to be patient.   _____ _____

10. I do not demean or belittle my child.   _____ _____

11. I affirm and acknowledge my child.   _____ _____

12. I do not continually express
    disapproval.   _____ _____

13. I communicate the facts and explain
    the issues in terms that my child can
    understand.   _____ _____

14. I communicate positive expectations to
    my child.   _____ _____

15. I help my child understand and sort
    out problems.   _____ _____

16. I encourage my child to find solutions
    to his or her own problems whenever
    possible.   _____ _____

17. I am willing to allow my child
    sufficient time to think over issues
    before responding.   _____ _____

18. I am not autocratic when I
    communicate with my child.   _____ _____

19. I avoid using threats.   _____ _____

10. I am reasonable in my expectations.   _____ _____

21. I am willing to look at my own
    shortcomings.   _____ _____

22. I am willing to consider my child's
    criticism of me.   _____ _____

INTERPRETING THE CHECKLIST. Parents who can answer "yes" to most of the questions on the checklist are probably able to communicate effectively with their child. Despite attitudes that are conducive to effective communication and problem solving, these parents may still periodically experience episodes when communication is strained. Like their adult counterparts, most children go through emotional cycles. If they are unhappy, they may be less willing to respond to their parents' efforts at communication. Although a breakdown in the family communication system may be temporary and attributable to the child's emotional cycle, it may also reflect specific underlying problems which should be addressed. The checklist may help parents identify these underlying problems.

Parents who have answered "no" to most of the questions on the checklist must determine if they are comfortable with their attitudes about communication. If they are not, they may be able to make some changes. In the event they feel incapable of making these changes unassisted, they should consider professional counseling.

Expressing Disapproval and Criticism

No one enjoys being on the receiving end of disapproval and criticism. Children are no exception. As a group, children are subjected to more disapprobation than any other population. Traditional thinking supports the argument that a child's flaws must be pointed out and that the child will require a great deal of censure in order to make a successful transition from childhood to adulthood.

The ostensible goal of parental criticism is to change a child's behavior or attitudes. The traditional means for achieving this objective is to identify the child's errors in performance or judgment. When criticizing a child, the parent usually makes the following assumptions:

1. I am correct in my perceptions and judgments.
2. My child will accept my criticism.
3. My child will agree to change that which has been criticized.

Parents who make an effort to examine their assumptions dispassionately might discover that:

1. Their perceptions and judgments are not always accurate.
2. Their child will not accept their criticism.
3. Their child will not agree to change that which has been criticized.

Five factors can influence how an underachieving child responds to criticism: the age of the child, the implications of the child's underachievement, the manner in which the criticism is presented, the child's personality, and the type of behavior or attitude being criticized.

THE AGE FACTOR Because younger children have relatively little power, they must accept their parents' prerogative to criticize them and insist on changes in their behavior. They realize and, to varying degrees, accept that the consequence of noncompliance is usually punishment. Recognizing that they lack the power to resist openly, younger children may feel safer resisting their parents' authority in a devious or passively aggressive way. They may, for instance, "forget" to do something that their parents request, or they may do chronically shoddy or incomplete work.

Teenagers who want to resist their parents' authority may feel that they can be somewhat more blatant about refusing to comply with their parents' wishes. They may argue openly or withdraw to their rooms and slam the door. In extreme cases they may simply disregard what they are told, and do what they want. Although some teenagers openly express their unwillingness to comply with their parents' wishes, others manifest their resistance passively. For example, they might procrastinate and leave important projects to the last minute, knowing full well that they are exasperating their parents by doing so.

During this transitional period from childhood to adulthood, much of the teenager's energy is directed toward gaining peer acceptance, cultivating an identity, and projecting his image. Children normally experience certain rites of passage before they enter the world of adults. In our culture, some of the common symbols of this rite of passage include smoking, driving, dating, drinking, and asserting their independence. Despite their often expressed desire for independence, most teenagers are still uncertain about their identity and about the limits of their power. This confusion often frustrates teenagers, and heightens their sensitivity and vulnerability to parental disapproval and criticism.

When teenagers are criticized by their parents, they are forced to confront a reality that they might prefer to avoid. Their parents' prerogative to find fault underscores the fact that they do not have as much independence and power as they would like to think they have. The criticism and the expectation that they will automatically change their behavior confirm that they have not yet achieved the cherished status of adulthood. The resulting frustration can increase the temptation to reject the criticism.

The typical teenager wants as much control over his life as he can get. In families in which control is given up grudgingly by parents, an actual war for power may take place. The teenager may realize that he is not ready to assume total control over his life, but this realization does not deter him from reacting negatively to both the symbolic and practical implications of parental criticism.

THE UNDERACHIEVEMENT FACTOR Because the self-esteem of the struggling child is generally fragile and his defense mechanisms elaborate, the child's reactions to criticism may be even more extreme than those of other children. Severe learning problems and chronic underachievement significantly increase the risk of emotional vulnerability and insecurity, and to protect himself, the underachieving child may reject any and all statements which communicate disapproval or which dredge up painful associations with academic deficiencies.

Under the appropriate circumstances, the expression of disapproval by parents can be an effective tool for changing the behavior or attitude of an underachieving child. From time to time, virtually all children need to be criticized or punished. The child who chronically "forgets" to hand in his homework may well benefit from suffering some consequences for his irresponsibility. By the same token, the child's good behavior should be acknowledged and rewarded. A note from the teacher confirming that the homework has been handed in on time might serve as a ticket for watching TV that evening.

As they express disapproval to the underachieving child, parents must cautiously evaluate the nature of the child's behavior, the source of the behavior, the options available for correcting it, and the psychological implications of expressing disapproval. They may conclude that their child responds better to a reward system than he does to a punishment system.

THE PRESENTATION FACTOR The effectiveness of parental criticism usually hinges on how the criticism is presented. Parents who communicate aggressively with their child should not be surprised when they encounter resistance. If a child feels attacked or denigrated, he will probably respond by either overtly or covertly refusing to do what the parent demands. The child who responds with passive resistance may procrastinate about doing his homework or cleaning up his room, or he may make a halfhearted attempt to comply with his parents' wishes, knowing full well that his effort will not meet their standards. By resisting, the child is able to press his parents' hot button. He may unconsciously choose this way to get back at the parents because he realizes that they have most of the power and that passive resistance is far safer than active resistance. (Specific methods for dealing with active and passive resistance will be examined in Chapter 12.)

THE PERSONALITY FACTOR Some children handle criticism and disapproval better than others. The child's response to censure can provide insight into his personality. As a general rule, secure children accept and respond to criticism more positively than do insecure children. The more insecure the child, the more elaborate his defense mechanisms are likely to be, and the more predisposed he will be to resist or reject criticism.

Children who were exposed to inconsistent child-rearing practices tend to have a more difficult time dealing with criticism. If the parents fail to establish clear guidelines and rules during the child's formative years, the child will probably have problems handling rules, authority, and criticism later in life. Parents who give their child double messages (anger followed by guilt or anger followed by excessive sweetness) also increase the likelihood of confusion and resistance.

The family chemistry strongly influences how a child's personality evolves. Parents who wish to express disapproval effectively to a struggling child must take into consideration their child's personality and their own personality. If they tend to explode when they criticize and they conclude that their child is too fragile to handle anger, they might try to vent their anger before confronting the child. If they have a tendency to belittle their child and they realize that this causes the child to become defensive or discouraged, they might make a conscious effort to use positive rather than negative statements. Although parents have more prerogatives than children, they also have more responsibilities. One of these responsibilities is to create an atmosphere that is conducive to communication.

THE BEHAVIOR CLASSIFICATION FACTOR Some problems are easier to criticize than others. One child might accept his parent's criticism that her room is a mess and needs to be cleaned, and another might aggressively or passively reject the criticism. Like adults, children have hot buttons. Certain criticism may be psychologically threatening. An insecure child, for example, may be overly concerned about peer acceptance. Although struggling academically, he may nevertheless be very popular. This popularity can serve as an important refuge for the child. Unfortunately, his social preoccupation may interfere with his schoolwork. If his parents criticize him excessively about the time he spends with his friends, they will undoubtedly provoke resentment. In view of the child's academic struggle, his parents might be well advised to consider striking a deal: one hour of homework for one hour of social time.

Self-Defeating Parental Criticism

Harsh disapproval and criticism are usually counterproductive. Although the venting of pent-up frustration and anger can be an emotional safety valve for parents, the net effect on the child's behavior is often negligible. Parents who feel frustrated by their child's behavior can easily fall into the trap of becoming highly critical of everything the child does. The more frustrated they become, the more they criticize. The more they criticize, the more anger and resistance they elicit. A never-ending cycle of resentment and hostility is thus created. This cycle can have a disastrous effect on the mental health of the entire family.

Most underachieving and nonachieving children do not have access to the same safety valves that are available to their parents. An angry or frustrated parent has a license to express criticism. If he so desires, he can yell at a child or punish him. An angry or frustrated child, however, is rarely permitted to "blow off steam" in public. If he is critical of something his parents have done, he may resort to giving them the "silent treatment," but he is not allowed to pour himself a drink or take the car for a long drive. Nor is he permitted to quit school, refuse to do his homework, kick the dog, or hit his younger sister.

Usually, the only recourse for a frustrated or angry child is to resist, either actively or passively. Active resistance may assume the form of aggressiveness or rebellion, such as refusing to do chores or homework assignments. Passive resistance is more convoluted. It may manifest itself as irritating or self-defeating behavior. A passively resistant child may feel that his parents are unfairly pressuring him, or he may feel unable to fulfill their expectations. He may express his resentment by handing in his assignments late or by procrastinating about doing his homework or chores.

A child who is exposed to constant parental criticism and displeasure must inevitably begin to feel resentment and anger toward his parents. No one can be on the receiving end of continual disapproval without ultimately becoming angry. This anger will either explode in the form of hostility or implode in the form of depression.

Contravening a rule or a value that parents hold dear can be a very effective retaliatory weapon. Other weapons in the child's arsenal include lying, procrastination, laziness, and irresponsibility. Few children recognize the irony that their retaliatory weapon is double-edged and that one of the edges is pressing against them.

The options that parents have for dealing with resistance or self-sabotaging behavior become increasingly limited as the child grows older. Parental power inevitably decreases with time. Alienation and estrangement are unavoidable when parent-child relationships are predicated on fear. Parents can, of course, resort to traditional weapons in their own arsenal. They can punish, restrict, and rescind privileges. The long-term effectiveness of these means of maintaining control is questionable.

Most perceptive parents come to the realization that confrontations, showdowns, and "power plays" rarely resolve problems. Frontal assaults may intimidate younger children and force them into compliance, but they serve only to alienate and antagonize teenagers. Communication and negotiation are far preferable to war. (Methods for restructuring the relationship between parents and underachieving children will be explored in Chapter 13.)

Underachievement inevitably produces emotional fallout. Methods for recognizing and dealing with this fallout will be explored in the next chapter.

● PARENTING SUGGESTIONS

● *Avoid the pitfalls which prevent effective parent-child communication.*
  1. Do not become preoccupied with asserting or defending your position.
  2. Avoid becoming highly critical.
  3. Get in touch with your underlying feelings. Help your child to get in touch with his.
  4. Be sensitive to your child's feelings.
  5. Do not allow intense feeling to undermine the ability to reason and problem-solve.
  6. Avoid and resist manipulative behavior.

● *Remind yourself that children can reason.*

Even younger children can comprehend complex issues if the issues are explained clearly. Gear your explanation to the developmental level of the child. Avoid talking down to the child. Experiment with metaphor.

● *Express your disapproval or criticism cautiously.*

Insecure underachieving children often are defensive. Highly critical parents exacerbate this insecurity. Parents who feel the need to criticize their child should make every effort to express their concerns without being demeaning, insulting, patronizing, or accusatory.

● *Communicate your expectation that the child will prevail over his difficulties.*

Children are very aware of and responsive to their parents' perceptions. If they perceive that you understand their problems and that you are convinced they can "win," they in turn will become convinced they can win.

● *Avoid adversarial relationships with your child.*

Showdowns, standoffs, and shoot-outs are O.K. in cowboy movies, but they are not O.K. in parent-child relationships. Finding a common ground is requisite to communication, problem solving, and agreement.

● *Learn to identify resistance and aggression.*

Your child's behavior is a barometer of his feelings. Resistance, procrastination, self-sabotage, and sarcasm are signals of resentment or anger manifesting itself in passive aggression. Bullying, fighting, teasing, and rebellion are signals of anger manifesting itself in active aggression.

● *Allow your child the opportunity to make mistakes and learn from them.*

Children acquire wisdom and maturity by experiencing life. Their need to develop independence is natural and normal. Help your children avoid major mistakes, but permit them to acquire their own truths.

- *Motivate your underachieving child to participate actively in solving his learning problems.*

  Your job is to support, encourage, and illuminate without smothering or creating dependence. This is, of course, no easy assignment!

Chapter

11 Performance Standards for the Underachieving Child

Peter: Too Nice to Discipline

Peter's cheerfulness and big, friendly smile surprised me. The nine-year-old knew that the purpose of the conference was to discuss his poor grades and his irresponsibility. He also knew that his parents were very upset with him.

Peter's father appeared stern and angry as he sat down at the conference table. His mother seemed nervous. I had the impression that she was quite intimidated by her husband.

I had tested Peter three months previously for a learning disability. The diagnostic evaluation had indicated no significant learning deficiencies. The fourth-grader's academic skills were at or slightly above grade level in all areas. His classroom teacher, however, reported that he was floundering in school. She indicated that he had chronic deficiencies in the areas of concentration, neatness, and attention to detail. His assignments were invariably sloppy and incomplete.

At my recommendation, Peter was enrolled in a two-hour-per-week learning assistance program specifically designed for underachieving children with deficient memory, concentration, and organizational skills. The program also provided accelerated learning assistance tailored to the needs of bright children with subtle academic deficits.

To our dismay, Peter had shown no improvement during the three months he had attended the center. The quality of his work in school was still below his potential ability level, and he remained highly distractible and disorganized. The few homework assignments that he bothered to complete were invariably sloppy and handed in late.

Peter's grades were all in the C− range. His IQ, however, was 141. Because of his distractibility and careless mistakes, Peter had been placed in the lowest reading and math groups in his regular classroom. Reducing the level of expectations had not improved his performance. He still was struggling to keep up with his class.

I asked Peter to tell me how he felt he was doing in school.

PETER: Not too good.
LJG: Can you tell me why?
PETER: I have trouble paying attention.
LJG: What happens?
PETER: I suppose I get bored.

At this point his father interjected.

FATHER: It's the same thing at home. He never listens. You tell him to do something and you have the impression that his mind is a million miles away. He invariably forgets what you tell him to do.

MOTHER: You're very hard on him, John. You get exasperated and lose your temper.

FATHER: The boy is nine years old. He should be able to remember more than one thing at a time.

MOTHER: I know he's forgetful, but he's only a child.

Throughout this exchange I observed that Peter was smiling. I could not decide if he was oblivious to the fact that his father was criticizing him or if he had heard this dialogue so many times that he knew the script by heart. I also considered another possibility: perhaps Peter enjoyed the negative attention he was receiving.

As the conference progressed, the respective roles of each member of the family became clear. The father was the disciplinarian. He was demanding of himself and of everyone in the family. His love and respect had to be earned. As a comptroller for a major corporation, he prided himself in being performance oriented.

Peter's mother felt that she had to compensate for her husband's exacting standards and critical nature. Each time her husband censured Peter, she would make an excuse or rationalize his behavior. Although she too was frequently disappointed and exasperated by her son's irresponsibility, her love was unconditional.

Both parents found it difficult to discipline Peter because he was never a behavior problem in the traditional sense. He was always pleasant, easygoing, happy, and cooperative. Because of their divergent parenting styles, Peter's mother and father had failed to agree on a consistent standard for behavior and performance. Peter had turned this inconsistency to his own advantage by developing a system of playing one parent off against the other. He knew that if he acted irresponsibly, his father would get upset. Once his father became angry, he could then count on his mother rescuing him and making excuses. Everything was predictable and orderly. Peter was like a sound engineer sitting behind a master console in a recording studio. He simply pressed buttons and the tapes began to roll. Although his actions were willful and calculated, he was not consciously aware of the motives for his actions. The behavior had been acquired early in his childhood, and his maneuvers were now so automatic they had become like conditioned reflexes.

Like many children who acquire too much power, Peter was caught in a paradox. Although the power he had assumed did not make him happy, he was unwilling to relinquish it. Being in charge provided order and structure. The predictability of his parents' responses to his behavior provided him with a surrogate for security he would have normally derived from consistent parenting.

The status quo would have to change for Peter to begin achieving in school. Each member of the family needed to examine his or her respective role in the family system. Addicted to being in charge, Peter would need to be certain that his parents would consistently assert their power before he would give up his own power.

I began the examination process by asking Peter's parents to list those specific behaviors which they would like to see changed. We then discussed their reasons for desiring these changes. I turned next to Peter and asked him if there were any behaviors that he himself wanted to change. After some hesitancy, he proceeded to list several. I was quite surprised by his forthrightness. After some discussion, we decided to focus on six goals that everyone felt were reasonable and fair: completing all assignments, handing them in on time, redoing illegible or sloppy work, making his bed each morning, feeding the dog without having to be reminded, and setting the table for dinner.

A simple monitoring and reward system was designed. Peter agreed to show his assignments to his parents each evening so that they could help him decide whether or not they were neat. If there was a disagreement, he consented to abide by their decision. Peter also agreed to write his assignments in a notebook and to ask the teacher to initial the assignments each afternoon, thus confirming that he had correctly written them down. The teacher would also initial a form indicating that the assignments had been handed in on time.

Points were to be awarded when Peter attained each of the six goals for the day. Every evening after dinner a family meeting would be held and the points earned for the day would be posted on a chart. The reward, a new dirt bike, was to be purchased and set up in the living room behind a chair. It was not to be used until all the required points had been earned.

The incentive system worked. Peter began to discipline himself, to concentrate in class, and to remember what his parents told him to do. His father made an effort to become less critical, and his mother made an effort to become less placating. Peter felt less and less need to sit behind the studio console and press buttons. The family standards, expectations, and guidelines were clear and unequivocal, and this clarity provided Peter with a new sense of security.

During the transitional period, Peter would occasionally revert to his old habits and would test his parents to see if they still "meant business." These testing incidents became less frequent once Peter became certain that his parents were committed to the new performance standards.

Peter earned the bike. His grades and performance in school improved dramatically. Within four months, he was placed in the highest reading and math groups. Although his parents had initially feared that they might have to "bribe" him indefinitely, they discovered that their son's basic attitude about himself had changed. The point system was abandoned eight months after our conference. Peter no longer needed extrinsic rewards. A simple acknowledgment sufficed. Structure, clear and unequivocal guidelines, and consistent parenting methods permitted Peter to make the transition from an underachiever to an achiever.

Establishing Limits

Peter's manipulative behavior did not develop suddenly. His behavior was the product of years of confusion on his part and years of inconsistency on his parents' part.

Two basic equations can be used to represent the cause-and-effect phenomenon of manipulative behavior:

Underachievement   ▶   Manipulative Behavior

or

Manipulative Behavior   ▶   Underachievement

In the first instance, underachievement is responsible for the manipulative behavior. Children in this category have probably experienced a great deal of defeat and frustration. Such children may use charm, irresponsibility, or misbehavior, to compensate for their deficiencies and deflect attention from their limitations.

In the second instance, manipulative behavior is responsible for the child's underachievement. Children in this category are generally confused by their parents' inconsistent child-rearing practices. Like Peter, they attempt to compensate for their uncertainty about the rules and guidelines by controlling the dynamics of the family. Because children cannot overtly seize power, they may try to do so covertly. They may play one parent off against the other, or they may do poorly in school knowing that poor performance is guaranteed to elicit attention and highly predictable responses from their parents. This manipulative behavior is the means by which the child attempts to provide a surrogate for the order that is lacking in his environment. With practice, the manipulative child can become so adept that he responds like an athlete on the basketball court who makes his "moves" almost instinctively.

The process of acquiring manipulative behavior begins early in a child's life. Young children are amazingly perceptive. Even a one-year-old has the uncanny ability to perceive ambivalence and inconsistencies in his parents. If he senses these qualities in his parents, he will be confused and distressed. Young children want their parents to be in charge. Their parents' certainty provides them with a sense of certainty.

Young children begin to test their parents between the ages of one and three. The phenomenon is a natural component in the child's development. By testing, the child is attempting to define the limits of his power. During this phase, the child need only look at his parent's face to discern immediately whether or not the parent "means business." A mother may admonish a two-and-a-half-year-old child not to touch a porcelain dish on the coffee table. Despite the warning, the child slowly moves his hand toward the dish. As he does so, he looks at his mother to gauge her reaction. If she backs down and permits him to touch the dish or if she herself moves the dish (to remove it from his path), she is sending a mixed message. The mother is telling her child with her words that he must obey her, but with her actions she is showing that she expects him to break her rules. Because he is confused, the child will attempt to determine his mother's real intentions by testing her again and again. If he ultimately concludes that she is indecisive, he may never stop testing rules and limits.

The self-control capabilities of a one-year-old must be differentiated from those of a two-and-a-half-year-old. A parent who removes a dish from the path of a one-year-old is being both practical and reasonable. A toddler cannot reasonably be expected to have developed the capacity to control his natural curiosity about how things work. This curiosity compels him to examine new objects so that he can better understand them. By touching things, picking them up, putting them in his mouth, and dropping them, the child learns to identify and classify. This examination process is an integral part of the child's intellectual development.

Although a one-year-old cannot be expected to control his inquisitiveness, a two-and-a-half-year-old can be expected to exert restraint when admonished by a parent. At this critical juncture in his development, the child must accept that there are limits to his freedom.

Establishing rules and guidelines for a young child is one of parenting's most compelling responsibilities. At times, this process of defining the rules will be painful for both the child and parent. Periodic collisions between the child's desires and those of his parents are inevitable. If these collisions are handled improperly, they may deteriorate into a protracted struggle for power.

The Function of Parental Power

Rules serve a vital function. They help a young child define the "do's" and "don'ts." This sense of order is vital to the child's emotional development. It provides him with a frame of reference which allows him to sort out, define, and evaluate the overwhelming quantity of stimuli in his environment.

As a child matures, he gains increasing power over his life. Equipped with greater experience and emotional maturity, he will begin to make more independent choices. He will decide if he should ride his skateboard down a steep hill or if he should smoke the cigarette offered to him by his friend. In the process of wrestling with his choices, he may elect to reject some of his parents' do's and don'ts. If they are to be able to make intelligent choices later in life, children must begin to develop a reference system. This schema of values, rules, and guidelines is imprinted during early childhood. For example: "We don't interrupt other people. We are all expected to help with the chores around the house. If children want pets, they are responsible for feeding them. Bedtime is 9:30 on school nights." Knowing the guidelines provides security and stability for a child.

Parents do not have to be despotic in establishing rules and limits. They simply need to communicate to their child that they have a responsibility to provide order, and that they take this responsibility very seriously.

Parents who insist on power for power's sake will face continual shoot-outs and showdowns with their children. At some point, highly autocratic parents will begin to lose the battles. Their children will no longer be cowed by brute force. Autocracy produces either alienated and hostile children or children who are so crushed and insecure that they lack the strength to break away from their parents' control.

Although reason and communication are far more effective tools for changing a child's behavior than are power and confrontation, there are times when an authoritarian response is both appropriate and necessary. For instance, parents may decide that bedtime on school nights must be at 9:30. They may explain their reasons, then make it clear that the issue is nonnegotiable. Parents who are not firm in asserting their appropriate authority undermine their credibility.

During early childhood, children must recognize and accept that parents are in charge and that parents make the rules.

Later, when they are older and can offer convincing, non-manipulative arguments for changing or bending the rules, their arguments should be heard and considered.

When parents fail to win the power struggles during the early testing phases of their child's life, they place the child's sense of order and security in jeopardy. Confusion, frustration, and insecurity frequently result. The natural power hierarchy in a family is prescribed by the child's emotional and physical dependence on his parents. Instability results when the hierarchy is inverted. Usually, the child who concludes that his environment is unstable will attempt to create his own system of order and structure. Peter's system clearly illustrates this phenomenon. Some children who are unhappy and confused by the lack of stability and consistency compensate with more extreme behavior. They may rebel against all authority. Such children often end up in juvenile court.

Most underachieving children have difficulty managing their academic and intellectual resources, and have an especially compelling need for a clear definition of their parents' position on such issues as effort, responsibility, neatness, and studying. When parents do not provide these guidelines, they increase the risk that their children will remain underachievers.

Parents who affirm their proper position in the hierarchy during the early phases of their child's development significantly reduce the probability of a protracted power struggle. As the child matures, he and his parents will most likely discover that they can resolve many of their conflicts without having to resort to power. Communication, reason, and context-appropriate compromises should suffice.

Some parent-child disagreements, of course, do not lend themselves to negotiation. A teenager who has a permit to drive only during daylight hours when accompanied by an adult clearly cannot be permitted to drive the car alone or at night. The situation is clearly nonnegotiable. Parents who have established their authority should have little difficulty insisting on compliance with their wishes and with the law. On an unconscious level, a developing child wants his parents to insist on obedience to rules which are fair and reasonable.

The Indecisive Parent

Parents who are hesitant to assert their authority when appropriate create a power vacuum. Their children usually interpret the parents' hesitancy as a lack of commitment to their own rules, and they respond by continuing to test the limits. Children raised in such an environment often have difficulty learning to conform to the rules at home, in school, and in society. They tend to be more self-centered, more demanding, and more defiant than children whose parents are committed to their beliefs, their values, and their rules.

Chronic parental indecisiveness is usually interpreted by children as weakness. Because children look to their parents as a source of strength, they will be confused and perhaps even resentful of this perceived weakness. The child may respond in several stages to his parents' indecisiveness:

1. He may begin to challenge the family's rules.
2. He may lose respect for the rules.
3. He may lose respect for his parents.
4. He may challenge his parents' right to discipline him.
5. He may conclude that no one has the right to control him.

The child at stage two may express his confusion and frustration by becoming passively resistant. He may remain at this stage, or he may proceed to stage three and become aggressively resistant or even defiant. The child who ultimately arrives at stage five is probably aggressively defiant. If he is unmanageable, he is a high-risk candidate for juvenile delinquency.

Some parents are indecisive about rules and guidelines because of guilt, fear, or misguided love. They may equate love with limitless tolerance. Unwittingly, these parents are signaling to their child that they lack faith in his capacity to conform to reasonable standards of behavior and performance.

Such parents are in effect saying, "This is the rule. I know you want to break the rule, and I will allow you to do so because I love you and I know that you aren't able to follow the rule." The child cannot help but conclude that he is incapable of conforming to any exacting standard of behavior or performance.

If a child is ultimately to survive and achieve in a competitive world, he must learn how to handle power appropriately. He can learn these lessons only in a context of order and structure. Just as the child must accept that there are conventions which govern math, grammar, and punctuation, so too must he learn that there are conventions which govern behavior. He cannot take another child's toy, strike a child with a sand pail, throw temper tantrums in a restaurant, or be disrespectful to his parents without having to suffer consequences.

Establishing Standards

Determining a reasonable and consistent standard of performance for an underachieving child who has difficulty conforming to standards can pose a severe challenge to the parents. Many difficult questions and issues must be confronted. For example, can parents reasonably demand that a child with poor fine-motor control write legibly? Can they reasonably expect that a child who is distractible or overactive pay attention in class?

The parent who says to a child, "This report seems sloppy to me. I have seen you write more legibly, and I would like you to redo it," is not being a tyrant. The parent is actually affirming the child's ability to produce quality work. The child may not appreciate what the parent is demanding because redoing the report will involve extra work. The message is, nevertheless, impacting on the child's unconscious mind. It may not be reasonable to expect that the child's handwriting be perfect, but it is reasonable to insist that the child get into the habit of doing the best job that he is capable of doing.

Parents who accept sloppy work are confirming in the child's mind that he is capable of producing only inferior work. The child hears his parent saying: "This is not very good. But we have to make allowances because we can't expect you to write legibly and neatly."

Appropriate allowances for learning deficiencies must, of course, be made. The child with fine-motor problems or concentration problems will have to struggle much harder to produce legible work than the child who does not have these problems. But the struggle can be a powerful ego-building experience, especially when the child realizes that he is capable of producing work that is far superior to that which he was previously producing.

Before parents can determine what is reasonable to expect from their underachieving child, they need data. Schoolwork, parent-teacher conferences, achievement tests, report cards, and diagnostic tests can provide the basic information requisite to establishing fair performance standards for the child.

Careful observations of the child can provide invaluable information about his capabilities. His work, his study habits, and his attitudes must be factored into the process of determining a reasonable performance standard. As parents and teachers wrestle with establishing a standard, they must confront a central issue: What is the underachieving child capable of doing if he makes an effort? Sometimes this information can be acquired by means of strategic subterfuge. In the dialogue below, a parent is attempting to establish a performance standard for a nine-year-old child who hands in chronically sloppy and illegible work.

PARENT: Cory, are you satisfied with this report?
CORY: Yes.
PARENT: Is it the best work you can do?
CORY: Yes.
PARENT: I'd like to try an experiment. I would like you to copy the first paragraph of your report in your very best handwriting. I would like it to be as perfect as possible. Take as much time as you need. Will you do that for me?

CORY: O.K.

PARENT: This is super! It's so good that I am
           going to take the paragraph and put it
           inside this plastic sleeve. When you do
           reports in the future, we can compare
           them with this paragraph. If we agree
           that the assignment is not as neat and
           legible as this one, I will ask you to re-
           copy the assignment so that it is up to
           the standard of the one in the plastic
           sleeve. Does this sound fair?

CORY: Yes.

Some parents and professionals might react negatively to
this strategy. They may feel that the child has been "conned."
This perception is, of course, accurate. There are, however,
six pragmatic reasons which in appropriate contexts justify the
selective use of this type of strategy:

1. It provides important data.
2. It permits the establishment of fair performance criteria.
3. It reduces the potential for disputes.
4. It reduces resistance.
5. It reduces the need for continual criticism.
6. It provides invaluable insight into the degree to which
   effort can affect the quality of the child's performance.

Parents should not be surprised if the child who has a long
history of underachievement resents the imposition of a more
rigorous standard. Rigorous standards require effort. The underachieving child who has become habituated to substandard
performance, who procrastinates, and who is sloppy, lazy, and
irresponsible will not be overjoyed by a new and more exacting
set of guidelines.

Habits of underachievement, like habits of overeating, do
not change overnight. In time, these habits become integrated
into a child's personality, and must be taken into consideration.
The longer a child has been an underachiever, the more en-

trenched his behavior patterns will be. Children, like adults, tend to rationalize their shortcomings.

Because the underachieving child with sloppy, illegible handwriting may be fearful of a tougher standard and perhaps resentful of his parents' attempts to monitor him, he might argue, "Well, my teacher allows me to write like this!" In cases where the pattern of resistant, manipulative, or avoidance behavior is chronic, outside professional support will probably be required.

Parents must use their discretion in establishing a performance standard. The standard cannot be arbitrary, and must reflect a realistic assessment of the child's capabilities. As a general rule, parents should attempt to raise the level of their expectations gradually. Unrealistic expectations can defeat the parents' efforts to improve the child's level of performance and can have a disastrous effect on the child's mental health.

The Guilt Factor

Guilt is a primary source of parental inconsistency and indecisiveness. A mother may fear that she is responsible for her child's learning problems because she had a difficult pregnancy or childbirth. A father may feel responsible for his daughter's learning problem because he also had a learning problem as a child, and he is convinced that he has passed this problem on to his daughter.

Sometimes the origins of a parent's guilt may be difficult or painful to identify. A parent may be hesitant about establishing firm rules, because as a child she felt that her own mother was unfair, excessively demanding, or tyrannical. Because of this unpleasant association, she may feel compelled to resist becoming like her mother. Each time she is tempted to impose a rule or guideline, she experiences guilt feelings. Although her behavior may be understandable, it is a disservice to her child who requires clear and unequivocal parental guidance.

Parents who feel guilty when they discipline their children or assert their standards tend to be excessively tolerant of their children's behavior and performance. In their zeal to protect their child from pain, these overcompensating parents often do not provide clearly defined standards, and thus unwittingly encourage an underachieving child to remain an underachiever.

Parents who feel guilty may fear that they are in some way harming their child when they insist that he work diligently and responsibly. The child may interpret his parents' indecisiveness as a license for him to do inferior work.

Guilt-ridden parents frequently defend their child even when the child does not need defending. They may attempt to take over any job which is the least bit challenging or unpleasant for the child. Although they may rationalize that they are protecting the child from pain, they are actually endorsing the child's use of avoidance, compensatory, or manipulative behavior. Their unwarranted guilt feelings serve no positive function and can seriously distort their relationship with the child. This distortion can in turn prevent the underachieving child from fully developing his emotional and intellectual capabilities. Parents who feel guilty when they assert their authority could best serve their child and themselves by seeking professional counseling.

Problem Ownership

A basic issue must be examined by the parents of all underachieving children: What is the most effective and appropriate response to my child's learning, attitude, or behavior difficulties? Parents have several options:

1. They can rescue their child.
2. They can assume ownership of his problems and attempt to resolve them.
3. They can do nothing.
4. They can help the child find a solution to the problem.

Powerful maternal and paternal instincts incline many parents to exercise options one or two. The origins of the temptation to protect a child from pain can be found in the role that parents must assume during the early phases of their child's life. During this period of total dependence, parents become accustomed to providing for all of the child's needs. They nurse him when he is sick, and they comfort him when he is frightened or upset.

The responsibility to provide basic support for a young child is quite distinct from the attempt to control all aspects of a child's life. Although a developing child will continue to need help, guidance, and emotional support, he must learn that he is expected to participate actively in the process of identifying and resolving problems which belong to him. Parents who do not begin the process of transferring responsibility to their children in early childhood are failing to prepare them to assume responsibility for their own lives. These children will have a difficult time making the transition from emotional dependence to emotional independence. In extreme cases, they may remain emotionally reliant on their parents for their entire lives.

When parents intentionally or unintentionally encourage dependence in their child, they give him a vote of no confidence and discourage him from growing up. The child will respond accordingly.

Many parents of underachieving children argue that they cannot be oblivious or cavalier about their children's problems. This is, of course, true. Parents cannot overlook a sick child's pain or discomfort, and the problem of finding medical assistance is clearly theirs.* This responsibility, however, does not make them responsible for solving all of their child's problems.

A clear signal that a parent has taken ownership of his child's problem occurs when the pronoun "we" is used. Parents who say, "We are having difficulty with our spelling" or "We received poor grades on the last report card" are deluding themselves when they rationalize that they are helping their child. In reality, they are taking over their child's problems, and they

---

*See Thomas Gordon, *Parent Effectiveness Training*, 1970, for a more complete discussion of the issue of problem ownership.

are creating an emotional dependence which may persist far beyond elementary school.

Some parents take the opposite tack. They react to their child's poor academic performance by attacking him. Although the example given below may seem extreme, it is not an uncommon reaction when frustrated parents have reached the boiling point:

> I'm fed up with your laziness and irresponsibility. You are never going to make anything out of your life if you don't clean up your act and get down to work. You had better shape up or you are going to end up working behind the counter at a hamburger stand.

Such a frontal assault is preordained to elicit resentment, hostility, fear, or guilt. The chances of such a statement changing the child's attitude or performance are minimal. The parent's approach does little to help the child understand, identify, or resolve his problem. Let's examine an alternative approach:

> I am concerned about your grades. People without a college education or technical training are finding it extremely hard to find jobs. Are you at all concerned about your grades? If you are, do you see any way that your Dad and I can help you?

In this example, the parent has expressed her concern without assaulting her child. She has chosen her words carefully so that they are neither demeaning nor threatening. Because the issue is presented in a nonaccusatory manner, the potential for resentment and resistance is reduced. The mother is in effect saying, "O.K., these are the facts and where do we go from here?" She has begun the process of helping her son recognize and take ownership of his problem. She is also signaling that she and his father are more than willing to provide assistance.

Despite the parent's diplomatically chosen words, it would still be unrealistic to expect the child to respond, "Oh, yes, get me a tutor, please!" Most youngsters need time to reflect before they will change their attitudes or perceive a solution to a problem. The issue may require several discussions before a mutually acceptable strategy is possible.

Parents can discover creative ways to reexamine a subject without giving the child the impression that they are harping. Let's assume that the child in the above example is unwilling to acknowledge that he has a problem with his grades. He continues to do poorly, and his mother feels it is imperative that she discuss the issue again. She might say:

> Several weeks ago I talked to you about grades. At the time, you denied that you were having difficulty in school. I just received a note from your English teacher, and he indicates that you are failing. Now if you were a parent of a fifteen-year-old and you received a note like this from your child's English teacher, what would you do?

When an underachieving child agrees to take ownership of his learning problem, he is taking a major step. This step is particularly symbolic if the child has never previously participated actively in problem solving. We all have a natural tendency to avoid looking at issues which are unpleasant or difficult to resolve. Examining these issues usually requires introspection and self-confrontation. This can be an especially painful experience for an underachieving child.

The quality of parent-child communication is usually the pivotal factor in determining whether a child participates in problem solving. Parents will need to draw upon their intuitive and creative parenting skills. They will have to develop their parental antenna, for their ability to "read" their child is essential in helping him to understand the issues and in motivating him to prevail over problems. Sometimes simple encouragement is all that is needed. Sometimes an incentive may be appropriate. Sometimes just listening and honestly expressing feelings is the most effective means for encouraging the child to participate in solving problems.

By modeling their own problem-solving ability, parents help their child recognize that practical solutions to problems can be found. Parents who verbally attack their child are modeling a flawed approach to solving problems. Unfortunately, an impressionable child may conclude that confrontation is the only way to deal with problems. There is a distinct possibility that when the child becomes a parent himself, he will adopt the same flawed approach with his own children.

Parents must be willing to provide emotional support and encouragement as the child struggles with self-confrontation. They must also be willing to accept that the child may be on an emotional roller coaster during this period. Parents who encourage the development of rational problem-solving skills are helping their child to take charge of his life. The acquisition of these skills is a prerequisite to emotional maturity and independence.

Emotionally Charged Encounters

When parents decide to change their rules, standards, or guidelines in midstream, they increase the likelihood of confrontations with their children. This is especially true in the case of the underachieving child who has settled into a pattern of counterproductive, self-defeating behaviors and attitudes. Although the child may be unhappy, he has probably become habituated to his situation. The parents' proposed new standard may be fair and reasonable, but to an insecure child the prospect of change can be very unsettling and threatening. He may resist the changes either overtly or covertly.

In many respects, overt resistance is easier to handle than covert resistance. The child's resentment and anger are visible, and parents have the opportunity to identify, sort out, and resolve the issues. Covert resistance can be insidious and defeat the best-intentioned efforts of parents to define and deal with the underlying problems. Complex defense mechanisms are hard to penetrate. For example, a child may go through the motions of studying, but may refuse to concentrate or pay attention to such details as deadlines, neatness, or organization. Although some of this behavior may signal a need for specialized learning assistance, the behavior may also reflect a conscious or unconscious expression of resistance and anger. Chronic passive or covert resistance usually requires professional treatment.

Confrontations are inevitable when a child openly resists his parents' attempt to establish a new performance standard. These confrontations can become highly emotional if parents insist that their child change entrenched behavior or attitudes.

Under certain conditions, intense encounters between parents and a child can provide a beneficial emotional catharsis. Pressure from pent-up resentment, frustration, and anger reaches the boiling point and explodes. Tears may be shed and feelings hurt, but if parents handle these encounters with restraint, sensitivity, and fairness, the storm passes and an equilibrium is reestablished. Once the dust settles, the potential exists for confronting and examining the issues and emotions with more objectivity. Misunderstandings can be resolved, and the relationship between parents and child may actually be enhanced.

Although angry confrontations can sometimes help liberate an emotionally grid-locked family and permit individual family members to develop greater sensitivity to each other's feelings and perspectives, such encounters usually work at cross-purposes with problem solving. The triggers for these encounters may be significant, or they may appear to be trivial. A word, a facial expression, a body position, or a seemingly innocuous statement can trigger an outpouring of negative feelings.

Scripted, repetitive, emotionally charged parent-child encounters usually indicate a pattern of unresolved misunderstandings and communication breakdowns. A child may continually leave his homework to the last minute. In so doing, he creates a great deal of stress in the family as he scrambles to complete his work. Despite constant reminders from his parents, he remains seemingly oblivious to his responsibility to allow sufficient time to get the work done. One day his mother's anger explodes, and all of her suppressed resentments spill out. It is possible that the child may be so frightened by this expression of anger that he begins to take more responsibility. It is also possible that the explosion of anger will have little or no effect on changing the child's behavior.

Recurring, explosive confrontations with children are generally a nightmare for everyone involved. The feelings of the participants in such encounters can get badly bruised. As the intensity level rises, parents and children frequently stop listening to each other.

Children who feel attacked during angry encounters have three choices: they can become assertive, defensive, or passive. A child may back down simply because he recognizes that he lacks the power to confront his parents aggressively. Although he may appear to acquiesce to his parents' demands, in order to placate them, he may not really be willing to cooperate. If the child feels that he is being treated unfairly, he may simply sublimate his anger. This anger will eventually manifest itself in passively aggressive ways. The child may, for instance, continue to leave his homework to the last minute, but he may be more surreptitious about it. In effect, the child has simply realized that he must hide his resistance for his own protection.

In most angry encounters, specific catalysts can be identified which cause a predictable chain reaction. When one person makes a particular comment, the other will respond in a scripted way, as if each person's role has been written into the family drama. For example:

PARENT: You never take the time to check over your work.
CHILD: You're always complaining about everything I do.

Typical triggers which can cause communication to break down include:

1. Excessive disapproval or criticism
2. Inconsistent application of rules
3. Preferential treatment of another sibling
4. Psychological abuse
5. Physical abuse
6. Hypocrisy ("Do what I say, not what I do!")
7. Inability on the part of the parents to express love

Sometimes a child's anger will result from a distortion in his perceptions of reality. A child may conclude that he isn't loved as much as his sister or that he is a disappointment to his parents. Or he may decide that he is a bad person because he senses feelings within him which are unpleasant or frightening. These negative feelings can distort the child's perspective. Because the child may have no other available target, he may direct his frustration and anger toward his parents. His anger may manifest itself as argumentativeness or, in the case of younger children, as temper tantrums. If the child manifests his anger passively, he may sabotage himself, resist authority manipulatively, or repeatedly press his parents' "hot buttons."

Learning how to respond appropriately and effectively to the angry, the resistant, the self-sabotaging, or the uncommunicative child can test the mettle and emotional resources of any parent. The test can be even more severe when the child's behavior reflects deep-seated family or emotional problems.

The following guidelines may help parents deal with potentially explosive confrontations.

EVALUATE THE SITUATION Explosive anger is by its very nature spontaneous. Parents do, however, have the option to control their anger. Verbal or physical abuse is invariably destructive, and parents have a solemn responsibility to resist any temptation to resort to this type of behavior. Parents have an equally solemn responsibility to seek professional help when they feel that they cannot control their anger.

Under certain circumstances, the verbal expression of anger may be justified. During calm periods, however, parents should examine the nature of their anger and decide if the cathartic effect justifies the potential damage they might be doing to their relationship with their child. If they rationally conclude that the recurring expression of anger provides little or no benefit, then they must strive to develop a system for redirecting situations which are clearly leading to an angry confrontation. They might say, "Time out. I feel that we are both getting angry. Let's talk about it tomorrow after we have had some time to think." Or: "I feel myself getting angry. I would like both of us to discuss the issues and express our feelings without getting angry. Do you agree to this?"

It is, of course, easy to talk about strategies for dealing with anger when one is not angry. But parents who perceive patterns of anger can plan ahead. They can run imaginary video or audio tapes in their minds in which they conjure up the recurring scenario and see (or hear) themselves handling the situation more constructively.

FIGHT CLEAN Fighting is rarely an effective means for changing behavior or resolving problems. Some children argue with their parents for symbolic reasons. The argument is their means of asserting their growing independence and increasing maturity. Other children argue in order to express their frustration. They may be frustrated because of problems in school or because they feel that they are being unfairly controlled. Upset because they lack power, they may use confrontations as a vehicle for asserting their rights.

Parents sometimes initiate confrontations with their children because they want to assert their own prerogatives. They may feel a compelling need to control their child, and they may use an argument as a vehicle for affirming this power. Parents may also precipitate a confrontation because they are experiencing frustration in either their dealings with their child or in other areas of their lives. If parents aren't getting along with each other, or if one parent is having job-related problems, they may unconsciously focus on the child's deficiencies and, in so doing, deflect their attention from their own unresolved problems.

Misbehavior sometimes requires an angry reprimand. The option to express anger, however, is not a license to abuse a child. If parents and children must argue, then parents have a compelling responsibility to keep the fighting clean. Clean fighting means not attacking the child physically or psychologically. An angry parent who yells, "You left the door open again. You're an idiot! Sometimes you act so dumb that I can't believe you're my child," may be irreparably harming his or her relationship with the child. An alternative might be: "I get furious when you leave the house and forget to lock the door. If the television or the stereo is stolen, the whole family suffers, including you!"

SEEK ALTERNATIVES TO EMOTIONAL CONFRONTATIONS Families that communicate and examine feelings, ideas, and issues resolve problems far more effectively than families that argue. The emotionally charged confrontation is usually a highly inefficient and ineffective means for changing behavior and attitudes. Although parents may intellectually appreciate the value of communication, they may find it difficult to break the confrontational cycle.

Just as the habit of emotionally charged confrontations can become increasingly entrenched, so too can the habit of effective communication. Parents, not children, have the responsibility for developing an effective communication system in the family. With sufficient desire, effort, and practice, a counterproductive system can be replaced with a new and more efficient one, and a family tradition of dialogue can be substituted for a family tradition of angry encounters.

Parents who want to communicate with their children can schedule time for discussing important family issues. They can also resist the temptation to become angry should the discussion encounter a snag. Experimentation will permit parents and children to devise a practical system for dealing with problems and disagreements. Practice will enable them to become increasingly proficient and comfortable with the new system.

The underachieving child with emotional problems demands special parenting skills and insight, and this will be the subject of the next chapter.

• PARENTING SUGGESTIONS

• *Establish limits for your child.*

The child who isn't taught to respect limits will continue to test limits. Parents who are indecisive about rules upset a natural sense of order and stability vital to the child's emotional development.

- **Establish realistic performance standards for the underachieving child.**

  Underachieving children often develop counterproductive work habits which can become entrenched. Parents who set a fair and reasonable performance standard for their child and who then insist that he work up to this standard are giving him an important vote of confidence.

- **Express your disapproval or criticism cautiously.**

  Insecure children are often defensive. Highly critical parents exacerbate this insecurity. Parents who feel the need to criticize their child should make every effort to express their concerns without being demeaning, insulting, patronizing, or accusatory.

- **Do not allow guilt to prevent you from being a consistent parent.**

  Children want their parents to be self-assured and consistent. Their parents' emotional security allows them to develop emotional security. Unwarranted guilt serves no positive function.

- **Do not take ownership of problems which belong to your child.**

  Parents who help their child find solutions to problems are preparing him to meet challenges later in life. Conversely, parents who attempt to solve all of their child's problems are creating emotional dependence and, possibly, an ongoing symbiotic relationship which could emotionally cripple the child.

- **Resist frontal assaults.**

  Children who feel personally attacked will probably become defensive and resistant. When parents are able to express their concerns diplomatically, they create a context conducive to communication and problem solving.

- *Avoid emotionally charged encounters.*

  Little is accomplished when parent-child encounters become acrimonious. Identify the verbal triggers which can set off an emotionally charged encounter and make every effort to avoid them.

12 Emotional Problems and Underachievement

Mark: He Had Placed His Fears in a Cigar Box

The frail-looking eight-year-old entered my office carrying a cigar box under his arm. Although the boy seemed friendly, he did not appear to be aware of me or his surroundings. When I asked Mark what was in his box, I could tell that he was not listening. Despite my efforts to engage him in conversation, he remained detached and unresponsive. Distracted by some pencils that were on my desk, he began to play with them and soon became totally preoccupied.

As part of the diagnostic procedure, I asked Mark to draw a picture of a person for me. He proceeded to draw a child whose head was resting on a block above which was suspended the blade of a guillotine. At this point, I asked Mark to wait in the outer office with my secretary.

Mark's parents explained that their son never went anywhere without his cigar box. The objects inside were little trinkets whose significance they had never understood. Mark would not let the box out of his sight, nor would he voluntarily show the contents to anyone.

Mark, now a second grader, had been nonfunctional in school since kindergarten. After being tested by a school psychologist in first grade, he had been placed in an educationally handicapped class. Although his teachers reported that he was never a behavior problem, they also indicated that he never voluntarily participated in any class activities. Mark would sit at his desk either drawing or playing with little objects. He could barely read. His math skills, however, were quite advanced, and he seemed to enjoy math.

The other children in school had completely rejected Mark because they considered him "weird." During recess, he would usually wander off by himself. After school, he would spend most of his time playing alone in his room. His parents reported that he frequently talked to himself and seemed to live in his own private world. Although he permitted parent-initiated affection, he himself never initiated any form of physical contact.

I could see that the results of the diagnostic evaluation would be inconclusive. The trinkets in his cigar box, his isolation, and his draw-a-person were blatant indications of a severe emotional problem. I was stunned that the boy's parents had either not recognized the symptoms or had chosen to disregard them. I was also stunned that Mark's pediatrician had not referred the child for a psychiatric evaluation. When I inquired about this, his mother explained that the family had moved four times during the previous eight years and that Mark had had several pediatricians. Their son was seldom sick and was always well behaved in the doctor's office.

I inquired if any of Mark's teachers had ever suggested a psychological evaluation. Mark's mother reluctantly admitted that all of his teachers had expressed serious concerns about his behavior. The school psychologist who had tested Mark in first grade had found indications of an emotional problem. She had recommended a workup by a psychiatrist. Because they had moved so often, they had never followed up on her recommendation.

It was apparent that Mark's parents were unable or unwilling to accept the staggering evidence of their son's emotional problem. They had grasped at the fact that Mark was not a behavior problem at home or in school, and they had used this as a rationale for overlooking his bizarre behavior.

Mark's need for treatment was desperate. I recommended

to his parents that he be comprehensively evaluated at a facility that could offer a complete range of diagnostic and treatment services. This evaluation would ideally include a workup by a pediatrician, a neurologist, a child psychiatrist or clinical child psychologist, an educational psychologist, a social worker, and a learning disabilities specialist.

I expressed my concerns about his mental health in very clear terms, and I was unequivocal on four issues: (1) Mark had serious emotional problems. (2) His emotional needs took precedence over any academic problems he might have. (3) His emotional problem would not disappear of its own accord. (4) He desperately required psychotherapy.

Before leaving my office, I was able to extract a promise from his parents that they would make an appointment at a hospital-affiliated child development clinic.

Nonachieving Children with Emotional Problems

Eight-year-olds who fantasize about guillotine blades suspended above their heads are relatively rare. When children have such fantasies, they are signaling that they have serious psychological problems.

Severe emotional problems generally incapacitate a child academically and socially. If the child's distortions about himself and his world are extreme, he may never develop the ability to function in the real world. Mark was a case in point. Isolated by his fears and nonadaptive behavior, he had retreated into a private world of symbolic trinkets and images of death and execution. His inability to relate to other human beings and to his surroundings was so complete that he was forced to create his own secret universe. This universe was both his fortress and his prison.

One could only speculate about the meaning of the trinkets Mark had placed in the cigar box. Perhaps by placing them there, he was attempting to maintain some semblance of control over the phantoms which lurked in his unconscious mind. The phantoms, however, would not be so easily placated. His draw-a-person evidenced their continuing hold on his mind.

Mark's mental illness was at the extreme end of a broad spectrum of psychological problems which can undermine a child's capacity to achieve. Although children with subtle-to-moderate emotional problems may not be as academically or socially incapacitated as Mark, they will probably require support in the form of therapy or special educational programs. Their level of functioning will depend on the severity of their problems, the effectiveness of the therapy they receive, and the skills, patience, and empathy of their parents and teachers.

Less severe emotional problems may escape early diagnosis. Children with more subtle problems may be perceived by their parents, teachers, and peers as peculiar, eccentric, or simply creative. Some may act out, and others may be shy. Although these children may struggle socially and academically, they are able to make sufficient accommodation to the system to slip through the diagnostic screen. Their problems may simply be overlooked or disregarded. The seriousness of the situation may not be appreciated until these children become teenagers. At this stage, their nonadaptive behavior may be so blatant that it can no longer be dismissed.

In rare instances, emotional problems may actually serve as a catalyst for a child's creativity and achievement. For the vast majority of children, however, emotional problems have the opposite effect. They interfere with a child's ability to focus and direct his emotional, intellectual, and physical energies. An excessively fearful or self-conscious child, for example, might have difficulty reading aloud, recalling information, or following instructions. He may panic when taking a test or forget what he has studied, assuming that he was able to study.

The complex, cyclical interaction of emotional problems, underachievement, stress, and negative self-esteem are represented graphically on the following page.

Note that each component in the cycle affects the other components. Stress can cause emotional problems, learning problems, and/or negative self-esteem. Emotional problems can cause learning problems, stress, and/or negative self-esteem. Learning problems can cause emotional problems, stress, and/or negative self-esteem.

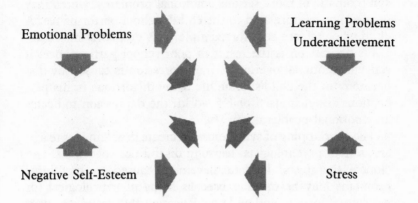

Emotional Problems

Learning Problems
Underachievement

Negative Self-Esteem

Stress

Emotional Overlay

Behaviors and attitudes resulting from poor school performance are generally referred to by educators as "emotional overlay." Many of the specific symptoms of emotional overlay have been examined in previous chapters: poor self-esteem, irresponsibility, frustration, counterproductive behavior, poor self-confidence, avoidance behavior, and compensatory behavior.

Distinguishing the counterproductive behaviors, attitudes, and feelings characteristic of emotional overlay from those characteristic of an emotional problem can be challenging because the behavioral symptoms of both conditions are similar and frequently overlap. The struggling, underachieving child with emotional overlay may be disruptive, resistant, distractible, and/or depressed. Despite these behaviors, the child may not have a profound underlying psychological problem. If the behaviors are the result of the child's learning problems or underachievement, they will usually disappear once the learning problems are corrected.

Behaviors symptomatic of emotional overlay may also be symptomatic of more serious emotional problems, which may or may not be unrelated to the child's school performance. A child who is depressed, for example, may do poorly in school. If his depression is the result of poor school performance, it reflects emotional overlay. If the depression is caused by disharmony in the child's home life or by distortions in his perceptions about himself or his world, the depression indicates an emotional problem.

The overlapping of symptoms can create problems for teachers, school psychologists, learning disabilities specialists, and clinical therapists. Underachievement caused by emotional problems may be misdiagnosed as being of neurological (or perceptual) origin, and underachievement that may be of neurological origin may be misdiagnosed as being an emotional problem.

Accurate diagnosis may be even more challenging in the case of a third type of underachieving child. This child underachieves because he has emotional problems *and* learning problems. A child who comes home from school angry or upset after failing an exam is manifesting a reaction to a setback. On the surface his behavior appears to reflect emotional overlay. Were the child to slip into a profound depression because of his setback or were he to vent his frustration by terrorizing his brother or brutalizing the family dog, his behavior would be symptomatic of an underlying emotional problem. To overcome his learning problem and his emotional problem, the child would require both learning assistance and psychological counseling.

Emotional problems do not necessarily affect all areas of a child's life. Mark's psychological problems, for instance, did not interfere with his capacity to do math. Unlike reading or spelling, math does not require a great deal of class participation or emotional involvement. Mark could do math computations at his desk without having to interact with the other children.

Severe mental illness in children is relatively rare. Even subtle forms of emotional stress, however, can divert the energies that are necessary for achievement. An insecure or self-conscious child, for instance, may be unwilling to ask questions in class when he is confused, or unwilling to volunteer information about the subject being discussed. If his fears and insecurities are extreme, they will undermine his self-esteem, his self-confidence, and his desire for achievement. The chronically self-effacing child is generally an underachiever.

Misbehavior

Chronic misbehavior is a primary symptom of an emotional problem. The unacceptable behavior may take the form of explosive anger, excessive profanity, lying, stealing, fighting, or cheating. A vital distinction, however, must be made between occasional incidents of misbehavior and chronic misbehavior. Every child occasionally misbehaves. Only unhappy children chronically misbehave.

As discussed in the previous chapter, some forms of misbehavior reflect confusion on the child's part about the family's guidelines and rules. Chronic or extreme misbehavior indicates more complex causal factors than a child's basic inclination to test the limits. The child with a violent temper, for instance, is telegraphing his internal conflict. Under normal conditions, anger does not reach the stage where it explodes into uncontrollable fury. When anger does reach this point, it poses a risk to the child and to others. The child manifesting such behavior is crying out for help.

Identifying Emotional Problems

The parents and teachers of children with psychological problems will usually recognize the emotional distress signals. Sometimes, however, the symptoms are unintentionally overlooked or intentionally disregarded.

The following Emotional Disturbance Checklist is designed to help parents determine if their child is manifesting symptoms of a possible emotional problem. Parents who suspect, after completing the checklist, that their child might be at risk emotionally are advised to consult their pediatrician or family physician. If the physician concurs with their concerns, he or she can refer the family to the appropriate mental health professional.

In evaluating whether or not your child displays the behaviors on this list, it is important to note that *all* children can experience occasional feelings of depression, anger, or fear without having emotional problems. These emotions may reflect temporary mood swings, caused by transitional events in the child's life, such as being punished, having an argument with a best friend, not making the cheerleading squad, breaking up with a girlfriend or boyfriend, or failing an exam. Even though the child's reactions do not necessarily signal a deepseated emotional problem, he or she may derive benefit from short-term counseling if the emotions persist beyond a reasonable period.

EMOTIONAL DISTURBANCE CHECKLIST*

	Yes	No
Behaviors in Young Children (approximate age 3–12 years)		
Cannot control emotions (temper tantrums, cries excessively)	_____	_____
Resists help from parents and teachers	_____	_____
Refuses to share	_____	_____
Shy, withdrawn, fearful in social situations	_____	_____
Excessive fear in leaving mother or home	_____	_____
Lacks ability to create friendships	_____	_____
Disruptive behavior in school	_____	_____

*I am indebted to Estella Lacey, Licensed Marriage, Family, and Child Counselor, for designing this checklist and the Family Problems Checklist that appears at the end of the chapter.

Inability to follow directions or rules

Need to control, bully, or fight with other
children

Chronic bedwetting

Inappropriate social behavior (destructive,
needs constant attention)

Chronic sleep disturbances

Chronic eating disorders

Chronic dissatisfaction and complaining

Behaviors in Older Children (approximate age 8–18 years)
Extreme moodiness

Demands immediate gratification

Violent outbursts and temper tantrums

Isolation (no social contacts)

Chronic manipulative behavior

Memory loss

Disorganized thinking*

Sudden change in friendships or peer groups

Lack of interest in play

Chronic inability to motivate self or use time
constructively

Unwillingness to accept constructive criticism,
help, or advice

Mistrust of authority figures (parents,
teachers, police)

Extreme critical attitudes (verbally attacks self
or others)

---

*This behavior may indicate serious mental illness.

Unwillingness to accept consequences of
behavior (denies, lies, or blames others to
avoid the truth)   _____ _____

Overeating or no appetite   _____ _____

Chronic physical problems (vomiting,
excessive tiredness, headaches, stuttering)*   _____ _____

Sudden change in personality or behavior   _____ _____

Disregards or discounts own abilities   _____ _____

Demonstrates no interest in personal
achievement   _____ _____

Exhibits extreme fears or anxieties   _____ _____

Chronic nightmares   _____ _____

Delinquent behaviors (steals, truancy, runs
away, picks fights, uses drugs or alcohol,
sexually promiscuous, abusive)   _____ _____

Verbalizes suicidal thoughts ("There is no
reason to live," "I wish I could die")†   _____ _____

Excessive inappropriate behaviors (silliness,
needs constant attention, shyness, inability to
make sense when communicating)   _____ _____

Rigid, judgmental, inflexible attitudes   _____ _____

INTERPRETING THE CHECKLIST. The symptoms and their
underlying problems may range from subtle to moderate to
severe. Some of the behaviors on the checklist could indicate
significant emotional problems. Others are symptomatic of less
serious emotional problems. The child who cannot handle being

---

*A physician should be consulted if your child manifests these symptoms.
They may signal a serious health problem.
†Parents should take all threats of suicide very seriously. Children who feel
overwhelmed by a sense of futility or who feel unable to cope with the
responsibilities of young adulthood may become convinced that suicide is
the only solution to their emotional discord. Parents perceiving self-destructive
tendencies should provide counseling support immediately.

criticized or reprimanded, for instance, may have a relatively slight emotional problem. Nevertheless, he would undoubtedly benefit from counseling if the behavior interferes with his ability to function academically or to relate socially.

Behaviors which are excessive, chronic, or persistent usually signal more serious psychological distress. Parents who discover a pattern of "yes" answers to the statements on the checklist should consult a qualified mental health professional before drawing any conclusions about their child's mental health.

Because parents are usually entwined in their child's problems, they may lack perspective and be unable to determine the urgency of the child's psychological needs. Parents who suspect that their child has an emotional problem will undoubtedly want to have the child professionally evaluated. Those who are concerned about the cost involved are advised to contact their local mental health association. This agency may provide diagnostic and treatment services at a reduced fee. The association can also advise parents about resources available in the community and about the fees charged for testing and counseling services. Parents should not hesitate to inquire about fees before they set up an appointment with a private practitioner. In some communities, public or private agencies charge sliding-scale fees.

Gina: Life Was Very Boring

It was quite obvious that Gina was unhappy about being in my office. Her mother had warned me on the telephone that her twelve-year-old daughter had been tested many times over the last six years and was highly resistant to the prospect of another test.

Gina grimaced when I asked her how she was doing in school. She replied that school was boring. She also informed me that her friends bored her. Her younger sister was a bore. Even TV was boring.

The child's attitude made the testing procedure grueling. She was not responsive to my questions and made no effort to solve the math problems or answer the reading comprehension questions. She slouched in her chair and gave the appearance that she was struggling to stay awake.

Gina grimaced again in response to my suggestion that she was angry because she was being tested. She replied that she wasn't angry, she was simply bored. Her compressed lips and clenched jaws belied her response. Gina's passive resistance and repressed anger made me suspicious about the results of not only my own diagnostic assessment, but also the other tests that had been previously administered in school. Although her scores on the school-administered achievement tests were extremely low, I suspected that Gina's actual reading and math skills were much higher than the tests indicated. Because of her low scores, she had been assigned to resource specialists for the last three years. Despite this assistance, Gina's grades were all in the D range. Both the resource specialist and her classroom teacher reported that she was unresponsive, uncooperative, and resistant.

While Gina completed a section of the test in another room, her mother explained that Gina continually complained about disliking her resource specialist. She also disliked her regular classroom teacher. In fact, her daughter had disliked every one of her teachers during the last seven years.

Gina and her younger sister Becky constantly fought. Gina would antagonize the seven-year-old and would let up only after she had succeeded in making Becky cry. The tension at home had become unbearable. When she was not fighting with her sister, Gina vegetated in front of the television. She had no friends. She resisted doing her chores and her homework, and she seldom finished any project that she began.

When she was six, Gina's parents told her that she was adopted. At first, she seemed to accept the situation, but by the age of eight she had become preoccupied with finding her "real" mother. Although she professed a desperate desire to meet her natural mother, she was, at the same time, furious with the woman for having abandoned her. She was also angry at her adoptive mother for having allowed her to be abandoned. Becky, who was also adopted, shared none of these feelings. She expressed no interest in meeting her natural mother.

Although I suspected that Gina had learning problems, I was certain that her poor performance in school was primarily attributable to her inner turmoil. Terrified by her own repressed emotions, she protected herself by means of passive resistance and emotional shutdown. Her boredom and lethargy served as a mask which she unconsciously used to hide her anger and pain from others and from herself. Only when she was fighting with her sister did she allow the anger to manifest itself.

Gina had completely blocked all feeling and emotion. In the process she had sacrificed her capacity to relate to others and to enjoy life. If left to her own devices, I feared she would withdraw more and more into herself. Her anger would continue to implode until it destroyed her.

When I proposed counseling to her mother, I could see her body stiffen. She informed me that she and her husband had already taken Gina to a psychologist. The psychologist had suggested that the parents would also benefit from participating in family counseling. This suggestion had infuriated the father, and he had refused to return. The mother had discontinued the therapy after two sessions.

The refusal by Gina's father to consider that his daughter's behavior was possibly linked to a family problem was quite revealing. By attributing all of the family's disharmony to Gina, he was able to avoid examining himself and the family dynamics. He had convinced himself that if Gina could only "get her head screwed on right," she and the family would not be arguing and yelling at each other. Although he had identified Gina as the source of all of the family's problems, he was unwilling to cooperate in the process of correcting the problems.

I encouraged the parents to consider another therapist. The entire family desperately needed counseling. Gina's needs, however, were the immediate priority. She required psychological support irrespective of her parents' willingness to participate. To allay the parents' reservations about therapy, I suggested that Gina see a psychologist who would work exclusively with her. It would be up to the psychologist to deal with the issue of family participation. Perhaps in time, the psychologist would be able to establish sufficient trust and credibility to motivate the parents to examine their own respective roles. One fact was clear: any attempt to treat Gina's learning problems without addressing her emotional problems was destined to fail.

Diagnosis and Treatment

Identifying a child's emotional problems can be a relatively straightforward procedure for a competent mental health professional. Gina's boredom was transparent, and any well-trained mental health professional would have recognized that her behavior camouflaged underlying frustration and anger.

Accurate diagnosis can be much more problematic when emotional problems involve atypical components or when the symptoms are extremely well camouflaged. In such cases, the indications of a child's emotional stress may be overlooked, misdiagnosed, or misinterpreted.

There are two standard procedures for identifying emotional problems. One method relies on the subjective assessment of the therapist. During the initial sessions, the therapist attempts to identify and interpret specific behaviors which would offer insight into the child's perceptions about himself, his family, his peers, and his world. By observing body movements and facial expressions and by listening to verbal statements, the therapist begins to understand the child's emotional responses and perspective. The child who whines, complains, withdraws, sulks, fights, or makes excessive demands is signaling emotional disharmony. Drawings which reflect pain, sorrow, fear, or anger also provide significant clues to a child's emotions. On the basis of the therapist's clinical observations, he or she will determine if there are sufficient indications of emotional distress to warrant therapy.

The second procedure for identifying emotional problems utilizes highly refined diagnostic tests. These tests have been developed to reveal the common emotional indicators of psychological discord. Because the tests can be graded according to specific criteria, they are considered by some therapists to be more objective and perhaps more reliable than a subjective assessment.

There are many effective methods for treating a child's emotional problem: individual psychotherapy, group therapy, behavior modification, family therapy, medication, psychoanalysis, or a combination of any of the above. Some therapists are eclectic and will employ whatever method seems appropriate. Other therapists are committed to a particular treatment protocol.

Several different approaches may be effective in treating the same problem. The wide range of treatment options can make the selection process bewildering and disconcerting. As they wrestle with the choice of a therapist and a therapy approach, parents will be forced to rely primarily on their intuition.

The efficacy of any treatment program hinges primarily on two factors: the skills of the therapist and trust. Parents who seek out a therapist whom they can respect, trust, and support significantly increase the likelihood that their child will benefit from the therapy. The family physician, the pediatrician, or a respected friend can be an excellent source of referral.

The amount of time required to resolve emotional problems will depend upon the nature of the problems, the child's receptiveness to treatment, and the support, empathy, and patience of the child's parents. Minor emotional or family problems may be resolved relatively quickly. Deeply enmeshed problems usually require a more extended period of treatment before meaningful changes in behavior or attitude occur.

Children with emotional problems may be resistant to examining their innermost feelings. Having to confront one's fears, pain, and anger can be quite threatening, and the child may use any number of excuses and arguments in his attempt to convince his parents that he should be allowed to discontinue therapy. These include:

1. It's not helping.
2. I don't like her (or him).
3. It's stupid.

4. She's mean to me.
5. I'm doing fine now and I'd like to try it on my own.
6. It's a waste of money.

These arguments can be very persuasive to a parent who is paying a great deal of money each week for a service whose value appears questionable. The child's sessions with the therapist are, of course, confidential, and because of this the parents may not fully understand the issues being examined and the progress being made. Children are sensitive to their parents' attitudes about therapy and can be strongly influenced by them. For this reason, it is essential that parents who have reservations about the efficacy of the treatment program discuss their concerns directly with the therapist.

The temptation to abandon the therapy may be very compelling, especially when the process seems to drag on with little seeming improvement. Parents who accede to the temptation and permit their child to discontinue therapy before the process is completed may be orchestrating a failure for their child with profound emotional implications.

Although a child's resistance can impede and prolong the therapy process, the resistance often dissipates as the child begins to work through his problems and begins to feel better about himself. The child who is initially highly resistant may actually begin to look forward to his therapy sessions. There may be recurring episodes of resistance when the child is dealing with particularly painful issues, but most children soon begin to value the trust, the empathy, the intimacy, and the support that are developed in the therapy sessions.

In addition to the symptoms described in the Emotional Disturbance Checklist, parents of underachieving or nonachieving children should be alert to three other relatively common behavior patterns which may signal an emotional problem: chronic active resistance, chronic passive resistance, and emotional shutdown.

Chronic Active Resistance

Chronic resistance to authority is atypical behavior and a clear symptom of emotional discord. The child's resistance may assume many different forms. The most common manifestations are argumentativeness, disrespect toward parents, disobedience, and, at the extreme end of the spectrum, antisocial actions and attitudes.

Resistance crosses a threshold when it assumes the form of belligerency. The argumentative, hostile, or rebellious child is acting out his unhappiness. His lack of respect for himself and for his parents must be differentiated from the psychologically intact child's occasional episodes of resistance.

Under certain circumstances, resistance by a child is a sign of emotional security. The child is willing to express his feelings openly and risk the possibility of a confrontation because he trusts his parents to react with fairness and reason. Although such "healthy" resistance, which does not involve subterfuge, deviousness, guilt, or deflected hostility, can serve a beneficial function, resistance that is defiant serves no positive function. In extreme cases, this behavior may assume the form of stealing, lying, or drug or alcohol abuse.

Parents must decide how much resistance they are willing to permit, and under what conditions. Their children must accept that there are situations in which active resistance will not be tolerated. Those who cannot accept reasonable limits are signaling underlying emotional or family problems. These children will probably require professional treatment. Parents who recognize that they are too entangled in the family drama to avoid repeated showdowns are advised to seek professional help.

Chronic Passive Resistance

Some underachieving children resist their parents in ways designed to avoid direct confrontation. Such children resist passively. Examples of this behavior include procrastination, irresponsibility, indifference, poor work habits, deceit, and avoidance. Because the passively resistant child is often out of touch with his emotions, he may deny that he is angry, resentful, or hostile. His behavior, however, offers a truer picture of his underlying feelings.

In some instances, a child's resistance may overlap both the passive and active modes. Although this child may not argue openly with his parents, he may punish them with actions which stop just short of overt misbehavior. The child who tends to mislead, deceive, unjustly accuse or falsely implicate others is manifesting passive/active resistance. (This behavior may also be described as passive aggression.)

The repressed and deflected emotions of the passively resistant child are often camouflaged, as Gina's affected boredom clearly illustrated. If they are to understand the child's attitudes and behavior, parents, teachers, and therapists must look beneath the surface. Because of the difficulty in identifying the emotions responsible for the behavior of a passively resistant child, parents may experience a great deal of confusion, frustration, and anger. The child may go through the motions of cooperating and complying, and yet he may have programmed himself to defeat not only himself but also the efforts of his parents and his teachers. He may, for instance, appear to be doing his homework diligently, but may neglect to do important components of the assignment.

Patterns of passive resistance tend to become entrenched after years of practice, and parents may not be able to alter the behavior without assistance. Usually, the parents are themselves deeply entangled in the child's behavior patterns. Professional intervention may be the only means for untangling the knots.

Emotional Shutdown

The underachieving child with emotional problems can easily become overwhelmed by frustration and hopelessness. He may feel powerless to control the course of his life and incapable of meeting his parents' expectations. The child who is convinced that all effort is futile may be very tempted to shut down emotionally.

A child typically shuts down his emotions in order to escape from despair. He detaches himself from his feelings and retreats into a private world where he feels protected. The protection is, of course, illusory, but the child is too involved in protecting himself to see that his behavior is magnifying his vulnerability and inadequacies.

The more vulnerable a child feels, the more he may be tempted to withdraw into a world where he can exert a semblance of control. Even the mildest parental or teacher criticism can have a devastating effect on an insecure child with low self-esteem.

Emotional shutdown assumes many forms. An unhappy child may spend a great deal of time isolated in his room listening to music or sleeping. In so doing, he may be able to escape temporarily from his unhappiness. The fantasy world that Mark created represents an extreme manifestation of emotional shutdown. Gina's chronic boredom and lethargy illustrated a less extreme example of the same phenomenon.

A child's behavior is a barometer of his feelings. Reading the barometer accurately can sometimes be difficult. In the case of emotional shutdown, however, the child's behavior is transparent. The child is waving a red flag signaling that he can no longer handle the stress that is being imposed on him or that he is imposing on himself.

Emotional shutdown should be considered a symptom of a potentially serious emotional problem. Parents who conclude that their child is becoming detached are strongly advised to seek a professional psychological or psychiatric assessment.

Family Problems and Underachievement

Families in distress produce children in distress. The strain produced by family disharmony will invariably take an emotional toll on all who are exposed to it. This disharmony can directly impact upon a child's capacity to achieve. Stress caused by separation, divorce, marital conflict, alcoholism, or physical or psychological abuse can immobilize a child emotionally, academically, and socially. This immobilization may be transitory or permanent.

Some children appear to respond to family problems with remarkable resiliency. Although they may be affected by the tension at home and may experience pain and trauma, they are somehow able to continue functioning both socially and academically. This resiliency, however, may be deceptive. The emotional implications of family problems do not always manifest themselves immediately, and the long-term effects may not be apparent until later in the child's life.

Situations beyond the family's control may be responsible for certain types of family stress; for example, loss of a job, sickness, financial difficulties, divorce, or the death of a family member. These situations are invariably painful and traumatic for everyone in the family, but in time the pain and trauma usually dissipate.

Recurring patterns of intense family stress can have lasting psychological implications. A child may see his parent fail at one job after another. As a consequence of this experience, the child's own attitudes about achievement may become jaded. He may conclude that failure and disappointment are inevitable and that effort is futile. Another child exposed to the same conditions may react differently. At an early age, he may decide that he will never allow himself to fail or be rejected. He may feel driven to achieve so that he can insulate himself from the rejection and defeat experienced by his parent.

There are many other types of negative family conditions which can affect children and their capacity to achieve. Repeated confrontations in which the parents demean their child will inevitably cause profound and lasting emotional damage. A careful examination of the family dynamics usually reveals specific catalysts that predictably trigger anger, resentment, confusion, and mistrust. Examples of behavior which typically elicits negative reactions include outbursts of hostility, disparaging criticism, unreasonable demands, unwillingness to communicate, irresponsibility, blaming, nagging, and distrust.

Destructive behavior patterns are usually deeply woven into

the family fabric. These behavior patterns can create serious obstacles to family bonding and communication. In an extreme example, a father who is an alcoholic may become abusive when he drinks. This behavior will drive a wedge into the family that can damage everyone. A child who is exposed to these conditions cannot help but be affected when he sees his father drunk or his parents continually arguing about the father's drinking. The child may ultimately become an alcoholic himself, or he may react by developing a profound aversion to alcohol.

The range of potential responses to psychologically oppressive conditions at home is vast, and it is impossible to predict with certainty how children will react to these conditions. But it goes without saying that such conditions in the home invariably affect a child's emotions, schoolwork, and social relationships.

Less extreme family stress patterns can also seriously impact on a child's emotions. A woman who is unhappily married may establish an unhealthy symbiotic relationship with her child. She may use the relationship as a surrogate for the emotional closeness that she lacks with her husband. Although she may be meeting some of her own emotional needs, she is creating a dependence which undermines the child's own emotional development.

The origins of both positive and negative family behavior patterns can be traced to the personalities of the parents. Each man and woman bring to their marriage their respective psychological strengths and weaknesses. A family chemistry evolves which tends to magnify these strengths and weaknesses. As the family grows, new personalities are poured into the cauldron and the family chemistry becomes more complex. A family system with distinctive and often predictable parent-child interactions begins to emerge.

Each family has its own unique chemistry, with specific catalysts eliciting specific reactions. In distressed families, the catalysts are sometimes highly destructive and assume the form of emotional and/or physical abuse, abandonment, or rejection. Parents who communicate to their child that he is intrinsically bad or unlovable are planting seeds which are ultimately destined to germinate into anger, resentment, or counterproductive behavior. Although other destructive catalysts such as nagging, disparagement, or distrust may be less extreme, they can nevertheless trigger emotionally debilitating family disunity.

Excessive parental absenteeism can also damage a child. The child whose parents are frequently gone or emotionally distant will usually begin to manifest symptoms of emotional deprivation. Young children are particularly vulnerable. Such children may never learn to trust their parents. They may generalize their lack of faith to include all adults, especially teachers. Distrustful children are typically insecure and often have difficulty acquiring social skills and creating friendships.

The child with family-based problems usually carries his stress from home to the classroom. It is not uncommon for the emotionally distressed child to be distractible, sloppy, irresponsible, and inattentive. These characteristics are, of course, also symptoms of a learning problem. Because of overlapping symptoms, the underachieving child with family-based behavior problems may be misdiagnosed as learning-disabled. The child may have specific learning deficits, but to treat these deficits without also addressing the family problem would be an exercise in futility.

The child who experiences emotional stress at home which he feels powerless to resolve may internalize his frustration and anger, and become depressed. Or he may vent his frustration in destructive behavior, such as fighting, bullying, defiance, or rebellion. One child may react to his father's continual absence from home or loss of a job by becoming angry and defiant in school. He may strike out at other children or become uncooperative. Another child may become shy and withdrawn. In extreme cases, emotional deprivation or abuse can lead to mental illness, delinquent behavior, or self-destructive patterns such as suicidal thoughts or drug dependency.

There is a reciprocal relationship between family problems and underachievement: family problems can cause a child to become a nonachiever or an underachiever, and nonachievement or underachievement can create or intensify family problems. A continual and seemingly unresolvable pattern of poor academic performance or social difficulty can cause the child and his parents to become demoralized. Concern and frustration can magnify the family stress, which will in turn magnify the child's academic problems.

The following Family Problems Checklist is designed to help parents identify conditions which might be contributing to their child's unhappiness and to his underachievement or nonachievement. Some of the statements in the list may not be applicable to a particular family and should be disregarded.

FAMILY PROBLEMS CHECKLIST

	Yes	No
1. Family members rarely interact or share time, activities, or interests.		
2. Family members prioritize their own interests and are not available to assist other family members.		
3. Family members are unable to create trust, to share, or to establish intimacy.		
4. Family members have difficulty addressing family problems until a crisis develops.		
5. Family members have difficulty recognizing or responding to each other's needs, thoughts, and feelings.		
6. Parents seek to satisfy their own emotional needs and disregard their children's emotional needs.		
7. Parents have difficulty establishing consistent rules and consequences for misbehavior.		

8. Family members are required to share everything: time, activities, and interests. _____ _____

9. Family members are required to participate and agree, or are considered disloyal. _____ _____

10. Family attempts to protect its members from all outsiders. _____ _____

11. Family discourages individualization, independence, and separation. _____ _____

12. Parents are unable to establish intimacy in relationships with nonfamily members. _____ _____

13. Family members can "read" the thoughts and feelings of others in family. _____ _____

14. Parents use "we" when referring to their child's actions. _____ _____

15. Parents communicate that the child is helpless to meet his own needs. _____ _____

16. Parents are unable to unite as couple and coparent. _____ _____

17. Parents cannot agree on parenting issues. _____ _____

18. One parent aligns with child against other parent. _____ _____

19. Parents put child in double-bind, no-win situations. _____ _____

20. Parents continually fight about children. _____ _____

21. Parents permit children to create distance between them. _____ _____

22. Father or mother absent from home. _____ _____

23. Parent places priority on "peace and quiet."   _____ _____

24. One parent places work above family commitment.   _____ _____

25. Raising children is the mother's job exclusively.   _____ _____

26. One parent becomes overly dependent on children and "overprotects."   _____ _____

27. One parent dramatizes and overreacts to minor events.   _____ _____

28. Separated parents use children to "get back" at each other.   _____ _____

29. Single parent is overworked and has little time for children's problems.   _____ _____

30. One parent abuses other parent physically or emotionally.   _____ _____

31. Parents abuse child physically or emotionally.   _____ _____

32. One child in family is selected for family ridicule or abuse.   _____ _____

33. Sexual abuse of child by adult family member.   _____ _____

34. Sexual abuse of younger child by older sibling.   _____ _____

35. Chronic fighting and disagreement.   _____ _____

36. Stepchildren or stepparents resent or fear one another.   _____ _____

37. Stepchildren refuse to relate to one another.   _____ _____

38. Children relate only to natural parent and consider other blended family members as intruders.   _____ _____

39. Stepparent never assumes parenting role. _____ _____

40. Drug or alcohol abuse has caused children to become fearful or distrustful. _____ _____

41. Parents have difficulty putting their own lives in order. _____ _____

42. Parents avoid responsibility. _____ _____

43. Parents are highly critical. _____ _____

44. Parents have unreasonable expectations. _____ _____

45. Children have placed excessive demands on themselves. _____ _____

46. Parents are compelled to deny that the family has problems. _____ _____

INTERPRETING THE CHECKLIST. Before a family can resolve its problems, it must be willing to acknowledge that it has problems. In some instances family disharmony may be caused by a complex web of factors. In other instances the disharmony may reflect a single, specific causal factor. A pattern of "yes" answers on the checklist, or even one yes answer, may signal a serious family problem which should be addressed and resolved before emotional damage occurs. Parents are advised to look at their responses objectively and determine if professional counseling is appropriate.

Virtually every family goes through periods of stress and pain. Although the upsets may be significant, they can often be resolved without professional help. Conditions which can create strain include poor health, physical or mental handicaps, financial problems, death of a family member, separation, divorce, job changes, and children leaving home. If, however, the stress and pain persist, outside intervention may be required.

A protracted period of family unhappiness can have tragic

emotional implications for everyone in the family. Although the child-rearing years and their attendant problems may seem interminable to parents, they are, in fact, quickly gone. Children soon grow up, leave their homes, and begin their own families. Those who leave angry and emotionally scarred stand a good chance of imposing the same destructive family system on their own children. To prevent the perpetuation of this unhappiness, parents have a compelling responsibility to identify and resolve the patterns of disharmony which are affecting their family.

If untreated, stress and disunity can undermine the emotional health of every family member. Children are particularly susceptible to the negative effects of unhealthy family dynamics. Their self-concept, happiness, and ability to achieve hang in the balance.

Children coming from conflicted families are seldom able to work up to their potential. Parents who acknowledge that their family is struggling with problems which they themselves cannot resolve are being courageous and responsible. Those who then seek professional help are providing their family with a precious and loving gift.

● PARENTING SUGGESTIONS

● *Attempt to distinguish between emotional overlay and emotional problems.*

The counterproductive attitudes and behavior associated with emotional overlay are the direct result of a child's learning problems and underachievement. Emotional problems which are unrelated or only tangentially related to learning problems often produce similar behavioral symptoms. These emotional problems may be responsible for the child's underachievement. If you are unable to determine whether emotional overlay or an emotional problem accounts for your child's academic difficulty, seek professional advice.

● *Be alert to the symptoms of an emotional problem.*

Monitor your child. If you conclude that the child appears to be having difficulty coping, communicating, or relating and you feel you cannot help him resolve these problems, consider having him evaluated by a mental health professional.

● *If your child is receiving therapy, support the therapist.*

Resolving emotional or family problems requires time. Do not abandon therapy simply because your child is resistant or does not appear to be making immediate progress. If you begin to have doubts about the therapy process, discuss these doubts with the therapist.

● *Learn to identify the symptoms of active resistance, passive resistance, and emotional shutdown.*

Your child's behavior is a barometer of his feelings. Active resistance may take the form of rebellion, fighting, and bullying. These are symptoms of underlying anger and unhappiness. Passive resistance may appear as procrastination, teasing, sarcasm, and self-sabotage. These are also symptoms of anger and unhappiness. Isolation, withdrawal into a fantasy world, and chronic boredom represent repressed anger which is manifesting itself as emotional shutdown. Parents are advised to consult their pediatrician or family physician and request a referral for a psychological evaluation.

● *Periodically assess the mental health of your family.*

Family stress can directly impact on the mental health of all family members. Children are particularly susceptible to the effects of family problems. Recurring counterproductive patterns of behavior should be identified and resolved. Outside intervention may be advisable.

13 Orchestrating Achievement

Danny: Doing Cartwheels in Class

I couldn't help smiling at the seven-year-old with the mischievous smile and shiny bright eyes who stared at me in wide-eyed amusement. Danny knew that he was "in trouble" because he had been misbehaving in school. Despite his mother's obvious concern and anxiety, I sensed that the meeting was a great adventure for him.

We had been working with Danny for six months. Every Thursday his mother drove one hundred and forty miles round trip so that he could receive highly specialized learning assistance that was not available at his private school.

Danny, who was now in first grade, had been struggling ever since he entered kindergarten. His distractibility, over-activity, and inattentiveness were compounded by significant reading deficiencies. The learning deficits included letter reversals, inaccuracies, omissions, and transpositions. Because she was concerned about his lack of progress, Danny's teacher had recommended retention. His parents had refused to accept her recommendation.

Although Danny had made dramatic academic gains since enrolling at our center, these gains had not transferred to the classroom. He was still struggling, and he seemed to be falling further and further behind.

From the content of the classroom teacher's note to me, I could tell that she was at her wit's end. To underscore her frustration, she reported that Danny had actually turned a cartwheel in class during the reading period.

Danny had settled into the role of class clown and class dunce. His behavior guaranteed him the negative attention of his mother, teacher, and fellow students. Punishment, extra assignments, and denial of privileges had had no effect on him. He seemed to enjoy getting into trouble and watching other people's reactions to his misbehavior. Their reactions were Danny's reward, and he was willing to give up his recess for the payoff.

Prior to the conference in my office, Danny's instructor at our center had shared an interesting insight. She had discovered that despite his apparent need for negative attention, Danny actually responded very well to praise. She had devised a checklist system which permitted her to acknowledge Danny when he paid attention, completed an assignment, or read accurately. She made a point of placing check marks on the chalkboard after Danny's name at least ten times during each hour. The system worked. Danny was functioning superbly in her class, and his attitude, behavior, and effort were beyond reproach.

I asked Danny's mother if she praised her son very often. She replied that, on the contrary, she was continually scolding him. She indicated that Danny's classroom teacher also scolded and punished him on a regular basis. Ironically, both she and the teacher found it difficult to remain angry at Danny because he was never disrespectful, malicious, or devious. He simply did things that got him into trouble.

My associate's success with Danny prompted me to suggest a very simple positive reinforcement strategy. During a subsequent meeting at school with Danny's mother and his classroom teacher, I recommended that the teacher place a wide strip of masking tape with a happy face on top of Danny's desk. Each time that she looked over and observed that he was paying attention or doing his work, she would signal him and he would put a check on the tape. At the end of the day, the teacher would total the number of checks and she would send a form home to Danny's parents informing them of how many checks their son had earned that day.

Danny's mother agreed to place a similar strip of tape on the refrigerator door. She promised to make a special effort to acknowledge her son for his good behavior and his contributions at home. Each evening the family would gather around the kitchen table and total the number of checks that Danny had received that day in school and at home. At these nightly meetings, Danny would be praised for his performance during the day. He and his parents would then establish realistic performance goals for the next day.

Within four weeks, Danny's mother reported a dramatic transformation in her son's behavior. He began to thrive on the positive reinforcement he was getting from his teacher and his parents. He especially seemed to enjoy the challenge of improving his daily score. The teacher was amazed by the improvement in Danny's work. He had begun to pay attention in class, and his parents no longer needed to nag him about completing his chores at home.

The other children soon became jealous of the attention Danny was receiving. They also wanted strips of masking tape on their desks. Their reaction surprised the teacher, who had been oriented toward sternness. The teacher discovered a simple truth about children and human beings in general: positive expectations and praise produce positive effort and performance.

Danny needed to remain on the check system for only six weeks. Because he was only seven years old, his negative behavior and attitude had not yet become fully integrated into his personality. When he occasionally misbehaved, he simply required a verbal cue in order to get back on track. The masking tape was soon phased out. It was no longer needed. Danny had become an achiever.

Comfort Zones

Whenever possible, reasonable people come in from the rain. Seeking refuge from a storm reflects basic common sense. Underachieving children are no exception. They too will seek refuge from a storm. They typically do so by creating a comfort zone.

A comfort zone is a place where a child can exercise a degree of control over some of the variables in his life. It provides precisely what the name implies—comfort—and such zones can serve a very utilitarian and psychologically healthy function. A child does not necessarily have to be insecure or vulnerable to create a comfort zone. Seeking a sanctuary from stress, frustration, or daily routine can be reasonable, practical, enjoyable, and therapeutic. A child who plans his day so that he can have time to work on a model airplane or watch his favorite TV program is creating a comfort zone. Another child who programs a baseball game into his day is also creating a comfort zone. The game provides him with an opportunity for relaxation, competition, social interaction and, perhaps, achievement. This opportunity to experience pleasure and success is a vital component in the development of self-esteem and emotional health. The benefits are particularly important in the case of a struggling, underachieving child who has deficiencies in some areas of his life.

Although the nature of each child's comfort zone will differ, most comfort zones incorporate many of the elements of a carefully staged and carefully scripted play. The child functions as playwright, director, and principal actor in this play. He memorizes his lines and "blocks" the action so that he and the other players in the drama know when to enter, where to stand, and what to do.

The need and desire to exert control over one's life is normal. However, children who are compelled to control everyone and everything in their lives are signaling their insecurity. In extreme cases, the child may retreat to his comfort zone to evade responsibility and perhaps even reality.

When used obsessively for escape, comfort zones function as a barrier to emotional growth and achievement. This is especially true when a child feels compelled to hide from problems which need to be confronted and resolved. Danny's attention getting was a case in point; it functioned as his comfort zone. Here he controlled the action. At will he could produce behavior which was guaranteed to elicit a response from his parents and teachers. Like a consummate chess player, he had developed a strategy that permitted him to "win" the game. Each win was, of course, a defeat. Had his parents not changed the dynamics of the game and the payoffs, he would have continued to push his pieces around the board as he had been doing. The fact that Danny was not consciously aware of his motives for creating the game did not make him any less calculating.

Some underachieving children with learning problems may find sports an attractive refuge. Although these children may derive important psychological benefits from their athletic success, they may be using sports to compensate for their academic deficits. Energies which should be directed toward resolving their learning problems are thus deflected. The potential psychological and educational implications of this diversion of energies can be serious.

Comfort zones can become too comfortable. Had the dynamics of Danny's comfort zone not been realigned, his need for negative attention might have become permanently integrated into his personality. The cute, mischievous seven-year-old might have ultimately evolved into a very "uncute" teenager with serious learning, attitude, and behavior problems.

Coaxing an underachieving child out of a counterproductive, but secure, comfort zone requires strategic planning on the part of teachers and parents. An insecure child will resist relinquishing his tried-and-true system of interacting with the world in the same way that a two-year-old will resist relinquishing his security blanket. Just knowing that the blanket is there can make the world less forbidding to a child.

The desire for safety and security is universal. At an early age, children instinctively gravitate to their comfort zones.

Insecure children tend to become overly attached to them. To abandon the certainties of an accustomed pattern of behavior for the uncertainties of a new pattern of behavior requires a great deal of courage. This courage is usually acquired in stages. At first, a child may be willing only to venture tentatively outside of his comfort zone. If he concludes that he can be safe outside, he may consent to venture further and further from the security of known actions and reactions into the insecurity of unknown actions and reactions.

Profoundly insecure children are usually terrified at the prospect of giving up control and relinquishing the security of their comfort zone. The responsibility for helping the child acquire the necessary courage to take this step falls on the shoulders of the child's parents and teachers. By engineering extensive opportunities for the child to experience success and acknowledgment, they can create an appealing alternative to the child's counterproductive comfort zone.

As a child becomes more secure, his need for a sanctuary should be less and less compelling. In one of literature's most famous allegories, Plato describes a man who is chained in a cave. He can see only the shadows of the outside world reflected on the wall of the cave. Ultimately, the man frees himself and with great courage ventures out into the bright sunlight and the potential dangers of an unknown world. For the first time he can actually see reality as it is, and he knows that he can never return to the cave.

Counterproductive comfort zones possess many of the same features as Plato's cave. A child chained by fears and insecurities can see only a distorted reflection of reality. Although he may be desirous of participating in activities and experiences denied him in his comfort zone, he may at the same time be terrified of breaking his chains and venturing out into the sunlight. The cave may be restrictive, but it is at least safe. If he is ultimately to free himself, the insecure, underachieving child will require the extensive support, patience, and understanding of his parents and teachers. Once he realizes that the outside world is exciting and that he can actually survive and flourish there, he will not want to return to his sanctuary.

Achieving Perspective

Achieving perspective on issues in which one has a great emotional involvement or investment can be very difficult. Proximity to the issues frequently interferes with objectivity.

Like authors, most parents can benefit from the services of an editor when they are in a jam. To the writer, a talented editor represents a precious resource. Because the editor is less emotionally involved in the creative process, his or her perspective is more detached and objective. This objectivity permits the editor to see problems and flaws that the writer may not be able to see. Although authors may not always be willing to accept an editor's criticism or suggestions, most writers realize that a good editor can frequently untangle knots that the author might not otherwise be able to untangle on his own.

"Entangled" parents can often profit from the objective opinion of a friend or a spouse not directly involved in a particular crisis. This other person may be able to offer invaluable insight into the problem and practical suggestions about how to resolve it. One of the many advantages of two-parent families is that parents can support each other. The benefits of this mutual support can accrue only when parents are able to communicate without pressing each other's hot buttons and without triggering defensiveness.

When communication between parents is healthy, it can help both parents achieve and maintain perspective even when both parents are intensely enmeshed in a problem. Parents who can calmly and analytically discuss the dynamics of recurring, explosive confrontations with their child are availing themselves of an important resource.

The quality of communication between parents will reflect the quality of *listening* that occurs. When parents listen actively to each other, they are not only hearing each other's words, they are also searching for the meaning behind those words. A mother who says to her husband, "I'm really fed up with Steve's behavior," may also be saying, "I'm really fed up with the fact that you are not helping me discipline our son." Or she might be saying, "I'm fed up with myself because I feel that I'm botching the job of being a good parent."

Because mothers and fathers often interact with their children in different contexts, they frequently perceive their children differently. Certain problems may occur when one parent is at work. A mother, for instance, may have more direct contact with the child's teacher and consequently may be more aware than the father of a child's social and academic problems, procrastination, irresponsibility, or deteriorating self-confidence. The father, on the other hand, may be more aware of the child's frustration on the soccer field or his problems with coordination.

Single parents are at a disadvantage when dealing with recurring problems. They do not have the luxury of a built-in support system. In the case of divorced parents, one parent may see the child only on weekends, at Christmas, and for four weeks during the summer. The geographically detached parent may not be as aware of the potential danger signals as the parent who interacts on a daily basis with the child.

If possible, divorced parents should attempt to share their concerns with their former spouse, assuming that they can communicate with each other. Alternative resources should be developed if communication with a former husband or wife is not feasible or if one of the child's parents is deceased. Single parents who find themselves on the "front lines" alone, and who cannot count on the support of a spouse, might attempt to share parenting problems and concerns with other single parents or with friends whose judgment they trust. Everyone needs a support system, even those parents who pride themselves on being "strong" and self-sufficient.

Parents who recognize that they are making habitual mistakes or that they are locked into a negative script with their child have need for a sounding board, someone who will be both sympathetic and hard-nosed. In the case of simpler problems, a spouse or an insightful friend may suffice. More complex problems may demand the skills of a trained professional. A child may have needs that even the best-intentioned and most dedicated parents cannot fulfill without assistance. Admitting the need for outside help is the mark of responsible, concerned parents.

A Healthy Foundation for Achievement

Children are at the same time remarkably resilient and remarkably fragile. In some respects, a child is like a newly planted sapling. If the young tree receives sufficient sunlight and water, it will grow and thrive. Its roots will spread, and the sapling will become less and less vulnerable to the elements. If, however, the sapling is exposed to elements which are too harsh, its root development will be stunted. Unable to absorb the essential nutrients from its environment, the young tree will either perish or become permanently blighted.

A child can also withstand a certain amount of exposure to negative conditions. But if he is exposed to conditions which are too harsh, his growth will be impeded. Unable to absorb essential nourishment from his environment, he too may become permanently blighted.

A child's roots are planted in soil composed of three basic elements: family, school, and friends. The primary nutrients— love, encouragement, praise, support, and affirmation—are provided by the family. If they receive sufficient emotional nourishment, most children will conclude that they are loved and appreciated. This conviction forms the foundation for the development of self-esteem and self-confidence. Unfortunately, children with emotional problems who do not like themselves often cannot accept the love and appreciation of others. Such children will require professional assistance before they can permit themselves to receive or give nourishment.

Another vital function of the family is to provide external structure in the form of rules, expectations, and values. During the course of his development, a child will internalize many facets of this structure. This process of internalizing structure is integral to the development of emotional stability. By establishing clear behavior guidelines, by communicating reasonable expectations, and by encouraging increasing independence, parents help their child organize his life, focus his energies, and develop his potential. These capacities are the basic building blocks of achievement.

School is the second stratum in which a child's roots are planted. For the child to thrive in school, he must become convinced that he is able to learn. In order to acquire this conviction, he requires tangible evidence of his abilities in the form of skill mastery, decent grades, and acknowledgment. Unresolved learning problems, family problems, and emotional problems invariably destroy the child's faith in his ability to learn and achieve.

Friendship is the third stratum in which a child's roots are planted. For a child to thrive socially, he must be convinced of his value as a person and his desirability as a friend. Children can sense when another child is confident and competent. The self-esteem that the achieving child projects makes his friendship appealing to other children. It is for this reason that the athlete, the cheerleader, and the good student are generally the most popular children in the class.

The child who is unable or unwilling to achieve is quite visible. Just as children tend to be attracted to those who are successful, they also tend to reject children who lack confidence and competence. It is a bitter irony that the struggling child who most desperately needs social acceptance is often the very child who is denied this acceptance.

The Family's Position on Success

The parental desire that their children thrive and achieve is universal. Having to witness a child stumble or fail can be one of parenting's most heart-wrenching experiences. Although the natural parental instinct is to protect the child, this instinct may actually work at cross-purposes with the child's emotional development. The experience of stumbling, or even failing, can provide an important opportunity for growth. By confronting obstacles, the child learns about reality. By struggling and prevailing over these obstacles, he learns the value of effort, and develops a sense of his own power.

At an early stage of their child's development, parents must determine their position on the issues of achievement and success. They must decide how they want to define achievement. As they wrestle with their attitudes about this central issue, they will be forced to examine their value system. They must decide if achievement is a sufficient goal for their child, or if they are determined that the child become a superstar. Are they content with conscientious effort and gradual improvement, or do they insist on total victory? Is a B grade acceptable if the grade represents diligence and conscientiousness, or do they expect their child to push himself to the limit so that he can receive an A? At the heart of these questions is an even more basic issue: Do parents consider achievement and success to be relative or absolute? As a general rule, parents who are guided by their child's best interest will usually take a position on these issues which is reasonable, fair, and realistic. Conversely, parents who are guided primarily by their own ego needs often lose sight of the fact that their child's ego needs may not be congruent with theirs.

Parents are not the only ones who must determine their position on the basic issues relating to achievement. The child himself will also have to decide how important achievement and success are to him. Although the child's position will probably be strongly influenced by the attitudes of his parents, it might also be quite different from theirs. A child whose parents have eschewed ostensible achievement and success may be driven to become a builder of empires. Another child whose parents are highly achievement oriented and possession oriented may choose to reject his parents' materialistic values and become a gardener.

Environmental factors and historical cycles play a significant role in determining the values of our youth. In the 1960s many young people whose parents were highly successful became hippies. Ironically, the children of many of these hippies are now attending prestigious colleges. Described as "yuppies" in the current vernacular, they are highly materialistic and achievement-oriented. The word that may one day be used to describe their own children has yet to be invented.

The rejection of parental values generally involves a complex mix of psychological factors. Resentment, resistance, fear of not meeting parental expectations, and hostility can easily jade a child's attitudes toward achievement and success. Other factors can also influence a child's values. The child may decide to reject his parents' values and priorities because he concludes that they are shallow or hypocritical. In this case, his rejection reflects a conscious decision to substitute a more meaningful value system.

The desire to achieve and succeed can be a potentially positive or potentially destructive force in a child's life. Hospitals are full of people whose desire for success became an obsession. In some cases, the rewards they expected proved to be an illusion. In other cases, the price exacted by success proved too costly.

Whatever a family's value system, achievement and the experience of success play a vital role in the development of a child's ego. The child who can achieve derives important emotional payoffs: pride, self-esteem, and self-confidence. The child who is unable to achieve is denied these experiences.

Creating Opportunities for Achievement

Achievement is rarely accidental. Children achieve as a direct consequence of effort, desire, and ability. In order to achieve, a child must be able to perceive himself as an achiever. He must establish goals, and he must actually see himself attaining his goals.

Achievement-oriented children often feel a compelling need to test their own limitations. Challenges are not only accepted, they are eagerly sought. Barriers which restrict or block achievement are perceived as targets. The high achiever will become fixated on the A that she wants in history, the music scholarship that she wants in college, the record that she wants to set in track, or the starting position that she wants on the varsity basketball team. Her fixation impels her to push herself beyond her limitations.

Underachieving children are often frightened by the prospect of testing their limits. Rather than desiring to break down barriers, they actually create boundaries for themselves. A typical underachiever might say to himself, "I might be able to pass, but I'll never get an A on the biology test." This self-imposed limitation reflects the child's life experiences and his perceptions about himself and the world. Negative experiences typically imprint negative expectations. The child who has become accustomed to frustration and defeat frequently conditions himself not to reach beyond the boundaries.

Parents may discover that when they ask an underachieving child to cross the boundaries, they elicit anxiety, fear, and resistance. Because the struggling, insecure child is reluctant to expose himself to the possibility of failure, he is equally reluctant to take the risks that are requisite to seeking success. Accustomed to marginal performance, he may need to be nudged, coaxed, and sometimes coerced into achieving.

The attitudes of parents and teachers play an instrumental role in the evolution of a child's self-perception. Parents and teachers who resign themselves to misbehavior, shoddy work, irresponsibility, and resistance encourage underachievement. Parents and teachers who struggle for insight, who express positive expectations, who provide support, and who refuse to accept misbehavior, shoddy work, irresponsibility, and resistance encourage achievement.

Intentionality

The achieving child actually has two IQ's. One is his intelligence quotient. The other is his intentionality quotient.

Achievers push themselves when others give up. They consciously recognize that their achievement hinges not only on the level of their effort, but also on their degree of intention. One need only observe a professional tennis match to appreciate the power of intentionality.

Intentionality is one step beyond desire. The child with intentionality will say to himself, "I not only want that prize, I will get it!" The achieving child with this attitude will read his essay over two or three extra times to find the grammatical errors and to improve the syntax. He will review his history notes one extra time before the midterm exam. He will check and recheck his math problems to find computational errors.

Underachieving children generally lack intentionality. They tend to give up when they encounter a setback or an obstacle. They may make an effort, but they typically balk at making the intense, sustained effort which might push them over the top.

Parents' recognition that their child lacks intentionality can be a source of great frustration for them. Motivating a child to want to achieve an objective intensely enough to struggle for it can be one of parenting's most challenging assignments.

Like so many other powerful human emotions, intentionality is directly linked to self-perception. A struggling child with negative self-perception seldom possesses the confidence to pursue a goal. Before parents can expect to raise the level of their child's intentionality, they must help him raise the level of his self-esteem. To do so, they must encourage him to gain insight into why he acts in certain ways and why he has erected barriers to achievement. Concurrent with encouraging introspection, parents must also create repeated opportunities for the child to experience achievement and success.

Insight can be attained only through a continuing process of self-assessment. Underachieving children must be encouraged to think about what they want, and how to achieve it. Parents can be instrumental in stimulating this analytical thinking process by asking such questions as:

What do you want to get out of your history class?

How do you propose to get the money for the new dirt bike?

What do you think you have to do to make the varsity squad?

How do you think you can get your father and me to trust you with the car?

What do you think you'll need to do to become a veterinarian?

What can you do to stop your brother from picking on you?

These questions can help a child understand that only through effort and intentionality are desired goals attained. The child who wants an A in history must begin to think about what she must do to make this happen. The fifth grader must come to the realization that he can have a new dirt bike only if he delivers newspapers after school. The teenager who wants access to the family car on Saturday night must begin to think about how he can convince his parents that he is responsible. The aspiring athlete must understand that she can make the varsity only if she practices intensely during the summer. The child who loves animals must recognize that she can become a veterinarian only if she improves her grades. And the child who feels oppressed by his older brother must examine whether or not he is doing anything to elicit his brother's antagonism. All children must ultimately appreciate that they have the power to influence events in their lives. This realization unlocks the door to intentionality and provides the foundation for achievement.

Competition

Achieving children tend to be competitive. Through competing they seek to test themselves, their resources, and the barriers which limit their potential achievement.

Competition does not necessarily involve other people. When two high school athletes vie for the starting quarterback position on the football team, they are competing as intensely with themselves as they are with each other. Each must discipline himself and practice long hours to develop and refine his skills. The same phenomenon occurs when students enter an essay contest or compete for a college scholarship. They are not only seeking the prize, they are also seeking an objective measurement of their ability.

Some achieving children are content to compete exclusively with themselves. The student who struggles to improve her French skills may not consciously compete with the other students in the class. She may push herself to master the language because she finds French beautiful, or she may want to prove to herself that she can learn to speak the language fluently. She may also be driven to do well because she recognizes that her grade could affect her acceptance at the college of her choice. The gymnast who practices four hours each day may do so because she wants to prove to herself that she has the ability to be an accomplished athlete. She may also practice because she is determined to make the Olympic team.

A child's level of competitiveness frequently determines his level of achievement. The impetus which drives children to compete is directly linked to their Self-Quotient. Those who seek to test themselves against others must feel that they can win and that they deserve to win.

Children's life experiences significantly impact on their attitudes about competition. Because they have had little success in life, underachieving children tend to avoid competition. Their track record undermines their confidence not only in their *ability* to prevail, but also in their *right* to prevail. By avoiding competition, underachievers protect themselves from having to confront their limitations and from having to experience frustration and possible defeat.

Before the underachiever will feel sufficiently secure to compete, his mind-set must be altered. Parents can help their child overcome a fear of competition by encouraging him to begin competing with himself. Helping the child establish realistic, individualized short-term and long-term goals is the first step in this process. A child who is struggling with spelling and who usually misses ten of the twenty words on his weekly spelling test might be encouraged to establish a goal of spelling at least twelve words correctly on the next test. To help their child attain this objective, his parents may have to do their own homework. They may need to seek out materials designed to aid the poor speller who has deficient visual or auditory memory. They may need to ask the resource specialist at school for suggestions or look in the library for books which offer creative memory techniques that can be used to improve spelling skills.

Once the child becomes comfortable competing with himself, he can take his first tentative steps toward competing with others. With parental support and encouragement, he may be willing to try out for the football team, the chess team, or the school play. He may even be willing to work toward an A in history or a scholarship to college.

Feeling Worthwhile

Achievement is neither an absolute nor an end unto itself. Achievement is simply one of many ways in which people express themselves. For one person, ultimate achievement may be attaining the presidency of a major corporation. For another, it may be developing competence in teaching kindergarten. Neither objective is intrinsically better than the other. Both serve as a stimulus for self-actualization.

Achievement is also a primary means by which a child validates himself. Although vitally important, school achievement is but one of many forms of self-affirmation. Other equally important testimonials to achievement include the child's capacity to love, to create, to relate to others, to find pleasure, and to find purpose and meaning in life. Achievement and a sense of self-worth are inextricably linked. One of parenting's most sacred missions is to help a child discover that he is worthwhile. This mission is especially compelling in the case of an underachieving child.

The child who respects himself, who actualizes himself, and who derives pride from his accomplishments is blessed. Those parents who discover how to help an underachieving child realize that he has the right to establish goals and the ability to achieve his goals have themselves achieved the highest level in the art of parenting.

Bibliography

Allman, Lawrence R., Dennis T. Jaffe, and Philip Whitten. *Abnormal Psychology in the Life Cycle*. New York: Harper and Row, 1978.

Greene, Lawrence J. *Kids Who Hate School*. rev. ed. Atlanta: Humanics Limited, 1983.

Greene, Lawrence J., and Leigh Jones-Bamman. *Getting Smarter*. Belmont, Calif.: David S. Lake Publishing, 1984.

Perls, Frederick S. *Gestalt Therapy Verbatim*. Lafayette, Calif.: Real People Press, 1969.

Index

Ability to achieve, 51–53
  differentiating potential from
    developed, 53–57
Accommodation to school's
  educational system, 156–58
Accountability, public vs. private
  school, 182
Achievement
  ability, 51–57
  and affirmation, 37–38
  and aptitude, 58–59
  and comfort zones, 276–78
  and competition, 287–88
  creating opportunities for, 284–
    285
  deserving, 93–95
  desire for, 74–76
  and ego, 76–78
  and environment, 27–28
  expanded model, 78–79
  and feeling worthwhile, 289
  foundation for, 281–82
  and health, 30–31
  and intelligence, 57–58
  and intentionality, 285–87
  learning, 21–24

and learning efficiency, 54–55
  model, 61–62, 78–81
  orchestrating, 273–75
  path to, 36–38
  pluses and minuses, 26–27
  selective, 24
  and self-image, 64–67, 71–74
  and smartness, 61–62
  and survival, 24–26
  zest and, 34–36
  see also Underachievement;
    Underachiever(s)
Acquired helplessness, 101–3
Active thinking, 148–49
Adolescents, communication with,
  205–8
Affirmation
  and achievement, 37–38
  need for, 37
Age, and communication of
  disapproval and criticism,
  211–12
Aptitude
  and achievement, 58–59
  measuring, 59–61
Assignments, recording, 159–60

293

Attention deficit disorder (ADD), 132
Auditory learning, 154–55
Auditory processing deficits, 132
Authority
    chronic active resistance to, 261
    chronic passive resistance to, 261–62

Barriers, surmounting, 88–89
Behavior
    classification, and
        communication of disapproval
        and criticism, 214
    and emotional problems, 251
    establishing limits, 223–25
Budgeting time, 158–59

Challenges
    allowing children to confront, 88–91
    and frustration, checklist, 91–92
Checklist
    challenges and frustration, 91–92
    communication, 208–10
    emotional disturbance, 252–55
    family problems, 267–71
    learning problems, 138–41
    remediation, 174–75
    study skills, 153–54
    underachievement, 40–42
Child
    identifying as underachiever, 40–42
    parents' role in assessing, 38–40
    younger, communication with, 199–205
Clinical learning assistance
    programs, 183–84
Comfort zones, and achievement, 276–78

Commitment, and achievement, 43
Communication
    with adolescents, 205–8
    barriers to, 197–99
    checklist, 208–10
    of disapproval and criticism, 210–14
    parent-child, 195–97
    with underachieving child, 189–95
    with younger children, 199–205
Competition, and achievement, 287–88
Complacent underachiever, 42–45
Concentration deficits, and underachievement, 39
Conceptual learning, 156
Concerned parents, excessively, and early identification of learning problem, 114–15
Confrontations, between parents and children, 237–42
Coordination, poor, 133
Costs
    clinical learning assistance programs, 183–84
    private schools, 181
Criticism
    expressing disapproval and, 210–214
    self-defeating, 214–16
Cultural influences, and underachievement, 46–47

Denial-oriented parents, and early identification of learning problem, 115–16
Desire
    to achieve, 74–76
    and achievement, 43
Developmental immaturity, and underachievement, 39

Diagnosis
  of emotional problems, 258–60
  of learning problems, 110
  problematic, of learning
    disability, 125
Diagnostic testing, limitations,
    128–31
Disapproval, and criticism,
    expressing, 210–14
Distractibility, 133, 134
Dyslexia, 132
  and underachievement, 108–9

Edison, Thomas, 202
Efficiency, learning, 54–55
Effort, without reward, 162
Ego
  and achievement, 43, 76–78
  damage, and frustration, 92–93
Einstein, Albert, 202
Emotional disturbance checklist,
    252–55
Emotional overlay, underachiever's,
    249–51
Emotional problems
  chronic active resistance to
    authority, 261
  chronic passive resistance to
    authority, 261–62
  diagnosis and treatment, 258–60
  identifying, 251–52
  and misbehavior, 251
  and nonachievement, 247–48
  shutdown, 262–63
  and underachievement, 46, 245–
    247, 255–58
Emotional shutdown, 262–63
Emotional stress
  and achievement, 26–27
  and learning, 55
  and learning problems, 182

Environment
  and achievement, 27–28
  and study skills, 151–52
Eye-hand coordination, 133

Family
  and child's achievement, 281–84
  problems, checklist, 267–71
  and underachievement, 46, 263–
    267
  see also Parent(s)
Feeling worthwhile, and
    achievement, 289
Fine-motor coordination, 40
Foundation for achievement, 281–
    282
Friends, as foundation for
    achievement, 281–82
Frustration
  and challenges, checklist, 91–92
  and ego damage, 92–93
  and underachievement, 85–88

Generalized underachievement, 45
Goals
  establishing, 161–62
  symbolic nature of, 28–30
Gross-motor coordination, 39–40
Guilt factor, and performance
    standards, 232–33

Handwriting, poor, 133
Health, and achievement, 30–31
Helplessness, acquired, and
    underachievement, 101–3
Hyperactivity, 133
  and medication, 113–14n
  and underachievement, 39

Identification
jam-ups, 80–81
of learning problems, 135–36
Immaturity vs. underachievement,
185
Impulsivity, 133
Inattentiveness, 39, 133
Indecisive parents, and
performance standards for
underachievers, 228–29
Inefficient learner, helping, 158–62
Informational learning, 155–56
Intelligence
and achievement, 57–58
measuring, 59–61
Intensity, and achievement, 43
Intentionality and achievement,
285–87
Intentionality quotient, 285–87
Intuition
about child's learning disability,
111–12
in choosing reading center, 180
and early identification of
learning problem, 114

Jam-ups, identifying, 80–81
Jenner, Bruce, 202

Kinesthetic learning, 155

Language, in communicating with
younger children, 200
Learner, inefficient, helping, 158–
162
Learning
to achieve, 21–24
and adjusting to school's
educational system, 156–58

assistance programs, clinical,
183–84
auditory, 154–55
efficiency, 54–55
styles, 154–56
Learning disabilities
defining, 131–33
early identification, 112–16
problematic diagnosis, 125
and underachievement, 108–9
underachievers in gray area,
125–28
see also Learning problems
Learning efficiency, and
achievement, 54–55
Learning problems
acquiring essential information
about, 136–38
checklist, 138–41
clinical assistance programs,
183–84
critical questions and choices for
parents in face of, 118–19
diagnosis, 110
diagnostic failures, 128–30
early identification of, 112–16
early indications, 133–34
educational testing and treatment
priorities, 130–31
hoping they'll go away, 168–71
impediments to early
identification, 135—36
persistence and perseverance in
face of, 116–18
private programs, 175–84
programs within school system,
171–74
remediation options, 167–68
resolving, 164–67
and retention, 184–87
special assistance programs in
school system, 171–74

treatment, 110
and underachievement, 46
and underachievers, 121–25
see also Learning disabilities
Letter reversal, 134
Light's Retention Scale, 186
Limits on behavior, establishing,
  223–25

Manipulative behavior, and
  underachievement, 223–25
Measurement, of intelligence and
  aptitude, 59–61
Medication, and hyperactivity,
  113–14n
Memory skills, 151
Minimal brain dysfunction (MBD),
  132
Misbehavior
  and emotional overlay, 249–51
  and emotional problems, 251
Model, achieving child, 61–62,
  78–81
Motor skills deficits, and
  underachievement, 39
Multimodality learning, 156

Nonachievement, 46
  and emotional problems, 247–48
Notetaking skills, 151

Organizational skills, 150–51
Outlining skills, 151
Overachievers, compulsive, 23
Overweight, and self-perception,
  98
Ownership, of learning problem,
  233–37

Parent(s)
  achieving perspective, 279–81
  and assessment of child, 38–40
  and child's frustration, 86–88
  communication with
    underachieving child, 195–97
  critical questions and choices in
    face of learning problem, 118–
    119
  early identification of learning
    disability, 112–16
  emotionally charged encounters
    with children, 237–42
  guilt feelings, and performance
    standards for underachievers,
    232–33
  indecisive, and performance
    standards for underachievers,
    228–29
  intuition about child's
    underachievement, 111–12
  manipulated by underachiever,
    19–21
  persistence and perseverance in
    face of learning problem, 116–
    118
  power, and performance
    standards, 225–27
  and problem ownership, 233–37
  self-defeating criticism by, 214–
    216
  see also Family
Passive thinking, 149–50
Paying price for success, 95–99
Perceptual deficits, and
  underachievement, 39
Perceptual dysfunction, 132
Perceptual processing deficits, 132
Performance standards
  establishing, 229–32
  limits, 223–25
  and parental power, 225–27

Performance standards (*cont.*)
for underachiever, 219–23
Perls, Fritz, 89
Persistence and perseverance, in
face of learning problem, 116–118
Personality, and communication of
disapproval and criticism, 213–14
Perspective, achieving, 279–81
Poor study skills
implications, 146–48
underachievers with, 143–46
Power, parental, and
performance standards, 225–227
Presentation, in communicating
disapproval and criticism, 213
Priorities, establishing, 160
Private schools, 180–83
Problems, defining, 160–61
Psychological risks, in retention, 186
Punishment, and self-image, 64–67

Reading centers, 177–80
Recording assignments, 159–60
Remediation
checklist, 174–75
options for learning problems
167–68
Resistance to authority
chronic active, 261
chronic passive, 261–62
Retention
communicating with younger
children about, 200–204
and learning problems, 184–87
Reward, effort without, 162
Rockefeller, Nelson, 202

School
as foundation for achievement, 281–82
private, 180–83
Selective underachievement, 45–46
Self-defeating criticism, parental, 214–16
Self-esteem
and retention, 186
and self-image, 67–71
Self-image
and achievement, 64–67, 71–74
and self-esteem, 67–71
Self-perception, and achievement, 98–99
Self-quotient (SQ), 69–71, 78, 88–89
Shutdown, emotional, 262–63
Sloppiness, 39
Smartness, and achievement, 61–62
Social pressures, and
underachievement, 44
Social stress, and learning
problems, 182
Special education, vs. private
school education, 181
Struggling child, finding help for, 39–40
Student
good vs. poor, 148–52
with poor study skills, 152–53
Study skills
checklist, 153–54
good vs. poor, 150–52
implications, 146–48
poor, identifying student with, 152–53
and underachievement, 143–46
Stuttering, and frustration, 87–88
Success, paying price for, 95–99
Superego, 77

Survival, and achievement, 24–26
Symptoms, of learning problems, 110

Tests of child's capabilities, 23
Thinking
  active, 148–49
  passive, 149–50
Time, budgeting, 158–59
Treatment
  of emotional problems, 258–60
  of learning problems, 110
Tutoring, 176

Underachievement
  and acquired helplessness, 101–103
  checklist, 40–42
  and communication of
    disapproval and criticism, 212–13
  diagnosis and treatment, 110
  early identification of problem, 112–16
  early recognition, 106–9
  and ego damage, 92–93
  and emotional problems, 245–247, 255–58
  and family problems, 263–71
  and frustration, 85–88
  and parental intuition, 111–12
  responsibility for, 233–37
  sources, 46–47
  types, 45–46
  see also Achievement;

Underachiever(s)
Underachiever(s)
  communicating with, 189–95
  complacent, 42–45
  compulsive, 19–21, 23–24
  educational testing and treatment
    priorities, 130–31
  emotionally charged encounters
    with parents, 237–42
  emotional overlay, 249–51
  function of parent's
    communication with, 195–97
  in gray area, 125–28
  identifying child as, 32–34, 40–42
  with learning problems, 121–25
  performance standards for, 219–223
  with poor study skills, 143–46
  and problem ownership, 233–37
  self-defeating actions, 19–21
  see also Achievement;
    Underachievement

Value system, family and child's
  achievement, 282–84
Visual learning, 155
Visual perception deficiencies, 132

Younger children, communication
  with, 199–205

Zest, and achieving child, 34–36
Zest quotient, 34–36

About the Author

After completing his graduate studies at the School of Education at Stanford University, Lawrence Greene pursued his clinical training in learning disabilities in Chicago. For the last sixteen years he has been the executive director of the Developmental Learning Center in San Jose, California. In addition to his clinical, counseling, and program-development responsibilities, he functions as an educational consultant and teaches courses and seminars for parents and teachers at several California colleges. He has taught at the Esalen Institute in Big Sur, California, and has trained teachers and learning disabilities specialists as part of the continuing education program at San Jose State University.